SOUTH AFRICA

Highlights

Philip Briggs

Edition 1

Bradt Travel Guides Ltd, UK
The Globe Pequot Press Inc, USA

About this book

There are many heavyweight guidebooks to South Africa bloated with long lists of budget hotels and overviews of public transport targeted at backpackers and independent travellers. This 'highlights' guidebook is more selective in the information it offers, and is written for the traveller on (or planning to go on) an organised tour. The book has two main aims: first, to help those considering a vacation to decide what they'd like to see and do, and therefore to construct their itinerary or liaise with tour operators in an informed way; and, second, to provide an entertaining, colourful and informative guide to carry on the trip itself. With that in mind, the book provides overviews of every town, reserve and city that ranks as a possible highlight, a quick summary of practicalities and a short list of recommended accommodation. The selections are made by Philip Briggs, who is one of the world's most-renowned guidebook writers on Africa. In addition, we have called upon the expertise of some of the leading tour operators – those who know best the accommodation South Africa has to offer – to recommend their favourite lodges and tented camps. Those tour operators were carefully chosen by Bradt and invited to contribute on the basis of their reputations for excellence; they also made a payment towards the production costs of the book.

These pages are unique in bringing together the selections of a top writer and top operators, ensuring this is the most useful guidebook available to those planning an organised tour to South Africa.

Lodge/camp accommodation

Accommodation in this guide has been carefully selected and reviewed by the following tour operators: Aardvark Safaris Ltd, Bridge & Wickers, Imagine Africa, Rainbow Tours, The Zambezi Safari & Travel Company and To Escape To. See pages 60–1 for more information on these operators, including details on how to book.

Author

Born in the UK and raised in South Africa, Philip Briggs has been exploring the highways, byways and backwaters of his adopted continent since 1986, when he spent several months backpacking on a shoestring from Nairobi to Cape Town. In 1991, he wrote the Bradt guide to South Africa, the first such guidebook to be published internationally following the release of Nelson Mandela. Throughout the rest of the 1990s, Philip wrote a series of pioneering Bradt guides to destinations that were then – and in some cases still are   otherwise practically uncharted by the travel publishing industry. These included the first dedicated guidebooks to Tanzania, Uganda, Ethiopia, Malawi, Mozambique, Ghana and Rwanda (co-authored with Janice Booth), all of which are now several editions old. Philip has visited more than two-dozen African countries in total and written about most of them for specialist travel and wildlife magazines including *Africa Birds & Birding*, *Africa Geographic*, *BBC Wildlife*, *Travel Africa* and *Wanderlust*. He still spends at least four months on the road every year, usually accompanied by his wife, the travel photographer Ariadne Van Zandbergen, and spends the rest of his time battering away at a keyboard in the sleepy village of Bergville, in the uKhahlamba-Drakensberg region of South Africa.

Author's story

My first book for Bradt was a guide to South Africa, published back in November 1991, less than two years after the unbanning of the ANC and the release of Nelson Mandela signalled the imminent dismantling of apartheid. For South Africans, those were days of considerable uncertainty but even greater hope, with the latter blossoming on 27 April 1994, the landmark day when Mandela won our first democratic election. Since then, South Africa has flourished as a tourist destination, and where that long-out-of-print 1991 guide introduced a partially reformed pariah to an initial trickle of post-sanctions backpackers, its newer counterpart builds on my innumerable subsequent trips to every corner of my home country, to provide people planning organised tours with a discerning overview of its many, and varied, highlights. That *South Africa Highlights* is published only a week shy of its predecessor's 20th anniversary is a pleasing coincidence – and an apt moment to publicly thank Hilary Bradt for taking a chance on this then-unpublished writer all those years ago!

Southern carmine bee eater (J&CS/FLPA)

Contents

List of maps

Feedback request

If you have any comments about this guide (good or bad), we would welcome your feedback. Please email us on ✉ info@bradt guides.com. Alternatively you can add a review of the book to ⌂ www.bradtguides.com or Amazon.

Introduction

It's been in the ether for as long as this writer can remember: 'South Africa: A World in One Country'. This evergreen slogan stood the South African Tourist Board in good stead throughout the last decades of the 20th century, and while it has since been abandoned by officialdom, you need only Google the phrase 'World in One Country' today to see how popular it remains with private operators marketing South Africa.

Of course, like most hyperbole, this sweeping statement is both a little bit silly and demonstrably untrue – there are no glaciers in South Africa, for instance, nor are there any historical monuments quite so overwhelming as the Pyramids of Giza or the Americas. But as tends to be the case with venerable clichés, the phrase also contains a significant kernel of truth. South Africa, however you look at it, is a country of quite exceptional variety.

One of the world's top wildlife destinations, South Africa supports all the iconic large mammals for which Africa is renowned. The vast Kruger National Park, stretching over 500km from north to south, harbours a rhino population larger than every other country in the world combined, while adjoining private reserves such as Sabi Sands and MalaMala are among the last places in Africa where a two- to three-night stay comes with a near guarantee of ticking off all the so-called Big Five (lion, leopard, buffalo, elephant and rhino), alongside a dazzling selection of less-celebrated bush-dwellers, from the streamlined cheetah and elegant giraffe to the comical warthog and perhaps a dozen types of graceful antelope.

(NS/D)

South Africa is even more remarkable when it comes to the 'smaller stuff'. Indeed, some ecologists have ranked it the world's third most important country in terms of biodiversity, thanks to its unusually high level of endemism. Contained entirely within South Africa, the tiny Cape Floral Kingdom alone contains something like 5% of the world's plant species, of which two-thirds are found nowhere else. Likewise, the country is home to more endemic and near-endemic birds than anywhere in Africa, making it a highly popular destination for birdwatchers.

No less diverse and fascinating is South Africa's unique cultural blend of indigenous, European and Asian influences. Modern cities include brash Johannesburg, Africa's most important economic powerhouse, and its more stately coastal counterpart Cape Town, often ranked alongside San Francisco and Sydney as one of the world's most beautiful cities. Yet within easy driving distance of Johannesburg, the limestone caverns of the Cradle of Humankind have yielded the world's richest

Zulu woman (AVZ)

collection of hominid fossils, representing more than three million years of continuous human habitation. Elsewhere, traditional Zulu and Ndebele cultural villages remind visitors of the cultural diversity that existed prior to the arrival of Europeans. So, too, does South Africa's immense wealth of prehistoric rock art, nowhere seen to better advantage than in the remote open-air galleries of the imperious uKhahlamba-Drakensberg Mountains, which run for hundreds of kilometres along the border with Lesotho.

A significant part of South Africa's cultural fascination is the immense progress it has made as a unified nation since 1994, when the first democratic election was won by Nelson Mandela and the ANC, following decades of oppressive and racially divisive apartheid rule. A visit to Johannesburg's Apartheid Museum or Cape Town's District Six Museum is essential not only to understanding the iniquities of South Africa's recent past, but also to placing its subsequent achievements in perspective. To take one glib example, it is remarkable to think that the global sporting pariah of the 1980s has since become one of only two nations worldwide to have hosted the rugby, cricket *and* football World Cups. And the good news is that tourism has played a large role in this transformation – indeed, it now generates some 10% of the national GDP, and provides direct employment to more than half a million South Africans of all backgrounds.

So, a World in One Country? Of course not, no single country ever could be. But whether you are talking about wildlife or culture – or more so perhaps its dazzling array of landscapes, from the sweltering, acacia-studded savanna of the Kruger to the windswept moorlands and crags of the uKhahlamba-Drakensberg, from the sun-drenched, palm-lined beaches along the Indian Ocean to the wave-battered cliffs of the Atlantic coastline, from the mesmerising red dunefields of Kgalagadi to the tangled green forests of the eastern coastal belt, from the autumnal purple winelands to the dramatic spring wildflower displays of Namaqualand – South Africa is truly a country of inspirational variety.

Introducing South Africa

History   5

Economy and infrastructure   19

1 Background

Modern South Africa has been shaped by its long and at times traumatic past. Its story began four million years ago, when our earliest recognisable human ancestors trod the open plains of the highveld, and it gathered momentum with the Dutch colonisation of the Cape in 1652, which led to numerous clashes between expansionist settler communities and the indigenous peoples. The discovery of the world's richest gold reserves near Johannesburg in the 1880s led to the Anglo-Boer War of 1899-1902, and the eventual merging of the crown colonies of Cape and Natal with two former Boer Republics to form the Union of South Africa in 1910. More recently, the racist doctrine of apartheid caused immense suffering among the indigenous population, and civil unrest in the 1980s. Following the dismantling of apartheid in the early 1990s, South Africa has flourished as a democracy, having held its third 'free and fair' general election in 2009.

South Africa at a glance

Location The southernmost country in Africa, enclosing the Kingdom of Lesotho, and bordered by the Atlantic Ocean to the west, the Indian Ocean to the southeast, Mozambique and Swaziland to the northeast, and Namibia, Botswana and Zimbabwe to the north. The Tropic of Capricorn runs through the north.

Size 1,221,037km^2 (25th largest country in the world and ninth in Africa)

Status Republic

Population 50 million (2011 estimate)

Life expectancy Has declined from 62 years in 1990 to 50 years today, mainly due to HIV/AIDS.

Capital Pretoria (population 250,000)

Largest municipalities Johannesburg (3.8 million), Cape Town (3.5 million), eThekweni (3.45 million, includes Durban), Ekurhuleni (2.7 million, includes Germiston), Tshwane (2.4 million, includes Pretoria) and Nelson Mandela Bay (1.1 million, includes Port Elizabeth). Johannesburg, Ekurhuleni, Tshwane and the smaller Emguleni all lie within the tiny province of Gauteng and form part of one extended urban conglomeration of over 8 million people.

Economy Diverse, but mining, agriculture, services, manufacturing and tourism are all significant contributors

GDP US$287 billion; per capita US$5,823 (2009 estimate)

Languages 11 official languages (see page 99) including English

Religion 80% Christian or syncretism (combining Christian and traditional beliefs), 1.5% Hindu, 1.5% Muslim, 17% other or none

Currency South African rand

Rate of exchange US$1 = ZAR7; £1 = ZAR11; and €1 = ZAR10 (August 2011)

Head of State President Jacob Zuma

National Airline South African Airlines (SAA)

International dialling code 27

Time GMT+2

Electrical voltage 220–240V 60Hz. Round, three-pin, British-style plugs (standard in the UK prior to 1962).

Weights and measures Metric

Flag Green Y-shape rotated 90° anti-clockwise, with a red band on top and blue underneath, separated by narrow white bands, and a black triangle separated from the arms of the Y by a narrow yellow band

Public holidays 1 January, 21 March, 27 April, 1 May, 16 June, 9 August, 24 September, 16 December, 25 December, 26 December; also Good Friday and Family Day (Easter Monday)

History

South Africa as we know it came into being in 1910, when the Cape and Natal colonies formed a union with two formerly independent Boer republics acquired by Britain at the end of the Anglo-Boer War. However, hominid fossils unearthed at the likes of Sterkfontein Caves indicate that South Africa has an unusually long record of human habitation, stretching back at least four million years. Ironically, the region's documented history only goes back to the late 15th century, when the first Portuguese navigators stopped at the Cape coast in the course of opening a maritime trade route between Europe and India, and events in much of the interior went largely undocumented until the Great Trek passed through in the mid-19th century.

Prehistory

Extensive fossil evidence places sub-Saharan Africa at the forefront of human paleontological research, and the obvious inference to be drawn from this fossil wealth – ie: that the entire drama of human evolution was enacted in the region – is supported by several other factors. These include the total absence of contradictory fossil evidence elsewhere, the confinement to Africa of our three closest living genetic relatives and their ancestral lines, as well as compelling DNA evidence that every person alive today shares an African origin.

Prehistoric rock art in the Game Pass Shelter, Kamberg, Drakensberg. (AVZ)

The most ancient hominid fossils derive from Kenya and Ethiopia, and the East Africa Rift Valley is widely regarded to be where the evolutionary lineages of humans and apes first diverged, perhaps six–eight million years ago. However, the dozen or so paleontological sites that comprise South Africa's Cradle of Humankind, a UNESCO World Heritage Site west of Johannesburg, have yielded more early hominid fossils than anywhere else on earth, including a wealth of Australopithecine remains dating back four million years, and 1.4 million-year-old remains of *Homo erectus* that stand as the oldest known fossils of their kind.

Southern Africa entered the Stone Age at least one million years ago; indeed, there is some evidence to suggest that this oldest of human technologies arose in the region. The earliest evidence of controlled fire usage – dating back a million years – comes from the Cradle of Humankind. Elsewhere in the country, the remote Border Cave (on the Swaziland border) is the site of the earliest known remains of anatomically modern humans *Homo s. sapiens*, dating back at least 150,000 years, and the world's earliest evidence of ritual burials, religious worship and counting tools.

The history of the bushmen stretches back for thousands of years. (AVZ)

The Neolithic hunter-gatherer ancestors of the earliest southern Africans to whom we can put a meaningful name (albeit a less than flattering one, as the terms 'Bushmen' and 'San', coined respectively by later Dutch and Bantu-speaking settlers, are both pejorative) entered the scene some eight to ten thousand years ago. With their slight build, wizened, yellow-brown skin, click-based tongue and rich artistic tradition, the Bushmen betray a very different ethnic, linguistic and cultural background to any modern South Africans. And southern Africa remained the sole preserve of Bushman-like hunter-gatherers until around 1000BC, when the pastoralist ancestors of the Khoikhoi arrived in the area with their fat-tailed sheep, followed centuries later by Bantu-speaking, cattle-herding and farming societies that originated in the Congo Basin.

By the time Europeans arrived in the area, two main groups of Bantu-speakers inhabited South Africa. The longer established of the two was probably the Nguni, a group that includes the modern-day Zulu, Xhosa, Ndebele and Swazi, and who occupied the eastern coastal belt as far south as the Great Fish River, living in scattered family kraals presided over by broad regional chiefdoms. By contrast, the Sotho lived on the *highveld*, often in large cities said to hold up to 20,000 people. As a result, the Bushmen had been driven from most of their traditional hunting grounds into more arid or mountainous areas – for instance, the Kalahari and uKhahlamba-Drakensberg – unsuitable for farming and cattle grazing.

The first European expedition to reach South Africa was led by the Portuguese navigator Bartolomeu Dias, who inadvertently rounded the Cape of Good Hope in a storm before landing at present-day Mossel Bay on 3 February 1488. Dias sailed as far east as the Bushman's River Mouth, erecting a *padrão* (large stone cross) there in March 1488, before he decided to abandon the search for a sea route to India, a mission that was completed by his compatriot Vasco da Gama ten years later. From this time onwards, European ships bound for East Africa and Asia frequently stopped on South African shores, often trading with the local Khoikhoi for fresh produce. However, occasional skirmishes, such as the incident when Captain d'Almeida and 50 of his Portuguese crew members were killed at Table Bay in 1510, discouraged permanent settlement for another 150 years.

The colonial era (1652–1910)

The first permanent European settlement in South Africa was established at Table Bay in 1652, when Jan van Riebeeck set up a refreshment station for the Dutch East India Company on the site of present-day Cape Town. Five years later, nine company men were granted pieces of land to farm – in effect the start of the Cape Colony – and by the late 18th century the Cape hosted some 15,000 settlers, who had spread north into the Boland and east as far as Algoa Bay (Port Elizabeth). These early settlers were mostly farmers of Dutch and French descent, and they depended heavily both on the local Khoikhoi and on imported Malay slaves for unpaid labour. Indeed, for most of the Cape Colony's first century or so of existence, slaves outnumbered free citizens.

In 1795, Britain, by then an important player in the Indian Ocean maritime trade, annexed the strategically positioned Cape Colony. The Cape was handed over to the Batavian Republic in 1803 and re-occupied by Britain three years later; it became a formal British Colony in 1815. The new administration quickly made itself unpopular with the existing

Dutch-speaking settlers, declaring English the official language in 1828 and outlawing the recruitment of slaves in 1833. Many Boers (Dutch-speaking farmers) were financially ruined as a result of this new law, and they packed up their wagons and headed north *en masse*. The Great Trek, as this northward migration became known, was not only pivotal to the peopling of modern South Africa, but it was also the cornerstone of the mid-20th century Afrikaner nationalist sentiment that lay at the core of apartheid.

Equally significant changes occurred almost simultaneously in the part of the interior known as Zululand. In the early years of the 19th century, a combination of drought and land pressure caused the region's formerly dispersed Nguni clans to be welded into three cohesive and militarised nations. By 1825, however, total domination of the area had been achieved by the Zulu King Shaka through use of revolutionary military tactics. During the 1820s, many tens of thousands of non-Zulus were killed by Shaka's men, and more still were driven away beyond the border of present-day South Africa, some ending up as far afield as the East African Rift Valley Lakes (this series of events, known as the Mfecane or Difaqane, is covered more fully in the chapter on Zululand, see page 175).

It is widely believed that the Mfecane temporarily depopulated large tracts of the South African interior, one consequence of which was that the Voortrekkers – the participants in the Great Trek – believed the land they arrived at was largely unoccupied. The exception of course, was Zululand itself where the Voortrekker party led by Piet Retief attempted

Dingane and the Voortrekkers

Catastrophically, both for Piet Retief and for the future course of South African race relations, the Voortrekker leader made an inadvertent diplomatic blunder by arriving at Dingane's capital at night, an act that his Zulu hosts associated with witchcraft. Alarmed by the ill omen, Dingane ordered that the entire Voortrekker party be massacred in front of its leader, and then ripped out the living Retief's heart, liver and other vital organs to use as *muti* (medicine) to ward off further bad spirits. While Dingane's actions were justified from a Zulu perspective, other Voortrekkers understandably saw the murder of the king's guests as plain treachery. The subsequent Boer-Zulu War culminated in December 1838 with the defeat of Dingane – along with the slaughter of at least 3,000 Zulu soldiers by Andries Pretorius's Voortrekker party – at the Battle of Blood River.

The 1800s saw the decline of the Zulu Empire, with first the Boer-Zulu War and then the invasion of the British. (ILNL/ME)

to negotiate a land settlement with Shaka's successor Dingane in February 1838 (see box, opposite).

Soon after the end of the Boer-Zulu war Pretorius established Pietermaritzburg as capital of a Boer Republic called Natalia. It was a short distance inland from the British colony of Natal, which had been founded in 1835 centred on Durban. In 1843 Natalia was conquered and annexed by Britain, causing the Boers at Pietermaritzburg to repack their wagons and trek northwards and westwards to join or found a number of short-lived polities that were eventually moulded into the Zuid-Afrikaansche Republiek (ZAR/Transvaal) and Orange Free State (OFS). By 1860, the map of southern Africa had taken recognisable shape, comprising four major territories – Britain's colonies at the Cape and Natal, and the ZAR and OFS Boer Republics – whose borders were similar to those of the four post-union provinces of South Africa.

The discovery of two immensely wealthy mineral deposits – diamonds in 1869 at what is now Kimberley, and gold in 1886 in the ZAR around present-day Johannesburg – had an incalculable influence on the subsequent course of South African history. Both deposits lay under Boer soil, but were eagerly coveted by their British neighbours, leading to the annexation of Kimberley to the Cape in 1871. One of the major beneficiaries of this coup was Cecil John Rhodes, a British immigrant who became a millionaire off the back of the diamond rush at Kimberley, and went on to found the legendary De Beers Mining Company in 1880 and to became Prime Minister of the Cape Colony in 1890. An ardent and proactive British colonist, it was Rhodes who initiated the Jameson Raid of 1896, an abortive attempt to wrest control of the ZAR, as their exports were by then were outstripping those of the Cape.

In the aftermath of the Jameson Raid, Rhodes resigned from politics, and Britain and the ZAR embarked on an ultimately unproductive bout of negotiations. Britain subsequently decided that its only option for securing the goldfields around Johannesburg was to initiate a full-blown war with the ZAR, one it believed it could easily win. British troops were amassed on the borders of the ZAR, which lead to a Boer ultimatum that played right into their aspirant conqueror's hands. On 9 October 1899, the ZAR declared that if the troops were not withdrawn within 48 hours, it would 'be compelled to regard the action as a formal declaration of war'.

The Anglo-Boer War was an unmitigated disaster. Britain expected it would be over by Christmas 1899; instead it endured for almost 30 months to become the longest, bloodiest and most expensive war fought by the British between 1815 and 1914. Furthermore, in order to force the ZAR to surrender, the British used tactics that left the Boers deeply embittered. Boer farms and crops were razed, and civilians were herded into concentration camps where conditions were appalling: measles and dysentery claimed the lives of 30,000 Boer women and children, as well as 15,000 interned Africans, many of them Boer servants. The war

Bronze replicas of ox-wagons used by the Voortrekkers at the Battle of Blood River, Blood River museum. (AVZ)

finally ended, following a Boer surrender, with the signing of the Treaty of Vereeniging on 31 May 1902. The Transvaal and OFS became British colonies, only to be amalgamated with the Cape and Natal in 1910 to form the self-governing Union of South Africa. Ironically, the union's first elected Prime Minister and Defence Minister, Louis Botha and Jan Smuts, had both served as Boer generals during the war.

The interests of the indigenous peoples were largely ignored during the colonial era. The Cape Khoikhoi, numerically depleted by settler firepower and smallpox, were progressively forced from their traditional land during the period of Dutch rule, and were gradually integrated into the Cape's Coloured Community as slaves (see below). Hunted as vermin by the European settlers, the San/Bushmen met a similar fate, though their territorial distance from the Cape and their nomadic hunter-gatherer lifestyle ensured it was a more gradual process. By the early 20th century, a handful of San still eked out an existence in the Namib and Kalahari, but none whatsoever survived in the uKhahlamba-Drakensberg, the world's wealthiest gallery of Bushman rock art – an artistic tradition whose extinction is so recent that it includes a last few fateful panels depicting the first European ox-wagons to roll into the area in the 1830s.

The Bantu-speakers fared better, since their territories were further removed from the Cape and their societies considerably more militarised. Throughout the 19th century there were clashes and battles between the settlers and various indigenous kingdoms: British and Xhosa along the Great Fish River; Boer and Zulu then British and Zulu in Natal; and Boer and Sotho on the OFS/Lesotho border. By the early 20th century, however, the colonial powers had formally allocated pockets of land to the various indigenous groups. The largest of these, Bechuanaland (Botswana), Basutoland (Lesotho) and Swaziland, were never integrated into South Africa but remained British Protectorates until 1962, when they were granted full independence. Other areas, such as the Transkei and Zululand, remained native reserves in the newly created Union of South Africa.

In addition to European settlers and indigenous Bantu-speakers, two other distinct cultural groups had come into existence by 1910. The so-called Coloured Community, which numbers about four million today, emerged in the former Cape Colony as a mostly Afrikaans-speaking, mixed-race group descended from a blend of Malay slaves, early European settlers, and various indigenous people. Meanwhile, in Natal a number of Indians were imported as cheap labour for the coastal sugar plantations in the 1860s. Having served five years' indenture, many stayed on to become successful traders and skilled labourers, and founded a 1.5 million-strong 'Indian' community still centred on KwaZulu-Natal today.

The rise of Afrikaner nationalism (1910–48)

The divide between English settlers and their Afrikans counterparts dominated South African parliamentary politics in the first half of the 20th century. Although the Union of South Africa was ruled by former Boer generals, the Anglo-Boer War had left a bitter legacy among the Afrikaner community, who felt they had been persecuted ever since the British arrived at the Cape. Indeed, many rural Afrikaners were forced to live in poverty and squalor having lost their farms, even their families, as a result of the British scorched-earth policy in the Anglo-Boer War. Another result of the war was that the goldfields were now largely in the hands of English settlers, who soon came to dominate Afrikaners on the economic front. Worse still in the view of many, was that Botha and Smuts chose to side with Britain when World War I erupted, a mere 12 years after the Anglo-Boer War ended, and only four years after union.

In 1924, disgruntled Afrikaners voted Barry Herzog's National Party (NP) into power, leaving the 'sell-out' Jan Smuts, who had become Prime Minister when Louis Botha died in 1919, on the benches. However, by 1934 Herzog had also acquired the sell-out tag and a 'purified' NP, led by DF Malan, splintered from the National Party. Herzog and Smuts formed the United Party (UP), which won the 1938 election and was led by Herzog. A year later, following the outbreak of another World War, a familiar issue reared its head. Smuts backed Britain and the Allies, Herzog supported neutrality, and many of their more vehemently anti-British supporters backed Germany as a matter of principle. Smuts's stance won the day, however, and he assumed leadership of the UP, to serve his second stint as Prime Minister. Meanwhile, Herzog re-joined the Malan-led NP, and took many of his UP supporters with him.

At this point, the guiding concern of nationalist Afrikaners was their own economic progression and cultural self-preservation in the face of British pre-eminence, rather than any overt desire to dominate other races. Nevertheless, the parliamentary parlour games of the first half of the 20th century paid scant attention to the interests of Black, Coloured and Indian South Africans, and resistance to White dominance solidified. The African National Congress (ANC), for instance, was founded in 1912, inspired by the policy of passive resistance protest espoused by Mohandas Gandhi. The future Indian leader arrived in South Africa in 1893 to work as a lawyer and went on to found the seminal Natal Indian Congress after being booted off a train for being

Statue of Mohandas Ghandi, Pietermaritzburg (SS)

an Asian in the wrong compartment. He had become a major thorn in Smuts's side by the time he returned to India in 1914.

After the war, many ANC-organised protests were ending in confrontations with armed police. In 1946, a strike by 70,000 Black miners turned into a blood-bath after police opened fire. For the first time, the predominantly White electorate was forced to focus on the racial issue that has dominated modern South African politics ever since. Indeed, by the time of the 1948 election, Smuts and the UP were talking about integration, albeit in a limited sense, while the NP campaign focused on the one-word philosophy that led to it being swept into power. That one word – literally meaning separateness – was apartheid.

The building of apartheid (1948–80)

The apartheid ideology rested on two main fundaments: firstly, that the differences between the country's racial and cultural groups were God-given and these groups should thus be encouraged to develop in isolation, and secondly that Western culture represents the pinnacle of human development. In practice, however, both the politicians who implemented the policy and the Whites who voted for them used apartheid as an ideological tool with which the existing misbalance of power between Black and White could be entrenched with even greater rigidity and control.

During their first three years in power, DF Malan and his NP passed a series of apartheid bills. At the core of this policy was the Population Registration Act, which allowed the government to classify all South Africans into four racial groups (Asian, Black, Coloured or White). The Group Areas Act forced every South African to live in an area that was designated for their specific racial group, while the Immorality and Mixed Marriages acts outlawed marriage and sexual intercourse between the races. In addition to those acts directly related to apartheid, the NP also passed the Unlawful Organisations and Suppression of Communism acts, a precursor of the draconian powers that were soon to be vested in the state.

Malan retired in 1954 but his successor JG Strijdom continued in the same vein, implementing the State Aided Institutions Act, which banned Blacks from using public facilities run by White institutions, and removing Coloureds from the Voters' Roll. It was also under Strijdom that the NP embarked on its programme of forcible resettlement, ejecting all Black and Coloured people from Cape Town's District Six, Johannesburg's Sophiatown and other city suburbs that had been re-zoned as Whites only. Strijdom died in office in 1958, to be replaced by HF Verwoerd, who declared South Africa a republic in 1960 and severed all links with the Commonwealth. Verwoerd started in earnest to implement the all-important Homelands Policy, which designated certain parts of the country to specific tribes as nominally self-governing territories. The Transkei, set aside for the Xhosa people, became the first self-governing homeland in 1962 (and was granted full 'independence' in 1976).

Monument to ANC leader Albert Luthuli, Cape Town (SS)

As the NP pursued its absurd policies, the ANC grew in international stature under the leadership of Albert Luthuli, who won the 1960 Nobel Peace Prize in recognition of his role in the non-violent struggle against apartheid. The ANC Freedom Charter, drawn up in 1955, asserted the organisation's belief in a non-racial democracy, and remains to this day the major reference point in the party's political philosophy. At this stage, the ANC remained deeply committed to passive resistance and peaceful negotiation, leading to the splintering off of the more radical Pan African Congress (PAC) under Robert Sobukwe in 1959.

The turning point for both the ANC and PAC came on 21 March 1960. The PAC had organised a peaceful demonstration to protest against the recently expanded Pass Laws, which meant that any Black found in a White area without their pass book could be, and usually was, arrested. In the township of Sharpeville on the Cape Flats, 15,000 protesters gathered around the police station and the police opened fire, killing 69 people. In the aftermath of this massacre, a State of Emergency was declared, the ANC and PAC were banned, and the ANC decided to abandon peaceful protest in favour of violent resistance. The ANC and PAC established bases in Dar es Salaam (Tanzania) and London, and the ANC formed the underground Umkonto we Sizwe (Spear of the Nation). Led by Nelson Mandela, Umkonto we Sizwe undertook acts of terrorism against government property such as police stations and post offices. Eventually its leaders were captured and put on trial, with Mandela, among others, being sentenced to life imprisonment in 1963.

Robben Island was home to many political prisoners during Apartheid. (SS)

Throughout all this, White South Africa remained largely oblivious. In the 1961 election, the newly formed Progressive Party, which ran on an anti-apartheid, pro-negotiation platform, won a solitary seat for Helen Suzman, who stood as the lone voice of reason in an NP-dominated parliament until 1974. In 1963 and 1966, the NP passed a series of bills that allowed the police to detain people indefinitely without trial, to place people under house arrest, and otherwise harass perceived enemies of the state. In 1966, Verwoerd was stabbed to death in the House of Assembly by a European later adjudged to be insane, and BJ Vorster took over as Prime Minister. The first years under Vorster were relatively sedate. The leaders of the organised Black resistance movements were either in exile or jail, or placed under house arrest, the gold price was strong and the economy buoyant. Virtually the only internal resistance during this period came from the Black Consciousness Movement founded by Steve Biko.

In Soweto on 16 June 1976, marchers protesting the use of Afrikaans as a teaching medium were fired at by police. A number of children were killed, and Soweto exploded. When the Soweto Uprising subsided more than six months later, 700 people had died, thousands of children had been detained, 500 teachers had resigned, and hundreds of buses, schools, clinics and other buildings in the townships had been gutted by angry protesters. Black Consciousness and related movements were banned, and Biko was forced underground, eventually to be detained by the police in Port Elizabeth. On 12 September 1977, Biko died in police custody, the most prominent of the many political detainees who had contrived to kill themselves by means as diverse as jumping through barred windows, hanging themselves, or slipping on a soap bar in the shower. An official inquiry was launched and the police exonerated, but few doubted that Biko had been murdered.

The Soweto Uprising and Biko's death changed the atmosphere in the townships. A generation of teenagers had had their schooling disrupted and Black education facilities, never very good in the first place, were irreparably damaged. Conciliatory attitudes and goodwill, especially amongst the youth, had been stretched to the limit by police and government actions. For all the loss of life, Blacks had won precisely nothing – if anything the State pursued a policy of martial rule to a greater extent than ever. In 1978, in the face of a complicated scandal involving the embezzlement of government funds, Vorster resigned, to be replaced by stalwart PW Botha.

The dawn of democracy (1980–94)

Initially perceived to be a reformist, Botha implemented a new constitution in 1983, one that offered nothing fresh to Black South Africans – who, according to apartheid theory, were officially citizens of one or other independent or self-governing homeland – but gave Coloureds and Indians a limited say in a new Tricameral Parliament. Although the 1983 constitution gained almost 70% support in a 'Whites-only' referendum, it initiated the split of the ultra-right wing Conservative Party (CP) from the NP, which realised it might lose power if it moved too quickly for its White electorate. Paralysis followed, and while Botha went on to scrap the Mixed Marriages Act and Pass Laws, and reform the Separate Amenities Act, the core policies of apartheid were left in place.

In the 1980s, apartheid had come to look increasingly retrogressive and immoral to the international community, for whom Nelson Mandela, by then imprisoned for two decades, had become a figurehead. As a result, a vigorous ANC campaign for sanctions led several countries to expand upon sporting and arms boycotts established in the 1960s and implement full economic severance. Meanwhile, two important new organisations emerged during the 1980s: the United Democratic Front (UDF) and Inkatha, the former a virtual internal arm of the ANC, the latter a Zulu-centric organisation led by Chief Mangosuthu Buthelezi. The NP continued with its repressive ways, especially after 1986 when in the face of steadily vociferous and violent opposition to apartheid, a national State of Emergency was declared, giving the security forces carte blanche to terrorise the townships. The economy took a tumble as a result of sanctions, unemployment soared, and hundreds of township

Nelson Mandela, shortly after his release from 27 years in prison. (AC/A)

dwellers met a violent death every year, not only as a result of state oppression, but also due to faction fighting taking place between UDF and Inkatha supporters.

Botha resigned in 1989 and was replaced by FW de Klerk, who led the NP to electoral victory in September that year on a typically ambiguous platform. However, de Klerk's appetite for reform was made abundantly clear on 2 February 1990 when he astonished most observers by lifting the ban on the ANC and 20 other organisations. Soon afterwards, Mandela was released after 27 years of imprisonment, the national State of Emergency was lifted, apartheid laws were peeled away one by one, and the ANC abandoned the armed struggle following exploratory talks with the ANC. A National Peace Accord, signed by most major parties in September 1991, was followed in December by the first CODESA negotiating forum between the ANC, NP and other major players. In March 1992, the last all-White referendum was held, and more than two-thirds of the electorate voted in favour of reform.

Following several setbacks, negotiations resumed in April 1993, overshadowed by the assassination days later of the prominent ANC leader Chris Hani. The perpetrators were brought to book within days, and the killing prompted new focus and momentum at the negotiating table. In June, CODESA settled on 27 April 1994 as the date of South Africa's first fully democratic election. The months that followed were marked by high levels of tension, as the right-wing underlined its disapproval with several bombings, and doomsayers inevitably predicted that the country would descend into chaos on, or shortly after, the big day. In the event, however, votes were cast in a peaceful, reconciliatory, even cathartic mood. The ANC secured a 62% majority, with the NP gaining 20% of the vote and Inkatha 10%, and – predictable as to be a formality – Nelson Mandela became the first Black president of a new South Africa.

The FNB Stadium in Johannesburg played host to the final of the 2010 FIFA World Cup. (PA/D)

The Mandela years and beyond (1994 to the present day)

The years since the 1994 election lack the sense of narrative that marked the preceding period. The country has held three further general elections, one every five years, all won convincingly by the ANC, though the opposition Democratic Alliance, led by Helen Zille (a former journalist credited with exposing the security forces' role in Biko's death back in 1977) regained control of the Western Cape from the ruling ANC in the 2009 elections. The ageing Mandela, who retired from the presidency in 1999, was replaced by his deputy Thabo Mbeki, who resigned as a result of party infighting in September 2008. 'Caretaker president' Kgalema Motlanthe took control prior to the May 2009 election, when Jacob Zuma became president and Motlanthe stepped down to become his deputy.

On the downside, South Africa is in the grip of the world's worst HIV/AIDS pandemic, with an estimated five million people now infected, and the government is widely perceived to have responded inadequately to this crisis, particularly during the Mbeki years. While sound fiscal policies ensured that the country was less badly hit than most by the ongoing global recession, unemployment stands at a hefty 25%, a mere 10% of the population are registered taxpayers, and the inflation rate has typically fluctuated between 4% and 10% since 1994 (comparable figures for the UK would be 8% unemployment, 40% registered taxpayers, and inflation rates between 2% and 5%). Also of deep concern is the high rate of violent crime, and the deeply flawed healthcare and education systems. True, these issues are the partial legacy of the 40-year period during which government money was frittered away on the construction of pointless homeland capitals, to fund destabilising wars in neighbouring countries, and to support the unwieldy bureaucracy required to run the apartheid system. Equally destructive, however, is the burgeoning level of corruption and cronyism that infects all tiers of government today.

It isn't all bad news, by any means. The ANC has made significant progress when it comes to the social uplifting of the country's poorest and most disadvantaged sectors. Some 66% of households now live in formal dwellings, as opposed to 47% in 1994, similar increases have been achieved in the provision of piped water and/or electricity, and more than 13 million South Africans receive social benefits of some form. Internationally, the country is no longer the pariah it was under apartheid; on the contrary, South Africa is now the most popular tourist destination in sub-Saharan Africa, attracting some ten million visitors annually (thrice as many as in 1994) and it has hosted several major international sporting events, notably the rugby, cricket and (most recently) FIFA world cups. Above all, and despite the country's fractious recent past, South Africa retains a large store of mutual goodwill and common sense when it comes to race relations and to making things work. For many, perhaps, the fact that South Africa – an infinitely more tolerant, open and progressive society under the ANC than it was before 1994 – has come so far without major disruption is cause enough for continued positivity about the future.

Economy and infrastructure

South Africa has the largest economy in Africa, and one of the fastest growing. The 2009 Gross Domestic Product (GDP) of US$287 billion represents an increase of almost 200% in the past 20 years, and it accounts for about 40% of the entire GDP of sub-Saharan Africa. To some extent, these figures say more about the overall poverty of Africa than they do about South Africa's relative wealth on a global level –

in 2009, the whole of Africa accounted for less than about 2% of the global GDP, and South Africa itself had a GDP comparable with that of Argentina, Denmark or Thailand. This figure is less impressive when you take into account the country's population, which places it 70th in the world in terms of per capita GDP.

In the 1960s, the South African economy had a growth and inflation rate that compared favourably with most Western economies. During the 1980s, by contrast, the economy stagnated, inflation hovered at around 15%, the exchange rate plummeted by a factor of 300%, and unemployment soared close to 50%. The main causes of this economic slump were political, as government funds were wasted on maintaining the inefficient apartheid system, while economic sanctions undermined global trade. Since the 1994 election, however, a full return to the global economy has boosted foreign trade and manufacturing, inflation has mostly hovered around 5%, and the foreign exchange rate, though subject to short-term volatility, has been reasonably stable in the longer term. The moral rehabilitation of South Africa has also led to a significant increase in tourist revenue, as indicated by a rise from fewer than one million foreign visitors annually in the 1980s to more than 10 million in 2010.

South Africa has long claimed to be the economic gateway to sub-Saharan Africa, boasting as it does the subcontinent's most advanced infrastructure, and – with sanctions no longer forming an obstacle to intra-African trade – it has grown into this role in the post-apartheid era. Indeed, South African business interests elsewhere in Africa include ownership of, or important management roles in, several other countries' mobile phone, satellite TV, tourism and manufacturing industries. It produces almost half of the continent's electricity, has by far the highest rates of telephone and car ownership in Africa, has more air traffic and tonnage of goods through its ports than the rest of sub-equatorial Africa combined, and the ratio of paved roads to land area is 15 times the continental average.

South Africa is one of the world's best-endowed countries when it comes to innate mineral wealth. Most famous perhaps is the prodigious gold that lies below the soil of Gauteng, which accounted for 51% of revenue raised by foreign exports in 1980, and ensured that South Africa was the world's largest gold producer throughout the 20th century, and still holds an estimated 40% of the known global reserves. The country is also well known for its diamond production; indeed, the Premier Diamond Mine in Cullinan is where the largest-ever gem-quality diamond was discovered – a 3,100-carat stone that was carved into several pieces which now form part of the Crown Jewels! In addition, around 90% of the world's known platinum reserves lie in South Africa, along with 80% of the manganese, 75% of the chromium, and 45% of the vanadium.

From being the dominant economic contributor in the apartheid era, mining has assumed a lower level of importance over the last few decades. By the mid-1990s it only accounted for 11% of the country's GDP, and this figure dropped to 5.6% in 2008. Another sector in relative decline is agriculture, which provided around 9% of the GDP in 1960 as compared with 2.3% in 2008. However, neither of these figures reflects a decrease in production, but rather a maturation from what was once largely a primary economy to one with better developed secondary and tertiary sectors. Important growth areas in post-

Diamonds are just one example of South Africa's vast mineral wealth. (SS)

apartheid economic diversification include the financial, real estate and business service sector, which now accounts for 22% of the GDP, as well as manufacturing (16%), IT and communications (9%) and tourism (7%).

Despite all this, South Africa displays striking disparities in wealth. The country ranks second in the world according to the 'Gini co-efficient', and while the correlation with race and poverty is not absolute it is very strong, with some 60% of Blacks living below the poverty line, compared with around 10% of Whites. Similar racial discrepancies occur when it comes to most other factors that affect material quality of life and/or longevity, whether it be land ownership, access to medical facilities, adult literacy or educational opportunities. In South Africa, finding the optimum balance between policies aimed at wealth creation and those aimed at wealth re-distribution is a problem likely to tax the government for years to come.

2 The Natural World

A country of immense natural beauty and variety, South Africa is by some accounts ranked third in the world in terms of biodiversity. To most wildlife enthusiasts it is best known as a safari destination, thanks to the presence of the iconic Big Five in sanctuaries such as the immense Kruger National Park and adjacent private reserves (probably the best place in the world to see leopards and rhinos). The country also provides many more unexpected delights, such as superb land-based whale-watching off Hermanus, the opportunity to hike in the bounteous green montane vistas of the uKhahlamba-Drakensberg, the breath-taking spring wildflower displays of the Western Cape and Namaqualand, a unique wealth of endemic and near-endemic birds ranging from the emblematic blue crane to the comic African penguin, the vast open spaces of the Karoo or red dune of Kgalagadi... all protected in a network of 500-plus reserves catering to all interest and budgets.

Geology, geography and climate

Farmland in Bergville at the base of the Drakensberg Mountains (AVZ)

The most southerly country in Africa is bounded by the warm rain-bringing Indian Ocean to the east and the south, and by the colder rain-inhibiting Atlantic to the west. The country's most important topographical feature is the escarpment that follows the coastline in a rough crescent, typically rising between 50km and 250km inland, and dividing South Africa into three broad altitudinal regions: the warm and low-lying coastal belt, the cooler *highveld*, and the escarpment itself. Altitude is an important factor in local climates, but so is latitude: while most of South Africa has a reasonably temperate climate, the far north of the country lies within the tropics and is atypically hot, particularly the *lowveld* of the northern Kruger National Park.

South Africa is a land of rare geological interest, providing a unique and almost complete overview of the earth's geological and evolutionary history. The northeast hosts some of the most world's most ancient rocks, with early Pre-Cambrian formations such as the Archaean Basement and Barberton Greenstone Belt estimated to be about 3.5 billion years old. The latter greenstones hold the fossilised relics of the very earliest micro-organisms to have inhabited the earth, whilst the somewhat younger Karoo Basin of the southwest has yielded the world's largest collection of proto-mammalian reptiles, a unique fossil record documenting the emergence of early mammals over a period of 50 million years.

In such venerable company, South Africa's most significant mountain range, the uKhahlamba-Drakensberg, feels like a geological infant. Running along the eastern border of KwaZulu-Natal, its escarpment, which only took recognisable shape in the past 5–10 million years, is capped by a formidable basaltic plateau whose length of more than 200km is breached by just one solitary and remote road, the Sani Pass, which is only accessible by 4x4. The uKhahlamba-Drakensberg is the tallest African mountain range south of Kilimanjaro, boasting several dozen peaks that top 3,000m, the tallest being the 3,482m Thabana Ntlenyana in Lesotho. The 3,282m Mont Aux Sources, which lies on the Lesotho border about 3km behind the escarpment, is – as its name suggests – the country's most important watershed, being the source of five different rivers, including the two largest, the eastward-flowing Thukela and westward-flowing Orange.

Most of South Africa has a temperate climate, though parts of the Northern Province and Northern Cape become very hot in summer, as does the humid coastal belt north of Durban. Summer falls between October and March, while winter falls between May and August. The Western Cape has a winter rainfall pattern, but the rest of the country receives almost all its rain during the summer. Rainfall is highest in the east, most of which averages around 1,000mm annually, while on the west coast and in the Kalahari it drops to below 250mm. Overall, however, South Africa is a rather dry country, as reflected by a paucity of natural lakes, and even its moister regions are prone to periods of extended drought.

Habitats and vegetation

South Africa is a land of varied habitats and exceptional floral wealth. The Cape Floristic Kingdom, the smallest of the six such entities recognised globally by botanists, lies entirely within its borders and the country as a whole hosts a remarkable 10% of the world's known plant species. Most of these species are associated with a particular habitat, a term that might refer to something quite small and specific, such as a lily-covered pool or isolated rocky hill, or to a more generic landscape like the vast tracts of *bushveld* in the northeast. Learning to recognise habitats and their associated flora will greatly enhance a visit to any national park or nature reserve, whilst also helping predict what wildlife might be seen in a given location and assisting in the identification of similar-looking species.

Savanna woodland

Savanna woodland is a loosely defined term that in sub-Saharan Africa is generally used to describe relatively moist habitats where the grassy ground layer is partially shaded by an open canopy of fire-resistant shrubs or trees. Roughly a third of South Africa can be characterised as

Different forest types

Several different forest types are recognised in South Africa. These include the Afro-montane 'mistbelt' forests, which stretch inland from the eastern coastal belt to the coastal forests of Zululand and the Garden Route, and are distinguished by the presence of large hardwood trees such as black stinkwood *Ocotea bullata* and Outeniqua yellowwood *Podocarpus falcatus*. Elsewhere, many watercourses and other wetland habitats sustain ribbons of riparian forest, often dominated by the fever tree and various leafy *Ficus* species, to provide a corridor supporting forest wildlife in non-forested habitats. Accessible examples of this important niche habitat are the Kruger National Park's Sabie and Luvuvhu rivers, where the forested banks provide refuge for bushbuck, nyala and various forest birds, as well as attracting large numbers of elephant.

savanna woodland, including most of the Kruger National Park and its surrounds, northern KwaZulu-Natal, and Limpopo and the Northwest Provinces. Savanna is probably the natural climax vegetation type in these and other relatively moist, low- to mid-altitude parts of Africa with clearly defined dry and wet seasons. However, some ecologists suggest that open savanna dominated by fire-resistant trees is the result of centuries of deliberate burning by pastoralists seeking to stimulate fresh growth to feed their cattle, aided and abetted by the tree-shredding activities of elephants.

Highly characteristic of the African savanna are thorn trees of the genus *Acacia* (recently split from their Australian counterparts and controversially reassigned to the genera *Senegalia* and *Vachellia*, but we have chosen to stick with the more familiar name until this debate is resolved). These include large trees such as the flat-topped umbrella thorn *A. tortilis* (known as the *haak-en-steek* – hook and stab – in Afrikaans), the camel thorn *A. erioloba*, the monkey thorn *A. galpinii*, and common hook thorn *A. caffra*, as well as the groundwater-loving, jaundice-barked fever tree *A. xanthophloea*, and a number of more shrub-like species.

In the northern Kruger National Park, the mixed acacia savanna of the south is replaced by a near-monospecific cover of mopane woodland. This is dominated by the mopane tree *Colophospermum mopane*, noted for its hard, termite-resistant wood and diagnostic butterfly-shaped leaves, which transform from green summery hues into autumnal yellows and greens as winter approaches. It is a major food source for the protein-rich mopane worm *Imbrasia belina*, a caterpillar that is roasted and eaten as a delicacy by locals. Other savanna trees include the sausage tree *Kigalia africana*, which has a thick, evergreen canopy and gigantic, sausage-shaped pods that are eaten by elephants and used by locals as gourds. Often associated with rocky slopes in savanna settings, the candelabra tree *Euphorbia candelabra* is a superficially cactus-like succulent with an inverted umbrella shape that grows to more than 10m in height.

The Africa savanna can support immense herds of grazing ungulates, including mixed herds of wildebeest, zebra and antelope such as still occur in the central Kruger. Other large grazers associated with lightly wooded savanna include eland, red hartebeest, tsessebe, reedbuck and oribi, while more thickly wooded areas are favoured by impala, buffalo, giraffe and warthog. Predator populations are proportionately dense, particularly lion, spotted hyena and black-backed jackal. More open savanna habitats support a limited avifauna but are often notable for the presence of heavyweights such as ostrich, kori bustard, secretary bird and southern ground hornbill, alongside ground-dwelling plovers, larks, longclaws and waxbills. More densely wooded savanna supports a greater avian variety, with conspicuous perching birds such as rollers, shrikes, bee-eaters and raptors occurring alongside the more active sunbirds, parrots, hornbills, starlings, and helmet-shrikes, as well as the relatively secretive bush-shrikes, owls, woodpeckers, cuckoos and batises.

View of the indigenous forest at the Kaaimans River valley, Wilderness National Park. (AVZ)

Indigenous forest

Forest differs from woodland by having a closed canopy and a dank, jungle-like feel, often comprising several tall, vertically layered sub-canopies that cast a permanent shadow over a tangle of undergrowth, epiphytes and vines. Indigenous forest accounts for a paltry 0.25% of South Africa's surface area, a figure that has declined greatly in recent decades, but it has the most diverse fauna of the country's terrestrial habitats. It is of particular interest to birdwatchers as it is the main habitat of localised bird species such as the hefty, conspicuous and noisy *Bycanistes* hornbills, the colourful turacos and trogons, various forest barbet and tinkerbirds, and a miscellany of inconspicuous and secretive warblers, thrushes and bulbuls. The invertebrate diversity of the forests is incalculable, with butterflies being very well represented.

Semi-desert and desert

The western half of South Africa receives a significantly lower rainfall than the east due in part to the influence of the cold Benguela Current, which ensures that annual precipitation varies from 50mm to 500mm depending on the exact location. The only true desert in the country is the Springbokvlakte in the Orange River Valley, which abuts the Namibian border and is protected in the remote Richtersveld National Park. In addition, parts of the Kalahari, notably the tall, red dunefields protected within Kgalagadi Transfrontier Park, are desert-like in appearance, though they are classified as semi-desert and are technically part of the savanna biome.

The country's most important arid ecosystem is the Karoo, a 400,000km² basin that has been in place for 250 million years, experiencing periods of glaciation, flooding and intense volcanic activity, and which is rich in fossils dating back to the time of the dinosaurs. The Karoo is divided into two distinct vegetation biomes, of which the more noteworthy is the smaller, more westerly and drier Succulent Karoo. Extending northwards into Namibia, this is the world's most florally diverse arid area, hosting almost 4,000 plant species of which some 70% occur nowhere else in the world. It also supports around 30% of the world's succulent species, including striking oddities such as the quiver tree *Aloe dichotoma* and Halfmensboom (Half-human tree) *Pachypodium namaquanum*, and is renowned for the peerless spring flower displays that transform the stony Namaqualand region into a sea of colour throughout the months of August and September. Further east, the less ecologically interesting Nama Karoo supports a sparse cover of grass and deciduous shrubs.

Road through the desert in the Kalahari, Northern Cape (AVZ)

Dry-country wildlife tends to be thinly distributed, and is dominated by desert-adapted creatures such as gemsbok, springbok, Hartmann's mountain zebra and ground squirrels. It is also very rich in small predators, particularly brown hyena, aardwolf, bat-eared fox, black-backed jackal, black-footed cat, meerkat and yellow mongoose. Reptiles are well represented and display of a high level of endemism, with 15 lizard species, for instance, being regularly found in the Karoo, among them the peculiar armadillo girdled lizard *Cordylus cataphractus*, which has a heavily armoured body and spiny tail, and rolls into a tight ball when threatened. The arid west is also a stronghold for dozens of bird species that are endemic to southern Africa, among them the white-backed mousebird, Ludwig's bustard, Karoo korhaan, Karoo eremomela, Namaqua warbler, cinnamon-breasted warbler, Karoo scrub-robin, Karoo chat, pale-winged starling, dusky sunbird and half-a-dozen lark species.

African jacana (LD/D)

Aquatic

South Africa is rather poorly endowed when it comes to freshwater wetlands, a term embracing any habitat that combines terrestrial and aquatic features. The one major exception to this is the iSimangaliso Wetland Park in northeast KwaZulu-Natal, a vast protected area that incorporates Lake Sibaya (incredibly, the country's largest natural freshwater body) and three other Ramsar sites. Nevertheless, the significance of the country's isolated wetlands is almost impossible to overstate, both as self-sustaining ecosystems supporting fish, amphibians and other water-associated birds and mammals, and as a source of vital drinking water to most terrestrial creatures, including humans. Sadly, wetland habitats, more than any other, are frequently threatened by development, whether that be swamp drainage, industrial pollution, the disruption of riverine habitats to feed reservoirs or hydroelectric schemes, or the introduction of exotic species. However, it is equally true, in the case of a relatively dry country such as South Africa, that man's need for reservoirs and dams has created an enormous number of artificial wetlands as beneficial to wildlife as their natural counterparts.

Mammals exclusive to aquatic habitats include hippo, marsh mongoose and otters, but elephant and buffalo also regularly take to water, and most other species need to drink daily. More than 100 of South Africa's bird species are strongly associated with one or other wetland habitat, ranging from the swallows and martins that feed above lakes, to aerial anglers such as the pied kingfisher and African fish eagle, to the waders that peck in the shallows. And while a few water-associated birds, such as the Egyptian goose or cattle egret, might live in almost any aquatic habitat, others have more specific requirements. African finfoot and white-backed night heron, for instance, favour still or sluggish waters with overhanging vegetation, whereas many lapwings and migrant waders are associated with exposed sandbanks. Quiet, lily-covered pools are the haunt of the African jacana and pygmy goose.

Mountains, hills and cliffs

South Africa has plenty of large mountains, notably the Cape Fold Mountains around Cape Town, and the Mpumalanga Escarpment. But the largest montane habitat is the uKhahlamba-Drakensberg, the southernmost component in the Afro-montane eco-region, an 'archipelago' of high-altitude 'islands' that rise in isolation above areas of relative ecological contiguity. As with true islands, these scattered mountains are important centres of biodiversity and endemism, providing ideal conditions for fresh speciation, as well as niche habitats for conservative species that have become obsolete in the more homogenous lowlands. The uKhahlamba-Drakensberg and bordering parts of Lesotho comprise a 40,000km^2 hub of floral diversity known as the Drakensberg Alpine Centre (DAC). Of more than 2,000 plant species identified within the uKhahlamba-Drakensberg Park, almost 30% are DAC endemics, and more than 100 are listed as globally threatened.

These are split across three main altitudinal vegetation zones: montane, subalpine and alpine. Moist montane grassland dominates up to the 2,000m contour, but there are also stands of fire-resistant *suikerbossie* (sugar bush) protea shrubs that attract a wide range of sunbirds and the endemic Gurney's sugarbird, while gullies tend to support strips of Afro-montane forest and the riparian woodland associated with streams and gullies. From 2,000–2,800m, the subalpine zone comprises open or bushed grassland interspersed with patches of heath-like scrub reminiscent of the ericoid fynbos of the Western Cape, and equally prone to spectacular spring wildflower displays. More bleak is the alpine zone, where the undulating, windswept plateaux support a sparse cover of snow-resistant tussock grasses and pastel-shaded Erica and Helichrysum shrubs, but few plants taller than 50cm.

The country's most important watershed, uKhahlamba-Drakensberg, is the ultimate source of several significant rivers, including the west-flowing Orange and east-flowing Thukela (also known as the Tugela). While its bird checklist doesn't compare to the likes of Kruger, uKhahlamba-Drakensberg is an important site for endemics, providing refuge for about half of the bird species whose natural range is restricted to South Africa (and/or Lesotho and/or Swaziland). Possibly the most limited distribution of any uKhahlamba-Drakensberg endemic belongs to the cloud protea *Protea nubigena*, whose known range extends over less than 1ha of the Royal Natal Park, where about 100 plants (with up to 20 off-branching stems) stand at an altitude of around 2,400m.

The uKhahlamba-Drakensberg Mountains (AVZ)

A common sloping habitat consists of isolated rocky hills called koppies (meaning 'little heads') and the tall cliffs associated with parts of the escarpment. Both possess something of an island ecology, offering permanent or part-time refuge to a range of rock- and thicket-loving plants and animals that couldn't easily survive on surrounding plains. Koppies and cliffs are favoured by baboons, which seem to be more skittish and vocal in this rocky environment than on the open plains, and the rock-hopping klipspringers. Also present are bush and rock hyraxes, which often live alongside each other, with the former grazing around the rocks and the latter feeding mainly on acacia and other trees, which it readily climbs. An important part of the koppie food chain, hyraxes are the main dietary constituent of the mighty Verreaux's eagle that nest on the pinnacles, and are also taken by other raptors, as well as by leopards and smaller felids that take daytime refuge in the rocks, and the cobras and puff adders that live in the crevices between the giant granite slabs.

Fynbos

The coastal belt extending east from Cape Town is something of an ecological island thanks to its so-called Mediterranean climate, characterised by dry summers and rainy winters, a reversal of the trend elsewhere in southern Africa. The borders of this winter rainfall region coincide with – indeed, define – those of the smallest of the world's six floristic regions, which extends over a mere 90,000km^2 but supports at least 8,500 flowering plant species, two-thirds of which occur nowhere else on earth. As some measure of this region's extraordinary floral diversity, a greater number of indigenous plant species have been identified in the Cape of Good Hope sector of Table Mountain National Park than on the whole of the British Isles.

The region's predominant vegetation is a low, heath-like ground cover known as fynbos (fine bush), which can appear rather drab at first glance, but on closer inspection reveals a rich sprinkling of subtle pastel hues that explode into flamboyant colour during the spring wildflower season.

Fynbos endemics

The three most common fynbos families are the striking winter-flowering Proteaceae (including the King protea *Protea cynaroides*, the national flower), the heath-like Ericaceae and the reedy Restionaceae. High levels of endemism are noted among the region's invertebrates and cold-blooded vertebrates, and eight bird species are more or less unique to fynbos habitats, including the emblematic Cape sugarbird, whose long, curved bill is designed to drink protea nectar. Mammals that are largely endemic to fynbos habitats include the tiny Cape grysbok and the handsome bontebok, as well as the extinct bluebuck.

(AVZ)

Artificial habitats

A significant proportion of South Africa supports manmade habitats, from reservoirs and plantations to urban settlements and farmland. This isn't always bad news for wildlife. Johannesburg, for instance, is officially listed as the world's largest manmade forest, comprising an estimated

Zoo Lake, Johannesburg (SS)

10 million exotic and indigenous trees that collectively attract a far greater variety of small creatures than would ever have inhabited the area's natural cover of open grassland. Indeed, the leafier suburbs of this vast city must rank as one of the country's most rewarding areas for birdwatching. Likewise, artificial reservoirs create fresh habitats for aquatic creatures, urban settlements often sustain high densities of scavenging birds, and disturbed agricultural land is ideal for certain seedeaters and finches.

But let's not get carried away, these examples are very much the exception since all artificial habitats are created at the expense of an indigenous one: what used to be moist savanna is now cultivated monoculture, what used to be indigenous forest is now sterile plantation, what used to be an aloe-clumped grassy slope is now a subsistence farm. And while the arid regions of western South Africa are less overtly affected by human activity than their moister eastern counterparts, many are eroded or denuded by the overgrazing of livestock.

A related and more insidious threat to the ecological integrity of any given ecosystem is the inadvertent spread of exotics (ie: species that don't occur there naturally). These might sometimes be animals, such as the Indian mynas and house sparrows that breed profusely in an ever-increasing number of urban centres. More often, however, they are plants introduced deliberately for cropping, plantation or hedging purposes. Most such plants are poorly adapted to local conditions and cannot survive long or propagate without human intervention, but a small proportion will find local conditions to their liking, and these adaptable aliens – referred to as invasive species – often spread like the proverbial wildfire because here they aren't controlled by the natural enemies in their country of origin.

The spread of invasive exotics and associated loss of biodiversity has become a major global concern over the past century. And while South Africa is less compromised than much of the world in this respect (which is why so much wildlife still remains) it is no exception. Of an estimated 8,000 alien plant species planted here since the arrival of European settlers, at least 160 are regarded as invasive, and collectively they cover an estimated 100 million hectares, or 8% of the country's surface area. Worryingly, the most heavily affected province, with an invader cover estimated at 30%, is the Western Cape, where the unique fynbos and succulent habitats account for the majority of South Africa's 16,000-plus endemic plant species.

Wildlife

Like many African countries, South Africa is renowned for its diverse and prolific wildlife, which is protected in a network of around 500 conservation areas, ranging from vast national parks such as Kruger or Kgalagadi to smaller local reserves protecting niche habitats such as pockets of indigenous forest, mangroves and freshwater marshes. The most important and popular of these individual reserves are covered in the main regional body of this guidebook, but the following section provides an overview of what you are likely to see where, focusing mainly on the larger mammals central to the safari experience, but also providing a brief introduction to the region's extraordinary avifauna (which includes more endemic species than any other African country), as well as its reptiles and amphibians.

Cats

For most visitors to Africa, the success of a safari will rest largely on the quality of big cat encounters. Stealthy, secretive and inscrutable, the cats of the family Felidae are the most efficient of mammalian killers, the most strictly carnivorous, and they exude a singular fascination that might well be explained by the probability that our ancestors expended a great deal of time and effort in keeping out of their way.

The guaranteed showstopper on any first safari, the **lion** *Panthera leo* is Africa's largest terrestrial predator, weighing up to 220kg, and is present in several South African parks and reserves, notably the Greater Kruger, which hosts a population estimated between 1,500 and 2,000. The most sociable and least secretive of the world's 36 cats species, the lion typically lives in prides of up to 15 individuals, and is

Lions are a highlight on any safari. (AVZ)

unusual among felids in that it seldom takes to trees, and a fully grown male sports a regal mane. It is mainly a nocturnal hunter, favouring large or medium antelope such as wildebeest and impala, though giraffe and buffalo are also taken by larger prides. Most of the hunting is undertaken collaboratively by females, but dominant males normally feed first after a kill. Rivalry between males is intense and takeover battles are frequently fought to the death, so two or more males often form a coalition. When not feeding or fighting, lions are profoundly indolent creatures, spending up to 23 hours of any given day at rest. Your best chance of seeing action or interaction in is the cool of the early morning.

For more experienced safari-goers, the most prized carnivore is probably the **leopard** *Panthera pardus*, a powerful and stealthy black-on-gold spotted cat that can often get to within metres of its prey before it pounces, and habitually stores its kill in a tree to keep it from hyenas and lions. Its adaptability and intensely furtive nature has made the leopard the most successful of the big cats in modern Africa; it occurs in all habitats, favouring areas with plenty of cover such as riverine woodland and rocky slopes, and often lives in close proximity to humans for years without being detected. As might be expected, sightings are infrequent, the one exception being the Greater Kruger – indeed, the Sabi Sand cluster of reserves bordering the south-central Kruger is easily the best destination in Africa for viewing these normally elusive creatures.

Superficially similar to the leopard, the **cheetah** *Acinonyx jubatus* is the world's fastest land animal, attaining speeds up to 110km/h in short bursts. A diurnal hunter of the open plains, it can be distinguished from the thicket-loving leopard by its simple (as opposed to rosette) spots, streamlined, greyhound-like build, disproportionately small head and diagnostic black 'tear marks' below the eyes. Within South Africa, the most important cheetah stronghold is the Greater Kruger, where the population of 200 is centred on the plains around Satara and solitary adults or small family groups may be seen pacing restlessly across the plains, often stopping to survey the surrounds from a termite mound or fallen tree. The most reliable place in which to find cheetah, however, is the Phinda Resource Reserve, which supports a dense and very habituated population.

The serval is one of four smaller cat species found in South Africa. (AVZ)

Four smaller species of cat are present in South Africa. All are more widespread than the big cats, and are still well distributed outside reserves, but none is seen with much regularity on safari. The **serval** *Felis serval* has a similar build to a cheetah, with black-on-gold spots giving way to heavy streaking near the head, but its distribution is limited to areas northwest of Lesotho, where it favours moist grassland and riverine habitats. Present throughout the country but generally associated with more arid habitats, the **caracal** *Felis caracal* strongly resembles the European lynx with its uniform tan coat and tufted ears.

Similar in size and appearance to a household tabby, the widespread **African wild cat** *Felis sylvestris* is in fact ancestral to the domestic cat, with which it frequently interbreeds, causing some concern as to its long-term genetic integrity. Even smaller is the **black-footed cat** *Felis nigripes*, a southern African endemic, listed as vulnerable by the IUCN, with a black-spotted sandy coat. It is associated with sandy, semi-arid habitats where it is seldom seen, a result of its furtiveness as much as its scarcity.

Other carnivores

Africa's second-largest carnivore, weighing around 70kg, the blotched brown **spotted hyena** *Crocuta crocuta*, is highly conspicuous in several reserves, including the Greater Kruger, where it is particularly common around Skukuza and in the Sabi Sands region. It is a highly sociable creature, living in loosely structured matriarchal clans, and safari-goers who stand vigil outside a den entrance will often be rewarded with fascinating interaction and other behaviour. The smaller and more secretive **brown hyena** *Hyaena brunnea*, dark brown with lightly streaked legs and a paler mane, is a southern African dry-country endemic that's most easily seen in Madikwe Game Reserve but also occurs in Kgalagadi, Pilanesberg and Augrabies Falls. Both species have a characteristic sloping back, powerful jaws and a dog-like expression. Contrary to popular myth, hyenas are not exclusively scavengers – the spotted hyena in particular is an adept hunter capable of killing an animal as large as a wildebeest – while ancient charges of hermaphroditism stem from the false scrotum and penis covering the female's vagina. Much smaller than either of the above, the **aardwolf** *Proteles cristatus* is a striped insectivorous hyena associated mainly with dry-country habitats, but seldom seem.

The endangered African hunting dog can be found in Greater Kruger. (AVZ)

The **African hunting dog** *Lycaon pictus*, also known as the hunting or painted dog, is South Africa's largest canid, with a distinctively cryptic black, brown and cream coat. Formerly abundant in much of sub-Saharan Africa, but now reduced to an estimated 5,000 individuals in the wild, it is listed as 'Endangered' throughout its range, partly due to its susceptibility to diseases spread by domestic dogs, and partly as a result of human persecution. South Africa is an important stronghold for this highly sociable creature, with an estimated population of 400 in Greater Kruger boosted by small numbers in the Madikwe and Hluhluwe-Imfolozi game reserves.

The most common wild canid in South Africa is the **black-backed jackal** *Canis mesomelas*, an adaptable and opportunistic feeder with an ochre coat and prominent black saddle flecked by a varying amount of white or gold. It is still widespread outside protected areas and is often not particularly shy – indeed its yelping call is a characteristic sound of rural South Africa, where it is frequently persecuted by stock farmers. Also present in parts of the Kruger is the **side-striped jackal** *Canis adustus*, which has an indistinct pale vertical stripe on each flank and a white-tipped tail.

The region's only true fox, the **Cape fox** *Vulpes Chama* is a secretive species whose range extends from southern Angola to the Western Cape, where its presence is most often detected by its exclamatory nocturnal yapping. Its overall coloration is rather jackal-like, but the long, bushy tail precludes confusion with any other canid in the region. The loosely related **bat eared fox** *Otocyon megalotis*, a small, silver-grey insectivorous canid of arid country, is common in Kgalagadi and elsewhere in the Northern Cape, and is rendered unmistakable by its huge ears and black eye mask.

The most conspicuous of South Africa's small nocturnal carnivores are the **small spotted genet** *Genetta genetta* and **large spotted genet** *G. tigrina*, slender and rather feline creatures whose grey to gold brown coats are marked with black spots. Often seen on night drives, sometimes scavenging around lodges after dark, genets can be distinguished from all other carnivores by their exceptionally long, ringed tails. The colour of the tail tip (black for large-spotted, white for small-spotted) is the most reliable way to tell the two species apart. The related **African civet** *Civettictis civetta* is bulkier, shaggier and most likely to be seen along roads after dark, moving deliberately as it sniffs the ground.

Several species of mongoose occur in South Africa. Best known is the peculiar but endearing **meerkat** or **suricate** *Suricata suricata*,

Yellow mongoose, Kgalagadi Transfrontier Park (AVZ)

a southwest African endemic, most easily seen in Kgalagadi. It lives underground in close-knit gangs of 20 individuals and has unique monkey-like fingers with long claws used for digging, grooming and foraging, and often stands sentry on its hind legs, particularly when disturbed. Also endemic to southwest Africa, and common in Kgalagadi, is the **yellow mongoose** *Cynictis pencillata* that has a bushy orange-yellow coat and favours sandy environments, where it lives in sprawling burrows with dozens of entrance holes.

The **dwarf mongoose** *Helogate parvula* is a diminutive and highly sociable light-brown mongoose often seen in the vicinity of the termite mounds where it dens. The larger and equally sociable **banded mongoose** *Mungos mungo*, uniform dark brown except for a dozen black stripes across its back, is a diurnal species associated with most wooded habitats. Also quite common is the **slender mongoose** *Herpestes sanguineus*, with its diagnostic black tail tip, and the nocturnal **white tailed ichneumon** *Ichneumia albicauda*, which is easily distinguished by its bulk, solitary habits and bushy white tail.

The dwarf mongoose makes its den in termite mounds. (AVZ)

The widespread but seldom observed **ratel** or **honey badger** *Mellivora capensis* is a large, black mustelid with a puppyish face and grey-white back. It is an opportunistic feeder best known for its symbiotic relationship with a bird called the greater honeyguide, which leads the ratel to a bee hive, waits for it to tear it open, and then feeds on the scraps. Several other mustelids occur in the region, including the **striped polecat** *Ictonyx striatus*, a common but rarely seen nocturnal creature with black underparts and a bushy white back, and the similar but much scarcer **striped weasel** *Poecilogale albincha*. The **Cape clawless otter** *Aonyx capensis* is a brown freshwater mustelid with a white collar, while the smaller **spotted necked otter** *Lutra maculicollis* is darker with light white spots on its throat.

Primates

Dominated by savanna habitats, South Africa lacks the primate diversity associated with equatorial Africa and only three diurnal and two nocturnal species are present. The most imposing of these, weighing up to 45kg, is the **Chacma baboon** *Papio Ursinus*, which is easily distinguished from other primates by its far greater bulk, inverted

Chacma baboon (AVZ)

'U'-shaped tail, and distinctive, dog-like head. Omnivorous and highly intelligent, baboons live in large troops whose complex social structure is dominated by rigid matriarchal lineages, and they are usually very entertaining to watch, whether it's youngsters trying to climb, adults bickering or females grooming. They are still quite common outside the reserves and are frequently seen on the roadside in the uKhahlamba-Drakensberg area and the Cape Peninsula, where animals used to being fed by people frequently become dangerously habituated and have to be shot.

Equally sociable but far smaller, the **vervet monkey** *Chlorocebus aethiops* is probably the world's most numerous primate (aside from humans). It inhabits savanna and woodland, spending a high proportion of its time on the ground, and its light-grey coat, black face and white forehead band are diagnostic – as are the male's admirably gaudy blue genitals. The **Samango** or **blue monkey** *Cercopithecus mitis*, Africa's most widespread forest primate, occurs in suitably forested habitats in the eastern part of the country. It is common along the KwaZulu-Natal coast and in the far north of the Kruger National Park.

The **lesser bushbaby** *Galago senegalensis* is the most widespread and common of the country's prosimians, a group of diminutive nocturnal primates related to the lemurs of Madagascar. More often heard than seen, the lesser bushbaby is very common in savanna habitats, and can sometimes be picked out by tracing a cry to a tree and shining a torch into its eyes. The much larger **greater bushbaby** *G. crassicaudatus* occurs alongside it in several areas of South Africa, and is recognised by the terrifying scream it produces.

Buffalo and antelopes

The widespread **Cape buffalo** *Syncerus caffer*, closely related to the similar-looking Indian water buffalo, is Africa's only wild ox and most powerful bovid, weighing up to 800kg. Its imposing bulk ensures it has few natural enemies, though it is regularly preyed upon by lions in some areas, with the hunters occasionally coming off second best. Buffalo can adapt to most habitats, provided they are close to a reliable water source. Mixed-sex herds of 30–50 animals are typical, but older males often roam around in smaller bachelor groups, and herds of more than 1,000 are sometimes encountered in northern Kruger – their main stronghold – which supports some 35,000 individuals. Cape buffalo are also present in Addo Elephant National Park, the Pilanesberg and Hluhluwe-Imfolozi.

Cape buffalo and red-billed oxpecker (AVZ)

Africa's most diverse group of bovids, the antelopes are an unwavering feature of the South African landscape, thriving in every habitat from rainforest to desert, except where they have been eliminated by human activity. Several of the region's most striking species belong to the tribe Tragelaphini (spiral-horned antelopes), among them the **common eland** *Taurotragus oryx*, the world's largest antelope, which stands up to 180cm tall and can weigh more than 900kg. It is light tan-brown with faint white vertical stripes, and a bovine appearance accentuated by its short horns and large dewlap. Thinly but widely distributed, it is rare in the Greater Kruger and more common in Kgalagadi and the Pilanesberg, with the uKhahlamba-Drakensberg (in particular Giant's Castle) being an important stronghold.

Second in stature only to the eland, the magnificent **greater kudu** *Tragelaphus strepsiceros* has a grey-brown coat and up to ten vertical white stripes on each flank. It is most notable, however, for the statuesque male's double-spiralled horns, which can grow to be 1.4m long. An accomplished jumper, it can clear fences twice its shoulder height, which is one reason why it is the most common large antelope in many unprotected parts of South Africa. Small family parties are often seen in dense woodland along watercourses in the Greater Kruger and most other reserves.

Related to the kudus, the widespread **bushbuck** *T. scriptus* is an endearingly Bambi-like, medium-sized antelope that might occur in any non-arid habitat, and is still quite common in suitably wooded spots outside of protected areas. Very attractive, the male is dark brown or chestnut, while the much smaller female is generally pale reddish-brown and both sexes are marked with white spots and sometimes stripes.

A gemsbok's horns can grow up to over a metre long. (AVZ)

Intermediate in size to the greater kudu and bushbuck, the male **nyala** *T. Angasii* is a spectacular, dark chestnut-grey antelope with a grey-black leonine mane, light white stripes, yellow leg stockings and handsome, lyre-shaped horns that can grow to 80cm. Endemic to the eastern coastal belt of southern Africa, the nyala is strongly associated with the Zululand reserves of northern KwaZulu-Natal, where the population of 25,000 animals represents 70% of the global total. It also inhabits riparian forest along the Luvuvhu, Limpopo and Sabi rivers in the Kruger National Park.

The **gemsbok** or **oryx** *Oryx gazella* is a powerfully built, ash-grey antelope that stands 120cm high at the shoulder and has striking straight horns that grow to more than a metre in length, sweeping backwards at the same angle as the forehead and muzzle. Associated with arid environments, it can go without water for almost as long as a camel, obtaining all its needs from the plants it eats, and its body temperature can rise to as high as 45°C without the animal perspiring. Oryx are found in most protected areas in the northwest of the country and are especially common in Kgalagadi Transfrontier Park. Built to similar proportions, the **sable antelope** *Hippotragus niger* and **roan antelope** *H. equinus* both have restricted ranges in South Africa, the former being thinly distributed in the Kruger National Park and present in a few provincial reserves, while the latter is most likely to be seen in the Letaba area of Kruger.

Common in the Kruger and many other reserves, the **blue wildebeest** *Connochaetes taurinus* looks a bit like a buffalo from a distance (*wildebeest* is Afrikaans/Dutch for 'wild ox'), but its slighter build,

Black wildebeest, Mountain Zebra National Park (AVZ)

lighter coat and shaggy beard preclude confusion at close quarters. The **black wildebeest** *Connochaetes gnou*, darker and with a distinctive white tail, is a South African highveld grassland endemic that was hunted close to extinction in the 19th century and can now be found semi-domesticated in a few minor reserves. The related **red hartebeest** *Alcelaphus buselaphus*, associated mainly with the dry northwest of the country, is similar in height but more lightly built, with a yellow-red coat, heart-shaped horns (for which it is named), and an elongated face that gives it a somewhat morose demeanour. The **tsessebe** *Damaliscus lunatus*, reputedly the fastest of all antelope, is a darker, glossier and more handsome variation on the same body plan.

Endemic to South Africa and interbreeding freely where their ranges overlap, the **bontebok** *Damaliscus pygargus pygargus* and **blesbok** *D. p. phillipsi* are small, dark-brown hartebeests with white faces and legs. Regularly found in the fynbos of the Western Cape, the handsome bontebok was hunted near to extinction, and only 100 individuals remained in the wild prior to the creation of the eponymous national park near Swellendam in the 1930s. It has since been reintroduced to several of the conservation areas, including the Cape of Good Hope sector of Table Mountain National Park. The blesbok, a grazer of *highveld* grassland, is a widespread but now generally semi-domesticated resident of farms in the centre of the country.

The only gazelle found in South Africa is the **springbok** *Antidorcas marsupialis*, which strongly resembles the East African 'Tommy' with its fawn upper parts and cream belly separated by a black side stripe. It is the national antelope of South Africa and named for its habit of pronking (jumping to demonstrate fitness) when predators are in the vicinity. Despite its iconic status, the springbok is not as abundant as it was in the 18th century, when immense migrant herds were recorded in the Karoo. It is quite common in the Northern Cape, but naturally absent from the Kruger and other eastern reserves, where instead the superficially similar and highly gregarious **impala** *Aepyceros melampus* is found. A slender, medium-sized antelope with a chestnut coat that displays diagnostic black-and-white rump stripes, the impala is very common in many savanna reserves and the Kruger population alone exceeds 1,000,000.

The bontebok was pulled back from the brink of extinction after a successful reintroduction programme. (AVZ)

The grizzle-grey **klipspringer** *Oreotragus oreotragus* is almost exclusively associated with mountains and rocky slopes (its name is Afrikaans for 'rock jumper') and is commonly found in suitable parts of the Northern and Western Cape, as well as the uKhahlamba-Drakensberg. It boasts several unusual adaptations to this habitat, notably the unique capacity to walk on its hoof tips, coarse but hollow fur providing good insulation at high altitude, and binocular vision (a feature more normally associated with carnivores than herbivores) to help it gauge jumping distances accurately.

The **common waterbuck** *Kobus ellipsiprymnus*, one of the most visible species in the Kruger, has a shoulder height of up to 135cm and is easily recognised by its shaggy, grey-brown coat, pale rump, and the male's large, lyre-shaped horns. By contrast, the reedbuck are lightly built grassland dwellers with few distinguishing features: the **common reedbuck** *Redunca arundinua* is exceptionally common in parts of the iSimangaliso Wetland Park, while the chunkier and greyer **mountain reedbuck** *R. fulvorufula* is commonest in uKhahlamba-Drakensberg. The latter might be confused with the **grey rhebok** *Pelea capreolus*, a superficially similar but taxonomically enigmatic South African endemic with a woolly grey coat, distinctive, elongated, hare-like ears and several goat-like adaptations. Around 20% of the global grey rhebok population lives in the uKhahlamba-Drakensberg, and it is the second most commonly depicted animal, after the eland, in the park's ancient rock art.

The smaller **oribi** *Ourebia ourebi*, a localised grassland antelope with a sandycoatandadiagnosticblackglandular patch below the ears, is most common in the grassy southern uKhahlamba-Drakensberg foothills around Kokstad. The **Cape grysbok** *Raphicerus Malanotus* can be distinguished from other small antelope by its chunky build, tail-less appearance, and the combination of a flecked russet coat and white eye circle. It is endemic to fynbos and other thicket habitats in the Western Cape, and is reasonably common in suitable habitats such as Table Mountain National Park, De Hoop Nature Reserve and the Cederberg Mountains.

The grey rhebok can easily be mistaken for the similar-looking mountain reedbuck. (AVZ)

Smaller still, the **steenbok** *Raphicerus campestris* and **grey duiker** *Sylvicapra grimmia* are both rather plain, grey-brown antelope of wooded savanna habitats, with the latter being distinguished by the black strip running down its snout. The aptly named **red duiker** *Cephalophus natalensis* and **blue duiker** *C. Philantomba* are both secretive, slope-backed creatures found in eastern forests and coastal thickets. Also confined to well-wooded habitats in the subtropical eastern coastal belt are the tiny, rabbit-eared, tail-flicking **suni** *Neotragus moschatus* and fleck-coated, rump-raising **Sharpe's grysbok** *Raphicerus sharpei*.

Other large herbivores

The world's largest land animal, the **African elephant** *Loxodonta africana* (shoulder height 2.3–3.4m; weight up to 6,000kg) is intelligent, sociable and infinitely engaging, but also somewhat intimidating on account of its immense bulk, fierce trumpeting call and unpredictable temperament. Like humans, elephants are one of the few mammals capable of modifying their environment, and their habit of uprooting trees can cause serious deforestation and environmental degradation when populations are concentrated in restricted conservation areas. Elephants have two unique modifications in the form of a trunk and tusks, both of which have multiple uses. Female elephants live in close-knit clans in which the eldest member plays matriarch over her sisters, daughters and granddaughters, and mother–daughter bonds may last for up to 50 years. Males generally leave their birth group at around 12 years of age to roam singly or form bachelor herds. The African elephant is widespread and common in habitats ranging from desert to rainforest, though within South Africa it is all but restricted to the larger protected area in the east. The Kruger supports the country's largest population of African elephants, now estimated at more than 13,000, though some ecologists believe that culling or relocation will be required to protect the environment from this pachydermal overload. Elephants are also easy to see in Addo, Hluhluwe-Imfolozi, Pilanesberg and Madikwe among others.

The 'critically endangered' **black rhinoceros** *Diceros bicornis* (shoulder height 160cm; weight 1,000kg) is the more widespread of Africa's two rhino species, and was poached to extinction in most of its former range in the 1980s but since then numbers have recovered slightly. South Africa supports at least half the global population of black rhinoceros, with the best places to look for it being the southern Kruger and Hluhluwe-Imfolozi, but it's generally quite secretive and difficult to spot. South Africa is an even more important stronghold for the bulkier **white rhinoceros** *Ceratotherium simum*, supporting more than 90% of the global population of 20,000, more than half of which are centred on the Kruger, with most of the rest spread across the Zululand reserves. There is, incidentally, no colour difference between the two species: the misnomer 'white' derives from the Afrikaans weit (wide) and refers to its flattened mouth, an ideal shape for cropping grass. By contrast, the black rhino, a specialised browser, has a more rounded mouth and hooked upper lip.

The improbable-looking **giraffe** *Giraffa camelopardis* (shoulder height 2.5–3.5m; weight 1,000–1,400kg) is the world's tallest and longest-necked land animal, standing up to 5.5m high when fully grown.

White rhino (MS/D)

Quite unmistakable in appearance, it lives in loosely structured herds of up to 15 individuals and indulges in limited interaction, though the aggressive necking behaviour of males can be terrifying to watch. The giraffe is very common in southern Kruger and also in areas such as Hluhluwe-Imfolozi, Pilanesberg and Madikwe.

The **plains zebra** *Equus burchelli* (shoulder height 1.3m; weight 300–340kg), also sometimes referred to as Burchell's zebra, is a charismatic striped equid that ranges throughout most of East and southern Africa, where it is often seen in large herds alongside wildebeest. The southern race, distinguished by the paler 'shadow stripes' between the darker main stripes, is common in most savanna reserves in South Africa, especially the Kruger. Endemic to southern Africa, the **mountain zebra** *E. zebra* lacks shadow

Southern giraffes, Kruger National Park (AVZ)

striping and has a chestnut-tinged snout. Two races are identified: Hartmann's mountain zebra is centred on Namibia but a small number inhabit the extreme Northern Cape, while the Cape Mountain zebra is restricted to the Eastern and Western Cape. One-third of the global population of 750 Cape Mountain zebra lives in the eponymous national park, which was founded in the 1950s when fewer than 10 individuals remained and, like the closely related quagga, a dark-rumped zebra of the Western Cape, extinction beckoned.

There are only 750 Cape mountain zebra left in the world. (AVZ)

The **common hippopotamus** *Hippopotamus amphibious* (shoulder height 1.5m; weight 2,000kg) is the most characteristic large mammal of South Africa's rivers and lakes, where it remains common in protected areas, but is virtually extinct outside them. A bulky and lumbering animal, it spends most of the day submerged, but often ranges over long distances on land at night in search of food. Strongly territorial, herds of ten or more animals are presided over by a dominant male who will readily defend his patriarchy to the death. Hippos are likely to be seen in most large national parks and reserves with suitable habitats, and a pair is currently resident in Rondevlei Nature Sanctuary on the outskirts of Cape Town.

Africa's only diurnal swine, the **warthog** *Phacochoreus africanus* (shoulder height 60–70cm; weight 100kg) is a widespread and often conspicuously abundant resident of South Africa's savanna reserves. It has a grey coat with a thin covering of hairs, wart like bumps on its face, rather large, upward-curving tusks, and a habit of trotting off with its tail raised stiffly in the air. This last trait alone distinguishes it from the bulkier, hairier and browner **bushpig** *Potomochoerus larvatus*, which is possibly more widespread and common than the warthog, but infrequently seen due in most part to its nocturnal habits and preference for dense vegetation.

With the appearance of an oversized guinea pig but more closely related to elephants than rodents, hyraxes (shoulder height 35–30cm; weight 4kg) are often seen sunning themselves in rocky habitats and can become tame when used to people, as is the case at several lodges. The most commonly seen species is the diurnal **rock hyrax** *Procavia* *capensis*, but the nocturnal **tree hyrax** *Dendrohyrax arboreus* occurs in certain forested habitats, announcing its presence with an unforgettable banshee wail of a call. Like hyraxes, the **elephant-shrews** are a unique group of small, rodent-like mammals that hop like miniature kangaroos and have absurdly elongated and perpetually twitching noses. They are present but seldom seen in the Kruger National Park, as well as other *bushveld* reserves.

Surely the oddest of all African mammals, the **aardvark** *Orycteropus afer* is an exclusive insectivore that looks like a cross between a domestic pig, an anteater and a kangaroo. Widespread but strictly nocturnal and very seldom seen, one individual can snaffle up to 50,000 termites in one night with its long, sticky tongue. Not so much similar to the aardvark as equally dissimilar to anything else, the **ground pangolin** *Manis temmincki* is an unobtrusive and seldom observed nocturnal insectivore whose distinctive, scaled armour plating bears a superficial resemblance to the American armadillos, but this is probably a case of convergent evolution. Sightings are an extremely rare event.

Striped ground squirrel, Kgalagadi Transfrontier Park (AVZ)

As many as 80% of South African mammal species are bats or rodents of little interest to non-specialist safari-goers. One exception is the **Cape porcupine** *Hystrix africaeaustralis*, which ranks among the largest of rodents, weighing up to 27kg. It is covered in long, black-and-white quills that protect it from predators, and occasionally betrays its presence by rattling as it walks. Another large and seldom-seen nocturnal oddity, the **springhare** *Pedetes capensis* is a rodent rather than a type of rabbit, whose distinctive, kangaroo-like mode of locomotion means it is most often located when the spotlights pick out a pair of eyes bouncing up and down. South Africa also supports a diversity of squirrels, most commonly the **African bush squirrel** *Paraxerus cepapi*. Also likely to be seen on safari is the endearing **striped ground squirrel** *Xerus inaurus*, a terrestrial dry-country creature with a grey-brown coat and prominent white eye-ring.

Birds

South Africa is one of the world's top ornithological destinations. True, by African standards, a total checklist of 850 indigenous species isn't all that impressive, but this is amply compensated for by the relative ease of birding (both in terms of access to key areas and availability of birding tools such as field guides and CDs of common calls, see page 289) and the unusually high level of endemism. Indeed, a total of 31 species are found nowhere

Southern yellow-billed hornbill (AVZ)

else in the world, the highest number of any country in Africa, and that is without including a similar number of species that are near-endemic with ranges that extend only into the kingdoms of Lesotho or Swaziland (neither of which are commonly visited except as an extension of a trip to South Africa), or parts of Namibia and Botswana. Any good field guide to southern Africa will highlight these endemics, but it is worth noting for planning purposes that the key areas for visitors seeking these localised species are the fynbos of the Western Cape, the Karoo and uKhahlamba-Drakensberg/Lesotho border area.

For safari-goers seeking an introduction to Africa's more common birds, the Kruger National Park forms an excellent starting point, with the likes of lilac-breasted roller, yellow-billed hornbill, white-fronted bee-eater and African fish eagle drawing the eye of the unconverted. The dedicated birder could expect to tick 100 species in a day here, particularly in summer, and more than 200 over the course of a week's stay. The iSimangaliso Wetland Park and other Zululand reserves are also superb for birds, with water-associated species especially well represented. Another firm favourite, hosting several dry-country specials and a wealth of raptors, is the Kgalagadi Transfrontier Park. The best birding close to Johannesburg is in the Pilanesberg Game Reserve.

White-fronted bee-eater (AVZ)

Seasonal birdwatching

South Africa offers excellent birdwatching throughout the year, but the prime season runs from September to April, when resident populations are boosted by Palaearctic migrants, refugees from the northern hemisphere winter. It's been estimated that as many as six billion individual birds undertake this trans-Sahara migration annually, ranging from the diminutive willow warbler and chiffchaff to the somewhat bulkier white stork, along with innumerable flocks of European (barn) swallows and various waders, wagtails, raptors and waterfowl. The European winter also coincides with South Africa's rainy season, when several resident Ploceids (weavers and allies) undergo a startling, 'ugly duckling'-style transformation, shedding their drab eclipse plumage in favour of bright yellow, black and red breeding colours.

Reptiles and amphibians

Reptiles receive a lot of bad press, not entirely without foundation in the case of crocodiles and certain venomous snakes, but most of South Africa's 300 species pose no threat to humans. Furthermore, the ecological value of reptiles cannot be overstated. A healthy snake population plays a vital role in preventing plague-like outbreaks of rats and other fast-breeding rodents, while the geckos that skid around the walls of Kruger rest camps do much to control mosquito numbers, and crocodiles play a vulture-like role in devouring the carrion that might otherwise clog up lakes and rivers. At least 80 reptile species are endemic to South Africa.

Africa's bulkiest and longest-lived predator is the **Nile crocodile**, which weighs up to 1,000kg and has a lifespan similar to humans. Crocodiles have inhabited the lakes and rivers of Africa for 150 million years, and they are more closely related to dinosaurs than to any living

Beware of Nile crocodiles when taking a swim in a river or lake. (AVZ)

Namaqualand tent tortoise (AVZ)

creature. In South Africa, they have been exterminated from most unprotected freshwater habitats, but can still be seen basking toothily on sandbanks in the Kruger National Park and Hluhluwe-Imfolozi, although iSimangaliso probably harbours the country's densest population. River-dwelling crocodiles are said to be responsible for more attacks on humans than their lake-dwelling counterparts, but bathing in any lake or river is risky and it is best to seek local advice before jumping in.

Terrapins and **turtles** are well represented in South Africa. Most visible is the **leopard tortoise**, which weighs up to 40kg, has a mottled gold-and-black shell, and is often seen motoring in the slow lane of game reserve roads. Flatter and plainer brown than terrestrial tortoises, terrapins occur in freshwater habitats and are often seen sunning on partially submerged rocks or logs, or peering out from roadside puddles, particularly in the Kruger National Park.

The most numerous and conspicuous reptiles are **lizards**. The hefty **Nile monitor**, attaining a length of up to 3m, is common in aquatic habitats and is sometimes mistaken for a small crocodile. **Agama lizards** are typically 20-30cm long and have bright blue, purple, orange or red scaling, with the flattened head generally a different colour from the torso. The most diverse lizard family is the **gecko**, whose unique, adhesive toes enable them to run upside down on smooth surfaces – look out for the common house gecko, an endearing, bug-eyed, translucent white lizard that scampers up lodge walls in pursuit of insects attracted to the lights.

The most charismatic of lizards, **chameleons** are known for their abrupt colour changes (a trait that's been exaggerated in popular literature), but are no less remarkable for their protuberant eyes, which offer 180° vision and swivel independently of each other, and for the sticky, body-length tongue they unleash in a blink-and-you'll-miss-it lunge at a selected item of prey. The flap-necked chameleon is the most common savanna and woodland species, but ten species of dwarf chameleon, most very localised, are endemic to South Africa.

Snakes are common but secretive. Of the 150 known species in South Africa, fewer than 10% are on record as having caused a human fatality, and even these normally slither away unseen by approaching humans. The **rock python** is Africa's largest snake at up to 5-6m, and kills its prey by strangulation, wrapping its muscular body around its prey. The **puff adder**, a thickset resident of savanna and rocky habitats, is rightly considered the most dangerous of the region's venomous snakes, not because it is especially aggressive but because its sluggish disposition means it is more often disturbed than other species. Other dangerous snakes include the **cobras** and **mambas**, while the **boomslang** – in theory the most toxic of Africa's snakes – is back-fanged and very non-aggressive, for which reason the only fatalities recorded have been snake handlers.

South Africa harbours around 100 frog species, most nocturnal, and almost half endemic to the country. Male frogs attract potential partners with mating calls, which are unique to each species and often provide the most reliable clue to identification. Calling is most vigorous after rain, when safari-goers are often treated to an unforgettable evening medley of guttural croaks and ethereal whistles. The region's largest frog is the **African bullfrog**, which weighs up to 1kg and is generally associated with seasonal pools in the western half of the country. Small and distinctively patterned, the diverse '**tree frogs**' have long, broad-tipped toes adapted for climbing, and are associated with forest, woodland and reedy habitats. One of the region's most wondrous sounds is the ethereal popping chorus of the **bubbling kassina**, a 'tree frog' of marshes and moist grassland that is most vocal from November–March, especially after rain.

The flap-necked chameleon is the most common chameleon species in South Africa. (AVZ)

Marine wildlife

Boasting a 2,800km coastline divided between the warm Indian Ocean and the cooler Atlantic, South Africa supports a rich marine fauna. The coral and other areas offshore from KwaZulu-Natal are especially popular with divers and snorkellers, whereas the Western Cape coast is famed for offering the world's best land-based whale-watching. The most common marine mammal in the country is the **Cape fur seal**, which is often seen singly in harbours in the Western Cape, particular Kalk Bay and Lambert's Bay, as well as in Cape Town's Victoria & Alfred Waterfront. Island-bound breeding colonies of hundreds or even thousands of seals can be visited by boat from Hout Bay, Simon's Town and Mossel Bay.

Cape fur seal (S/D)

According to the IUCN Red List, some 42 cetacean (whale and dolphin) species have been recorded offshore from South Africa, and while many are confined to sub-Antarctic water, others are quite commonly seen close to shore. Most impressive are the **southern right whales** that gather in sheltered bays along the Western Cape coast between June and December – stunning views are regularly obtained from the whale-watching capital of Hermanus, or more occasionally from the east side of the Cape Peninsula. Elsewhere, there are good views of the larger **humpback whale** from the northern KwaZulu-Natal coast from June to October.

Common along the east and southern coast of South Africa, the **bottlenose dolphin** – named for its elongated upper and lower jaws, which create its characteristic smiling expression – is often seen playing in the surf or swimming in the wake of a boat. Associated with warm to temperate waters, the bottlenose is known for its friendly character and curiosity towards humans. It displays the only known use of tools by a marine mammal, as it sticks a marine sponge on its beak as protection when it forages in the sandy sea bottom. Also quite often seen off the east coast is the **spinner dolphin**, named for its occasional habit of pirouetting longitudinally when it leaps out of the water. On the Atlantic coastline, the endemic **Heaviside's dolphin** is particularly common in Lambert's Bay.

Southern right whales can be spotted off the Western Cape coast between June and December. (SS)

The northern KwaZulu-Natal coastline, protected by the iSimangaliso Wetland Park, is an important breeding site for marine **turtles**, representatives of conservative reptilian lineage that first appeared in the fossil record more than 100 million years ago and common to abundant until the late 19th century. Marine turtles have since suffered heavily from hunting (for food, skin and 'tortoiseshell'), accidental trapping, habitat destruction and pollution, so that all but one of the seven species worldwide is listed on the IUCN Red List. Five species are resident or regular visitors to the KwaZulu-Natal coast, but only two breed there: the soft-shelled **leatherback turtle**, the world's bulkiest marine reptile, measuring up to 3m long and weighing up to 900kg; and the smaller and more numerous **loggerhead turtles**, represented by about 500 breeding females in South Africa.

Among the cartilaginous fish most eagerly sought by divers are the **whale shark** (the world's largest fish) and the equally impressive **manta ray**, both harmless plankton eaters that occur in South African coastal waters. The region is also a stronghold for the legendarily aggressive **great white shark**, which can grow up to 8m long and is often seen during cage dives at selected sites in the Western Cape.

The Coelacanth – a living fossil

The oceanic waters off South Africa are home to the **coelacanth**, a peculiar 2m-long fish that was known only from fossils – and thought to have been extinct for more than 60 million years – prior to the discovery of the first living specimen near Port Elizabeth in 1938. Now considered to be the world's oldest surviving vertebrate species, the coelacanth also inhabits the underwater canyons carved into the continental shelf offshore from the Mozambique-South African border area, where the first documentary footage of these extraordinary 'living fossils' was captured in 2000.

3 Planning a Trip

Planning a trip to South Africa shouldn't be too daunting. This guide includes recommendations from some of the top safari operators, but a quick internet search will reveal any number of all-inclusive packages that range from large coach tours to bespoke self-drive visits, and pretty much everything in between. However, there are a number of factors that you might want to consider when investigating your options, settling on a suitable itinerary, and, as the trip draws closer, you start packing and preparing your paperwork. Among the most important of these are seasonal factors, with Cape Town being at its finest in the southern hemisphere summer and safari destinations such as the Kruger National Park generally offering the best wildlife viewing in the southern winter. Another useful planning feature is our selection of South Africa's Top 20 Attractions, which showcase the best of this varied country's cultural, scenic and wildlife highlights.

When to visit

Most of South Africa is warm and sunny for a large part of the year, and the country can be visited at any time. However, some seasonal factors are worth taking into consideration, bearing in mind that summer and winter are an inversion of the northern hemisphere, with winter falling between May and August and summer between October and March. One of the biggest local variables is rainfall, which splits the country into two distinct zones: a temperate, Mediterranean-like winter rainfall area comprising Cape Town and the Western Cape, and a warmer summer rainfall area that includes the rest of the country, where dramatic but short-lived afternoon thundershowers are typical.

Winter is the best time of year for wildlife spotting in Kruger National Park. (AVZ)

If game viewing is your top priority, then the time to be in South Africa is during the dry winter months, which offer the best conditions for spotting wildlife in the Kruger National Park, Sabi Sands and most other reserves. This is partly because the lack of temporary waterholes forces thirsty animals to concentrate along rivers and other perennial sources of drinking water, but it also helps greatly that the vegetation thins out, allowing far better visibility. Better still, the peak game viewing months of August and September are unpopular with foreign visitors so many private lodges offer substantial low-season discounts, and the vehicle traffic in public reserves such as Kruger is quite low (except during school holidays). If you visit at this time of year, you might want to think about concentrating any beach activities on the KwaZulu-Natal coast, which tends to be sweltering in midsummer but is often idyllic in winter.

By contrast, Cape Town is most climatically alluring in summer, though this is also the main tourist season and facilities can be very crowded. In winter the likelihood of a stay in Cape Town being dominated by rain is almost the same as the chance of fine weather, and the low tourist volumes (and cheaper hotel rates) arguably compensate. Another area that can be problematic in winter is the uKhahlamba-

Drakensberg, which gets very cold at night and where it often snows at higher altitudes. Scenically, most parts of the country are greenest and lushest in summer, while August and September is the best time to experience the spring wildflowers in Namaqualand. For birdwatchers, activity peaks October–May, when many Ploceids and other seasonally variable residents shed their drab eclipse plumage to emerge in full breeding colours, and avian variety is boosted by more than 100 species of Palaearctic and intra-African migrants.

Public holidays

The main effect of public holidays on tourists is that banks and offices will be closed, as will some shops. Generally, museums and other attractions with variable opening hours treat any public holidays as they would a Sunday, and many places close altogether on Christmas Day. When a public holiday falls on a Sunday, the Monday is normally taken as a holiday instead.

1 January	**New Year's Day**	9 August	**National Women's Day**
21 March	**Human Rights Day**	24 September	**Heritage Day**
27 April	**Freedom Day**	16 December	**Day of Reconciliation**
1 May	**Workers' Day**	25 December	**Christmas Day**
16 June	**Youth Day**	26 December	**Goodwill Day**

Movable dates: Good Friday, Family Day (Easter Monday)

Booking a trip

A choice that you will need to make when planning your trip is whether to book through a local ground operator or a tour agency at home. By using an agent in your home country you can plan an itinerary face to face, you may well get a cheaper flight to South Africa, payment is more straightforward, and (assuming the agent is bonded) you will have a significantly higher level of financial protection. Booking a package through an unbonded South African operator will usually be cheaper, but you will be less well protected in the event that something goes wrong and you will almost certainly need to buy additional travel insurance. However you book, the price of a safari is almost always inclusive of accommodation and/or camping gear, services of a vehicle and driver-guide, and all meals, park fees and pre-arranged activities – in short, everything except drinks, tips and other ad hoc purchases. It is, however, advisable to have this specified in advance.

Tour operators

Aardvark Safaris

📞 01980 849160 ✉ mail@ardvarksafaris.com
🖥 www.aardvarksafaris.co.uk (UK) & www.aardvarksafaris.com (USA)

Aardvark Safaris works with you to tailor-make your dream African holiday. With over 20 years' experience, we've slept in the beds, eaten the meals and walked with the guides. You can be confident that we have the expertise to fulfil all your holiday wishes. Offices in the UK and USA.

Bridge & Wickers

📞 020 7483 6555 ✉ southafrica@bridgeand
wickers.com 🖥 www.bridgeandwickers.co.uk

Some of our team have been exploring South Africa since apartheid ended. We have in-depth knowledge of all the iconic areas, plus little-known corners well off the beaten track. Our tailor-made holidays aim to surpass your expectations with genuine hospitality, superb safaris, stunning scenery and the related commitment to sustainable travel.

Imagine Africa

📞 020 7622 5114 ✉ info@imagineafrica.co.uk
🖥 www.imagineafrica.co.uk (UK) & www.imagineafrica.com (USA)

We pride ourselves on giving expert advice. We visit the lodges and hotels, have strong relationships with the owners and can give you the low-down behind the glossy images. Add competitive prices, award-winning service and financial protection and you're assured of an incredible holiday to Africa. US and UK offices.

Other UK-based operators

Africa Sky 🖥 www.africasky.co.uk. Bespoke holidays.
Audley 🖥 www.audleytravel.com. Tailor-made holidays.
Exodus 🖥 www.exodus.co.uk. Activity and adventure holidays.
Explore! 🖥 www.explore.co.uk. Small group adventures.
Journeys By Design 🖥 www.journeysbydesign.com. Luxury trips.
Naturetrek 🖥 www.naturetrek.co.uk. Expert-led wildlife trips.
Safari Consultants 🖥 www.safari-consultants.co.uk. Tailor-made safaris.
Steppes Travel 🖥 www.steppestravel.co.uk. Tailor-made holidays.
Tribes Travel 🖥 www.tribes.co.uk. Aims to offer inspiring trips.
Wildlife Worldwide 🖥 www.wildlifeworldwide.com. Custom-designed tours.

Rainbow Tours

☎ 020 7226 1004 ✉ info@rainbowtours.co.uk
🖰 www.rainbowtours.co.uk

From camping safaris and hidden gems to five-star luxury and urban chic, our honesty, enthusiasm and extensive firsthand experience has been recognised with four Best Tour Operator awards in the last seven years. With a decade of working collaboratively with our recommended lodges, local knowledge, service and value are our hallmarks.

The Zambezi Safari & Travel Company

☎ 0845 2930513 ✉ bradt@zambezi.com
🖰 www.zambezi.com

Zambezi specialises in arranging safaris along the course of the mighty Zambezi River and well beyond into the remotest corners of East, central and southern Africa. From authentic safaris to relaxing on pristine beaches, Zambezi serves adventurous spirits from all corners of the globe. Offices in the UK and the US.

To Escape To

☎ 0207 060 6747 ✉ escape@toescapeto.com
🖰 www.toescapeto.com

With offices in the UK and Cape Town, To Escape To offer the best of both worlds. A trusted UK company with eight years experience and ATOL bonding for your peace of mind, we offer local rates and first hand knowledge, enabling you to experience South Africa like a local.

Other US-based operators

Abercrombie & Kent 🖰 www.abercrombiekent.com High-end packages; also has UK-based offices.

African Travel 🖰 www.africantravelinc.com. South Africa packages.

Destinations and Adventures International 🖰 www.daitravel.com. Top-end custom-designed packages.

Explore Africa 🖰 www.exploreafrica.net. Customised packages. US and local offices.

Goway 🖰 www.go-way.com. Selection of South Africa holidays.

Micato Safaris 🖰 www.micato.com. Various South Africa packages available.

Natural Habitat Adventures 🖰 www.nathab.com. Focus on nature travel.

Your itinerary: 20 top attractions

The first step in planning an itinerary is deciding which places you absolutely must visit, perhaps starting with the brief synopsis of our 20 top attractions, below. Having done that, you will then have a basic route to discuss with your operator, who can help you sort out the logistics and add places along the way. One important decision, irrespective of the actual places you visit, is the broad divide between the 'bush', 'beach' and 'city' components of your trip – some visitors will favour an extended beach holiday punctuated by a two- to three-night safari to one major reserve such as the Kruger National Park or Pilanesberg, some will want to spend most of their trip to South Africa in game and nature reserves, while for others the urban attractions of Cape Town and Gauteng are paramount.

Cultural and historical

(SS)

1 Cape Town

Steeped in colonial history, the Mother City houses the country's oldest building, the Castle of Good Hope, as well as the Company's Garden founded by Van Riebeeck and a bevy of contrasting museums. The City Bowl is also a contemporary cultural melting pot, embracing the Malay-dominated Bo-Kaap, the grungy charms of Long Street, and any number of live venues hosting international and local talents.

2 Cradle of Humankind

A short drive west of Johannesburg, this sprawling World Heritage Site has yielded some of Africa's most important human fossil finds, as documented in the interactive Maropeng Visitors Centre and eerie Sterkfontein Caves.

(AVZ)

3 Apartheid Museum

'Today', reads the motto, 'apartheid is exactly where it belongs: in a museum'. This is that museum, and - situated just south of Johannesburg - it's an essential stop for anybody who wants to place modern South Africa in the context of its segregated recent past.

(AVZ)

4 Robben Island

Only 30 minutes by boat from Cape Town, the island where the likes of Nelson Mandela and Walter Sisulu were incarcerated by the apartheid authorities is now a UNESCO World Heritage Site and shrine-like museum.

(AVZ)

(SS)

5 Township tours

Whether it's sprawling Soweto outside Johannesburg, or the windswept Cape Flats west of Cape Town, a tour of one of the country's many townships exposes the meagre living conditions of most urban South Africans.

Coast

6 Cape Peninsula

Flanked by the Atlantic to the west and False Bay to the east, the mountainous sliver of land running south of Cape Town is peppered with scenic highlights, whether it be the magnificent Chapman's Peak Drive, the wave-battered cliffs of Cape Point, or the penguins that wobble endearingly on Boulders Beach.

(SS)

7 iSimangaliso Wetland Park

Hemmed in by the world's tallest forested dunes, the succession of deserted beaches running between the St Lucia Estuary and Kosi Bay are among the most beautiful anywhere in Africa. An important breeding ground for two species of marine turtle, this stretch of coast also shelters coral reefs alive with colourful fish, and offers excellent seasonal whale and dolphin viewing.

(AVZ)

8 Storm's River

The scenic highlight of the famous Garden Route is arguably the mouth of the Storm's River, protected by sheer cliffs on both sides, and traversed by means of a rickety wooden suspension bridge.

(AMO/A)

9 Whale-watching, Hermanus

The Cape Coast offers the world's finest land-based whale-watching, especially between July and November when southern right whales calve and breach in the deep coves below the quaint seaside village of Hermanus.

(AVZ)

10 Knysna

One of the prettiest towns in South Africa, Knysna's lovely lagoonside setting is complemented by its distinctly old-world character and funky, gay-friendly social scene.

(AVZ)

Safari

11 Greater Kruger

Simply one of the largest and finest game reserves anywhere in Africa, the Kruger National Park protects substantial numbers of all the Big Five. It's ideal for budget-conscious self-drivers, but those seeking a more luxurious guided safari are pointed to the exclusive Sabi Sands and other private reserves along Kruger's western border.

(AVZ)

12

Zululand reserves

Best known for its
pivotal role in global rhino
conservation, Hluhluwe-Imfolozi is
the biggest and best of half-a-dozen
excellent reserves scattered around
northern KwaZulu-Natal, while its
private counterpart Phinda is the place
to see cheetahs in South Africa.

(AVZ)

(AVZ)

13

Pilanesberg Game Reserve

All the Big Five are present in this smallish reserve
bordering Sun City, and while it doesn't quite match the
Kruger in terms of impact, this is countered for some by its
proximity to Johannesburg and the absence of malaria.

14 Addo and surrounds

Another malaria-free Big Five destination, easily appended to a tour of Cape Town and the Garden Route, Addo Elephant National Park is renowned for offering close-up encounters with the world's largest land mammal, while neighbouring Kwandwe and Shamwari provide a luxurious private alternative.

(SS)

15 Kgalagadi Transfrontier Park

Nudged up against the border with Botswana and Namibia, this remote and often-overlooked national park offers a combination of thrilling desert dunescapes and surprisingly good game viewing, with predators both large and small being particularly visible.

(SS)

Outdoors and scenery

16

Table Mountain

Offering fantastic views north over Cape Town and Table Bay, and south across the Cape Peninsula, this flat-topped South African icon can be ascended in a few minutes by rotating cableway, or more slowly by taking any of a number of scenic footpaths.

(SS)

17

uKhahlamba-Drakensberg Park

Running 200km along the Lesotho border, this vast mountain range has enough hiking and rambling options to keep you busy for months. A scenic highlight is the Amphitheatre in Royal Natal Park, while Giant's Castle harbours one of the region's most impressive and accessible rock art sites.

(AVZ)

18 Cape Winelands

There's hiking aplenty in the mountainous Winelands inland from Cape Town, but most visitors content themselves with the sedentary charms of the region's innumerable wine estates and old-world towns such as Stellenbosch and Franschhoek.

(AVZ)

19

Namaqualand

The spring wildflower displays in this succulent-rich semi-desert area north of Cape Town are well worth a diversion if you're here over August or September.

(AVZ)

20 Blyde River Canyon

Numerous day trails offer access to this immense forest-fringed canyon on the escarpment west of the Kruger National Park, while for the less energetic, there are viewpoints such as the Three Rondawels.

(SS)

Red tape

All visitors require a **passport**, valid for at least six months after the end of their stay, and with at least two full pages empty. No visa is required for tourist stays of up to 90 days by nationals from the UK, European Union, USA, Canada, Australia, New Zealand, Singapore or Japan. Visitors from most other countries do require a visa, which will be issued free of charge but must be applied for at least four weeks before the intended arrival date. A **multiple-entry visa** will be required by anybody intending to visit Lesotho, Swaziland or any other African countries and then returning to South Africa. A visa is not normally required to enter Swaziland, and if it is it can be arranged at the border. The USA, European Union and most Commonwealth nationals can enter Lesotho for up to two weeks without a visa, but other nationals must obtain a visa in advance.

Getting there

OR Tambo International Airport, about 25km east of **Johannesburg**, is the busiest flight hub in southern Africa. It has direct connections to most European and African capitals, as well as to the Americas, Asia and Australia, and it is also the main hub for domestic flights. A limited number of international flights land at **Cape Town** International, **Kruger** Mpumalanga and **Durban's** King Shaka airports, which are often more convenient options for those with no specific reason to pass through Johannesburg. The Airports Company South Africa (✆ 0867 277888; ✆ www.acsa.co.za) has detailed information about facilities at all major airports, excluding Kruger Mpumalanga (✆ www.mceglobal.net).

The most important carrier to South Africa is South African Airways (SAA; ✆ 021 936 1111; ✆ www.flysaa.com) with direct connections to most European and many African capitals, as well as to the USA, South America, Asia and Australia. Most of their international flights land at OR Tambo but they operate several connecting flights daily to Cape Town, King Shaka and Kruger Mpumalanga, and these can usually be booked as one routing through their website. Other international airlines include British Airways (✆ www.britishairways.com), Delta Air (✆ www.delta.com), Egypt Air (✆ www.egyptair.com), Emirates (✆ www. emirates.com), Ethiopian Airlines (✆ www.flyethiopian.com), Kenya Airways (✆ www.kenya-airways.com), KLM Royal Airlines (✆ www.klm .com), Lufthansa (✆ www.lufthansa.com), Singapore Airlines (✆ www. singaporeair.com) and Virgin Atlantic (✆ www.virgin-atlantic.com).

Tourist information

The **South African Tourism Board** has a detailed website (🖰 www.southafrica. net) and domestic call centre (📞 083 123 6789). It also has agencies in Sydney (📞 02 9261 5000), London (📞 08701-550044) and New York 📞 212-730 2929). Worth checking out are the nine provincial websites:

- 🖰 www.visiteasterncape.co.za
- 🖰 www.freestatetourism.org
- 🖰 www.gauteng.net
- 🖰 www.kzn.org.za (KwaZulu-Natal)
- 🖰 www.mpumalanga.com
- 🖰 www.northerncape.org.za
- 🖰 www.golimpopo.com
- 🖰 www.tourismnorthwest.co.za
- 🖰 www.tourismcapetown.co.za (Western Cape)

The **South African national parks** website (🖰 www.sanparks.org) has heaps of information about all the country's national parks, as well as a visitors' forum and a user-friendly, online accommodation-booking service. The websites run by the provincial conservation authorities for KwaZulu-Natal (🖰 www. kznwildlife.com) and Western Cape (🖰 www.capenature.co.za) are also very useful. Most larger towns have a tourist information office (sometimes called the Publicity Association), which can provide town maps, information on current events, museums and other points of interest.

Health and safety
with Dr Felicity Nicholson

Inoculations

You will be required to show a vaccination certificate for yellow fever upon arrival if you are coming from a yellow fever-endemic area. This may also include a transit in an airport as South Africa does not make a distinction. You do not need yellow fever vaccine for South Africa itself, and therefore if you are flying in from non-endemic areas then no certificate is required. It's important to be up to date on tetanus, diphtheria and polio, and you might also consider immunisation against hepatitis A, hepatitis B, rabies and typhoid.

Deep-vein thrombosis (DVT)

Prolonged immobility on long-haul flights can result in deep-vein thrombosis (DVT), which can be dangerous if the clot travels to the lungs to cause pulmonary embolus. The risk increases with age, and is higher in obese or pregnant travellers, heavy smokers, those taller than 6ft/1.8m or shorter than 5ft/1.5m, and anybody with a history of clots, recent major operation or varicose veins surgery, cancer, a stroke or heart disease. If any of these criteria apply, consult a doctor before you travel. Ensuring that you are well hydrated and trying to move around during long periods of travel can help to reduce the risk.

Malaria

This mosquito-borne disease is the biggest single medical threat to visitors to many parts of Africa. It is absent from most of South Africa, however it is present in the low altitude areas of Mpumalanga and Limpopo Provinces that border Zimbabwe and Mozambique, and which include the Kruger National Park, and in northeastern KwaZulu-Natal. There is a risk all year but it is highest from September to May. Most cases are due to *Plasmodium falciparum* and resistance to chloroquine is widespread.

If you intend to visit any of these malarial risk areas, precautions are strongly recommended. There is no vaccine, but several types of oral prophylactics are available, with Malarone (proguanil and atovaquone) being widely recommended for short trips, as it is very effective and has few side effects (though it is relatively expensive). Other possibilities include mefloquine and doxycycline, so visit a travel clinic for up-to-date advice about the most suitable option.

Travel clinics and health information

A full list of current travel clinic websites worldwide is available on ⏷ www.istm. org/. For other journey preparation information, consult ⏷ www.nathnac.org/ ds/map_world.aspx. Information about various medications may be found on ⏷ www.netdoctor.co.uk/travel. Other useful sites include ⏷ www.fitfortravel. scot.nhs.uk (a useful source of general travel health information) and ⏷ www. nc.cdc.gov/travel (includes updates on specific destinations and information for those with limited mobility and those travelling with children). Both the US State Department (⏷ http://travel.state.gov/) and the British Department of Health (⏷ www.nhs.uk/nhsengland/Healthcareabroad) also provide dedicated travel health information.

For on-the-ground advice on preventing malaria, plus other health issues to consider whilst on safari, see *Chapter 4*, page 82.

Women travellers

Although social attitudes across the board are relatively conservative and may occasionally be offensive to some women travellers, there is little to fear on a gender-specific level, especially on an organised tour. Dress codes are broadly comparable to Europe and North America, though a degree of circumspection is sometimes advisable: skimpy clothing might be considered offensive in Muslim areas such as the Bo-Kaap, whilst in other circumstances it could be perceived – however unfairly – as provocative. It's also worth noting that topless bathing in public areas is not broadly acceptable. More pragmatically, the range of toiletries available outside of larger towns – for instance in private reserves and rest camp shops – is somewhat limited, so ideally leave home stocked up with everything you need.

Disabled travellers

with Gordon Rattray ⌀ www.able-travel.com

South Africa is the continent's most inclusive destination. For most overseas visitors it may not be as barrier-free as they are used to, but public areas often show some consideration towards people with

Personal first-aid kit

Depending on where and how you travel, and for how long, a minimal kit might contain the following:

- A good drying antiseptic, eg: iodine or potassium permanganate
- A few small dressings (Band-Aids)
- Suncream
- Insect repellent
- Antimalarial tablets
- Antihistamine tablets and cream
- Aspirin or paracetamol
- Antifungal cream (eg: Canesten)
- Ciprofloxacin or norfloxacin, for travellers' diarrhoea
- Antibiotic eye drops
- A pair of fine-pointed tweezers
- Alcohol-based hand rub or a bar of soap in a plastic box
- Thermometer

disabilities and accommodation with accessibility features can usually be found. Where problems arise, South Africans like nothing better than getting stuck into a challenge, so you can always be sure of practical and enthusiastic help.

Most mainstream operators will try to cater to travellers with disabilities, but South Africa is also well covered by experienced and knowledgeable specialist safari companies (see below).

Specialised operators

Access 2 Africa Safaris ⁁ www.access2africasafaris.co.za
Endeavour Safaris ⁁ www.endeavour-safaris.com
Epic Enabled ⁁ www.epic-enabled.com
Flamingo Tours & Disabled Ventures ⁁ www.flamingotours.co.za

Further information

Bradt's *Access Africa: Safaris for People with Limited Mobility* is packed with useful advice and resources for disabled and senior adventure travellers, and has detailed descriptions of access in safari accommodation.

What to take

Clothing

Dress codes are casual and temperatures are generally on the warm side, so a good mix of comfortable, light clothing, similar to what you might wear on a warm summer's day in Europe, is advisable. Be warned, however, that winter nights can be chilly, especially at higher altitudes, and the Cape Town area often experiences wet and windy weather, so bring a couple of sweatshirts or similar, and possibly some sort of waterproof jacket. On safari, the ideal clothing is loose-fitting, lightweight, informal and made of natural fibres. Bright colours are a definite no-no when tracking wildlife on foot, and pale colours tend to show dust and dirt rather conspicuously. From dusk onwards it's advisable to wear closed shoes, socks, long trousers and long-sleeved tops to protect against mosquito bites. Most vehicle-based tours don't call for any special footwear, but decent walking shoes or boots are essential for foot safaris, forest walks and mountain ascents.

Photographic gear

Few people would consider going on safari without a camera and/or video recorder. It should be recognised, however, that wildlife

South Africa's stunning scenery offers some excellent photo opportunities. (SS)

photography and filming is a specialised field, and the fantastic footage and perfect still images that we're accustomed to seeing on television and in magazines are the product of patience, experience, planning, high-quality equipment and an element of luck (see also page 93). For decent results, an SLR camera is preferable to a 'point and shoot', and a high-magnification lens (200mm at the very least) is more or less essential. Zoom lenses (eg: 70–300mm) are generally more affordable and allow for greater compositional flexibility than fixed lenses, but they tend to lack the sharpness of the latter and to lose at least one

Binoculars

These are essential for viewing distant wildlife and obtaining close-up views of birds. For dedicated birdwatchers, 8x magnification is the minimal requirement, but 10x, 12x or (only for the steady of hand) 16x is even better. The trade-off between full-size binoculars (eg: 8x40, 10x50) and their compact counterparts (eg: 8x25, 10x30) is that the former have a wider field of vision and tend to show colours more brightly as a result of capturing more light, while the latter are considerably more portable and steady to hold, and they tend to be cheaper. On the whole, you will get what you pay for when it comes to binoculars: common problems with cheap or obscure brands include poor focussing or lens alignment, a distorting or prismatic effect, and dull or inaccurate rendition of colours. If your budget runs to it, it's worth paying a bit more and sticking with a recognised brand. Avoid gimmicky binoculars (with features like zoom or universal focus) at all costs.

Electricity

Mains electricity is at 220–240 volts 60Hz. So-called British Standard 546 round, three-pin plugs (the standard in Great Britain before 1962) are in the widest use, so if you are carrying electrical equipment with two-pin or square, three-pin plugs, be sure to bring a travel adaptor or two. Alternatively, you can buy an adaptor in any electrical appliance shop or at any international airport, and most of the larger hotels will sell or loan adaptors to you on request. The urban electricity supply is reasonably reliable, and upmarket hotels will almost always have a generator that kicks in during rare power cuts. Many wildlife lodges and camps are not on the mains grid but depend on generators, solar power or a combination of both, and it may only be possible to charge camera gear and other devices at certain hours, so it's a good idea to check the situation at reception and try to avoid letting batteries run down so low that they require urgent charging.

aperture stop at full magnification, making them less useful in low-light conditions. Magnification can be increased by using a converter, but with some loss of clarity and a further loss of one or two aperture stops for a 1.4x/2x converter. The bottom line, if you're serious about wildlife photography, is to buy the best long lens you can afford!

If you use a digital camera, make sure you have all the batteries, plugs, connectors and storage devices you need, as well as a universal adaptor. If you use film, this may not be readily available once you're on safari, so bring as many rolls as you are likely to need. Most first-time safari-goers and many experienced amateur photographers underestimate the importance of proper support in obtaining sharp wildlife shots: a beanbag is the most flexible and stable option for shooting out of a vehicle, and is easy enough to make yourself, ideally with a zip so you can fly with it empty and fill it up with whatever is available (beans, rice, dried corn) at the start of your safari. Make sure your camera bag is well insulated against the insidious dust associated with most African safari circuits.

Other essentials

Don't forget to bring suncream, a hat and sunglasses, a day pack to carry binoculars and field guides et al, a toilet bag containing razors, deodorant, tampons, lip salve and whatever other accessories you might need, and a basic medical kit (see page 74), and a penknife, torch and possibly alarm clock. Contact-lens users with sensitive eyes might be glad of a pair of old-fashioned glasses in the dusty conditions that often prevail on safari. A superb range of field guides is available locally, and you shouldn't have much difficulty locating anything you require, whether it be in airport bookshops, city shopping malls, or shops in lodges and rest camps.

It is advisable to take photocopies of passports and any other important travel documents and to store them separately from the originals in case anything is lost or stolen.

Finally, don't leave home without adequate **travel insurance**. This should include both medical insurance (specifically one that will fly you home in the event of an emergency) and a travel protection plan which would cover non-reimbursed travel expenses if an emergency occurs before or during your trip, causing it to be cancelled, interrupted or delayed. Check out ✆ www.worldtravelcenter.com and ✆ www. globaltravelinsurance.com for more information.

Organising your finances

People who visit South Africa on a pre-paid tour or safari generally don't need to carry a great deal of money on their person, as most costs will have been built into the package, including airport and other transfers, ground transport, services of a driver and/or guide as specified, pre-booked domestic flights, national park and other entrance fees, and accommodation. With meals, the most common arrangement is for city and beach hotels to be booked on a bed-and-breakfast basis, while upmarket safari lodges and tented camps tend to be full-board. However, some tours are booked on a full-board basis throughout, so check the arrangements with your specific operator. Certain exclusive lodges also include all drinks in the accommodation rate, but that is the exception not the rule.

Assuming that you are paid up in advance, you will only need enough cash to cover **day-to-day expenses** such as drinks, tips (see page 86) and curios, which are unlikely to tally up to much more than US$500. **Credit or debit cards** can be used to pay extras at most hotels, shops and restaurants, assuming that you have a widely recognised brand such as Visa, MasterCard or to a lesser extent American Express. Local currency can also be drawn from ATMs all over the country using the same cards. Failing that, hard currency cash – US dollars, British pounds, or euros – can also be converted into local currency at most banks, airports and many hotels. **Travellers' cheques** are more problematic to change.

(NC/R)

Entrance fees

Most entrance fees are quite moderate by international standards and will be included in the price of an organised tour. Individual travellers should note that all national parks charge a daily 'conservation fee', ranging from ZAR180 per foreign adult and ZAR90 per child for major parks to ZAR80/40 for smaller ones, while entrance fees to provincial and other game and nature reserves are generally between ZAR20 and ZAR50. If you'll be spending a lot of time in parks and reserves, consider buying a Wild Card, which allows unlimited entry to all national parks in South Africa and Swaziland and most provincial reserves on KwaZulu-Natal and the Western Cape. It costs ZAR1,310 for one person, ZAR2,195 for two people, or ZAR2,620 for a family of six (see ⁀ð www. sanparks.org for details).

Museum and gallery entrance fees are typically between ZAR10 and ZAR50. However, certain high-profile attractions are more expensive, for example a Robben Island Tour costs ZAR200 for an adult, ZAR100 for achild; the return cable-car ride up Table Mountain costs ZAR180/90; and the combined ticket for Maropeng and the Sterkfontein Caves (Cradle of Humankind) is ZAR190/110. Senior citizens, students and children get reduced admission rates at many places, but may be required to produce a student card or passport as proof.

4 On the Ground

On an organised tour, the ground operator and/or their appointed
guide will handle most day-to-day practicalities, whether it
be checking into a hotel, paying park entrance fees, locating a
suitable place to eat, or finding somewhere to exchange or draw
money. South African guides are generally very helpful and will
quickly assist you in dealing with anything that requires local
savvy; nevertheless, some advance knowledge about how things
work locally can be useful, and this chapter deals with a few
important points, from health and safety, to foreign exchange and
telecommunications, to tipping and shopping. It also includes a
section to help first-time safarigoers locate the wonderful variety
of creatures that inhabit South Africa's national parks and other
reserves, whether you explore them in a vehicle, or by stalking
through the bush on foot - with tips on visual location, the more
subtle craft of tracking spoor, as well as wildlife photography.

Health and safety in South Africa
with Dr Felicity Nicholson

South Africa is not an especially hazardous country health-wise, and standards of hygiene at most tourist facilities are high. Still, it is worth being alert to the more common health risks, and other aspects of health and safety discussed briefly below.

Malaria

Although malaria is absent from most of South Africa, it is present in the low-altitude areas of Mpumalanga and Limpopo Provinces, which border Zimbabwe and Mozambique and include the Kruger National Park, and in northeastern KwaZulu-Natal. Those intending to visit these areas should take all reasonable precautions. Even if on a course of prophylaxis, avoid being bitten by the nocturnal Anopheles mosquitoes that transmit the disease, by wearing a long-sleeved shirt, trousers and socks in the evening, and applying a DEET-based insect repellent to any exposed flesh (50–55% strength is optimal). Sleep under a net, or failing that in an air-conditioned room, under a fan or with a mosquito coil burning. Malaria normally manifests within two weeks of being bitten, but it can take up to a year, so if you display possible symptoms after you get home, go to a doctor immediately and ask to be tested.

Sunstroke and dehydration

Overexposure to the sun can lead to short-term sunburn or sunstroke, and increases the long-term risk of skin cancer. Wear a T-shirt and waterproof sunscreen when swimming. On safari or walking in the direct sun, cover up with long, loose clothes, wear a hat and use sunscreen (at least factor 30). The glare and the dust can be hard on the eyes, so bring UV-protecting sunglasses. A less direct effect of the tropical heat is dehydration, so it's important to drink more fluids than you would at home.

Travellers' diarrhoea

Many visitors to unfamiliar destinations suffer a dose of travellers' diarrhoea and South Africa is no exception. By taking precautions against travellers' diarrhoea you will also avoid more serious sanitation-related diseases such as typhoid, cholera, hepatitis, dysentery, worms, etc (though these are all very rare in South Africa). The maxim to remind you what you can safely eat is:

PEEL IT, BOIL IT, COOK IT OR FORGET IT.

This means that fruit you have washed and peeled yourself, and hot foods, should be safe, but raw foods, cold cooked foods, salads, fruit salads prepared by others, ice cream and ice are all risky. It is rarer to get sick from drinking contaminated water but it happens, so stick to bottled water. If you suffer a bout of diarrhoea, it is dehydration that makes you feel awful, so drink lots of clear fluids, ideally infused with sachets of oral rehydration salts, but any dilute mixture of sugar and salt in water will do you good, for instance a bottled soda with a pinch of salt added. If the problem persists for more than five days or there is blood with the diarrhoea, seek medical attention.

Bilharzia

Also known as schistosomiasis, bilharzia is an unpleasant parasitic disease transmitted by freshwater snails in lakes and rivers. It cannot be caught in hotel swimming pools or the ocean. If you do swim in a lake or river, you can test for bilharzia at specialist travel clinics, ideally six weeks or longer after exposure, and it is easy to treat at present. Avoid swimming in stagnant water, or at least avoid the reedy banks

Tickbite fever and quick tick removal

Ticks in Africa are not the rampant disease transmitters that they are in the Americas, but they may spread tickbite fever along with a few dangerous rarities. Tickbite fever is a flu-like illness that can easily be treated with doxycycline, but as there can be some serious complications it is very important that you visit a doctor.

Ticks should ideally be removed as soon as possible because leaving them on the body increases the chance of infection. They should be removed with special tick tweezers that can be bought in good travel shops. Failing that you can use your finger nails: grasp the tick as close to your body as possible and pull steadily and firmly away at right angles to your skin. The tick will then come away complete, as long as you do not jerk or twist. If possible douse the wound with alcohol (any spirit will do) or iodine. Irritants (eg: Olbas oil) or lit cigarettes are to be discouraged since they can cause the ticks to regurgitate and therefore increase the risk of disease. It is best to get a travelling companion to check you for ticks; if you are travelling with small children, remember to check their heads, and particularly behind the ears.

Spreading redness around the bite and/or fever and/or aching joints after a tick bite imply that you have an infection that requires antibiotic treatment, so seek advice.

– bathing in the centre is safer. Keep the time to a minimum and towel off thoroughly after coming out of the water.

HIV/AIDS

South Africa has one of the world's highest rates of HIV infection, with an estimated five million people carrying the virus. Other sexually transmitted diseases are also rife, so if you do indulge, use condoms or femidoms to reduce the risk of transmission.

Skin infections

Any mosquito bite or small nick is an opportunity for a skin infection in warm, humid climates, so clean and cover the slightest wound in a good drying antiseptic such as dilute iodine, potassium permanganate or crystal (or gentian) violet. Prickly heat, most likely to be contracted whilst visiting the humid Indian Ocean coastline, is a fine, pimply rash that can be alleviated by cool showers, dabbing (not rubbing) dry and applying talc, and sleeping naked under a fan or in an air-conditioned room. Fungal infections also get a hold easily in hot, moist climates, so wear 100% cotton socks and underwear and shower frequently.

Wild animals

Don't confuse habituation with domestication. South Africa's wildlife is genuinely wild: the lions that lie docilely in front of your minibus would almost certainly run away from or turn on anybody foolish enough to disembark in their presence, and elephant, hippo, rhino and buffalo might all bulldoze a pedestrian given the right set of circumstances. Such attacks are rare, however, and they almost always stem from a combination of poor judgement and even poorer luck. A few rules of thumb: never approach wildlife on foot except in the company of a trustworthy guide; never swim in lakes or rivers without first seeking local advice about the presence of crocodiles or hippos; never get between a hippo and water; never leave food in the tent where you'll sleep; and be aware that running away from a predator can trigger its instinct to give chase. See below for advice on rabies.

Rabies

Although rabies is less common in South Africa than other African countries, it has not been entirely eliminated and local outbreaks account for up to 20 human fatalities annually. To be on the safe side, assume that any warm-blooded mammal might be carrying rabies (even a stray village dog or habituated monkey), although most household dogs and cats are unlikely to be infected. So if you are bitten, scratched or licked over broken skin, scrub the wound with soap and running water and seek medical help as soon as possible. You might also think about having pre-exposure (Prep) doses of rabies vaccine before you travel. Three doses over a minimum of 21 days are advised. Prep will change the need for the expensive and hard-to-come-by rabies immunoglobulin, thus making treatment so much easier.

Though habituated to vehicles, wildlife in South Africa remains genuinely wild, and should be treated with respect. (AVZ)

Snake and other bites

Snakes are very secretive and bites are a genuine rarity, but certain spiders and scorpions can also deliver nasty bites. In all cases, the risk is minimised by wearing closed shoes and trousers when walking in the bush, and watching where you put your hands and feet, especially in rocky areas or when gathering firewood. Only a small fraction of snakebites deliver enough venom to be life-threatening, but it is important to keep the victim calm and inactive, and to seek urgent medical attention.

Car accidents

Road traffic accidents are the biggest threat to life and limb in South Africa. Indeed, according to the WHO, there are around 15,000 reported traffic fatalities here every year, around five times the number recorded in the UK, which has a larger population. From a tourist's perspective, a high proportion of these involve the recklessly driven minibus 'taxis' that ferry locals between towns, so the risk is lowered by sticking to tourist buses. On a self-drive safari, drive defensively, being especially wary of stray livestock, pot-holes and imbecilic or bullying overtaking manoeuvres. It is also a good idea to avoid driving at night and to pull over in heavy storms.

Banking and foreign exchange

The South African rand (ZAR), subdivided into 100 cents, currently trades at around US$1 = ZAR7, £1 = ZAR11 and €1 = ZAR10. Banknotes come in denominations of ZAR 10, 20, 50, 100 and 200, and coins are 5, 10, 20 and 50 cents as well as ZAR 1, 2 and 5 (many shops will refuse ZAR200 notes, however, due to the high incidence of forgeries). The easiest way to stock up on local currency is to draw it against an internationally recognised credit or debit card (Visa, MasterCard or to a lesser extent Maestro and American Express) from an ATM. There are plenty of ATMs at all airports and shopping malls, outside most banks and at many filling stations, and the usual withdrawal limit is

Tipping

Knowing when to tip, and by how much, is frequently a source of stress in a foreign country, particularly so when there's such a glaring gap in wealth between visitors and most locals. In South Africa, the rules of thumb are fairly straightforward. At restaurants, a 10% tip to the waiter would be standard, perhaps a little more or less, depending on the quality of service. Hotel porters usually expect a tip of around ZAR5 per item of luggage. On organised tours, this sort of thing is usually handled by the guide. It is customary to tip your guide and/or driver at the end of a tour, usually as a group rather than as individuals. There are no hard-and-fast rules relating to this, but a group tip equivalent to ZAR100-200 per day would be decent.

Upmarket lodges and camps operate on a full-board basis, and it's usually easier to sign drinks to the room than to pay cash, but you can always leave a tip for an individual waiter or bar person if you feel they deserve it, or add one to the bill. However, we often hear stories of a tip charged to a credit card not reaching the person for whom it is intended, so a direct cash tip might be preferable.

At most lodges, there's a tip box at reception where you can leave cash to be distributed amongst all the staff, a system that seems fairer on backroom workers in a country where hotel staff are very poorly paid.

around ZAR1,000 per day. Alternatively, hard currency cash can be exchanged for local currency at any bureaux de change (in the airport and most shopping malls) or bank, or at the reception of many tourist-class hotels. Credit and debit cards can usually be used to pay for most services directly, though they may not be accepted by smaller traders or at markets. A quirk of South Africa until very recently is that normal credit and debit cards could not be used to pay for petrol or other fuel; this is gradually changing, but at the time of writing, many filling stations will only accept cash (or dedicated garage cards issued by a South African bank).

On safari: locating wildlife

Television documentaries can create unrealistic expectations of an African safari. A top-notch wildlife film might be the product of years spent following one semi-habituated animal, and the high-speed chases and intimate wildlife interaction laid on for armchair safari-goers is seldom observed as easily in the flesh. It's a gap comparable to watching a sporting highlights package on TV and being present at a live match – the former is all action, punctuated with thrilling close-ups and slow-motion replays, but it lacks the immediacy and atmosphere of actually being there as events unfold.

Game drives

Most driver-guides will do all they can to ensure a safari runs smoothly, but especially in public reserves the onus is also on you to take a proactive role in game spotting, route planning, bird identification, deciding on photographic stops et al.

Most animals prefer to lie or stand in the shade during the heat of the day. (AVZ)

Timing

Whether you visit a private or public reserve, a typical day on safari is structured around a four- to five-hour morning game drive and a shorter afternoon drive, returning to camp in between for a leisurely lunch and siesta. A full-day drive may be enforced on days when you need to travel between different rest camps in the Kruger. Wherever possible, embark on your morning game drive shortly before sunrise, and plan your afternoon game drive so that you return to camp at the latest permitted hour.

Responsible wildlife watching

Avoid any activity that needlessly disturbs the wildlife or has a negative impact on the environment. Desist from littering, especially from throwing matches or cigarette butts into the bush, which could instigate an uncontrolled fire. Never feed the wildlife: monkeys and baboons in particular will quickly learn to associate humans with food and are often shot as vermin once they do. Hooting or yelling at wildlife to gain its attention is another no-no.

First and last light is when you are most likely to encounter secretive nocturnal predators such as leopard or serval, while the more conspicuous lion, spotted hyena and jackal are most active (and interactive) before the heat of the day kicks in. Other advantages to being out during the early and late light are the lower volumes of tourist traffic, the cooler temperatures, the higher level of avian activity, and the often sumptuous photographic light.

Guided night drives (or, more accurately, late afternoon drives that continue for an hour or two after sunset) in open 4x4s are now offered at most camps in the Kruger National Park and in several other public reserves, and they are a routine part of the daily schedule in private reserves. If you get the chance to join a night drive, take it. The main attraction is the opportunity to see a host of unusual creatures that are more difficult to locate in daylight – for instance bushbabies, genets, chameleons, brown hyena and aardvark. Even if you see little wildlife, the African bush possesses an unforgettable haunted quality after dark, and the sparkling night sky can be utterly mesmerising.

Where to look

Even the most experienced spotter might overlook a roadside lion if he is looking in the opposite direction or focussed on navigating a difficult stretch of road. Except in the early morning and late afternoon, most animals prefer to be in the shade, so scan the ground below isolated trees in open country, and try to look into thicker bush rather than letting your eyes follow openings through it. Be conscious of a 'ticking' mentality that informs the way some drivers conduct game drives – if you've seen and photographed one giraffe, for instance, your driver may decide not to stop for any other giraffes, no matter how distant or static that initial sighting was, or how photogenic a subsequent one is.

It's always worth stopping for a few minutes at any accessible river, reservoir or other watering point. Most animals need to drink at least once daily, so that from mid-morning onwards, perennial water bodies tend to attract a steady trickle of thirsty elephant, buffalo, zebra, giraffe and other ungulates, especially during the dry season. Should elephants be hovering at the water's edge, it's worth sticking around to see whether they actually get into the water and start playing, which can be great fun to watch.

Vegetated riverbanks tend to attract fewer transient drinkers than isolated reservoirs, but if you switch off the engine and sit for ten minutes at an apparently deserted riverbank scene you'll be surprised at what you see – a crocodile or hippo surfacing, a flash of brilliant colour as a kingfisher or bee-eater swoops from its perch, a bushbuck or kudu emerging from the tangled undergrowth, or a troop of monkeys erupting into treetop activity.

Following clues

Look for indirect signs of predator and Big Five activity. An aggregation of circling or roosting vultures will often point towards a recent kill, while vociferous agitation amongst an arboreal baboon troop or guineafowl flock might well be in response to a prowling predator.

Bearing in mind that many animals follow manmade roads in the same way that they would normally travel along established wildlife tracks, a trail of fresh paw prints laid on a muddy or sandy road, especially when located in the early morning, will often lead an experienced guide to the predator that made them, while a few gigantic steaming piles of roadside dung combined with torn-off branches and other destroyed vegetation is a sure sign that elephants passed through recently. Ironically, however, the most frequent and overt indirect evidence of an interesting sighting in some more popular South African parks requires no specialist bush knowledge to interpret, consisting as it does of a huddle of cars further along the road.

Guided walks

In most non-forested, non-montane national parks, visitors are confined to their vehicles except at lodges, rest camps, entrance gates and other designated spots. However, there is no more exciting way of seeing wildlife than on foot, and many private reserves now

Seeing wildlife up close on a game walk is a truly exhilarating experience. (JWLP/A)

offer morning game walks led by an armed local guide. This is a far more involving experience than a game drive, one that can transform what would otherwise be a relatively mundane sighting (yet another wildebeest or impala) into something altogether more immediate and inspirational, and that lends a definite edge to any encounter with elephant, buffalo, rhino, lion and the like.

No less important, walking in the bush provides a wealth of stimuli to senses that tend to be muted within the confines of a vehicle – on foot, you are far more conscious of sounds, smells and physical textures – and it provides the opportunity to concentrate on smaller creatures such as colourful birds, bugs and butterflies, and to examine all manner of environmental minutiae, from animal tracks to spider webs.

Animals that are habituated to vehicles are often less relaxed when they encounter human pedestrians, so dress in neutral colours such as green, grey or khaki, and desist from dousing yourself in perfume or any other non-functional artificial scents. Lightweight long trousers,

Tracks and signs

Hippo tracks
(C&TS/FLPA)

Even where large mammals seem to be uncommon, the bush is littered with their faecal spoor: the gigantic steaming pats deposited by elephant and rhino, the sausage-shaped scats of carnivores such as lion and jackal, the chalky-white, calcium-rich droppings of bone-chomping hyenas, and the neat piles of pellets that mark the territorial boundaries of a steenbok or duiker.

Sandy trails or dirt roads are often criss-crossed by all sorts of animal tracks. Most numerous are the near-symmetrical cloven-hoof marks of antelopes, a pair of teardrop-shaped segments that look like an elongated inverted heart split lengthwise down the middle. Most antelope prints are too similar to be identified by shape alone, but the possibilities can be narrowed down when certain factors such as size, number of prints and environment are taken into account. The print of a duiker is only 2cm long, an eland's is up to 14cm, and intermediate species tend to have proportionately sized spoor, with reedbuck, bushbuck and impala prints measuring about 6cm long, and wildebeest, oryx and hartebeest 11–12cm.

Of the other cloven-hoofed ungulates, a buffalo print is larger and more rounded than that of any antelope, while the giraffe's is squarer, more

socks and solid shoes provide better protection against thorns and biting insects than shorts and open shoes, and a sunhat and sunblock will protect against direct sunlight.

As a rule, it is more difficult to approach wildlife closely on foot, which means you are less likely to make use of a camera and more likely to regret not carrying binoculars. Where possible, those with specific interests such as birds or butterflies should ask for a guide with specialist knowledge. Also, be aware that on a game drive, noisy chatterers are likely to scare off any nearby animals and spoil the excursion for other guests, so say as little as possible as softly as possible. As for safety, the risk of being attacked by a wild animal is very small, but it is vital to pay attention during your pre-walk briefing and to listen to your guide at all times.

A walk with a knowledgeable and articulate guide will greatly enhance your understanding of the bush. You will be shown how to identify the more common and interesting trees, and may have some

elongated, and can be up to 20cm long. The print of a zebra comprises a large horseshoe in front of a pair of small antelope-like teardrops, while a hippo print looks like a gigantic, four-pronged fig leaf. Larger still, rhino prints look a bit like squashed heads with outsized ears, while oval elephant prints, up to 70cm long, are recognisable by size alone.

Look closely, and you may pick up the spoor of a carnivore, typically an inverted heart-shaped pad print below a quartet of oblong or circular toe marks. When trying to identify what made the print, look for a row of triangular claw marks above the toes – this is lacking in the case of genets and all cats other than the (non-retractably clawed) cheetah. As with antelope, print size is generally proportionate to the animal. A clawless, cat-like print of 10cm or longer is almost certainly the spoor of a lion, while a similar-sized print with dog-like claw marks would have been made by a spotted hyena. The print of a leopard, cheetah or African wild dog is typically 7–9cm long, and at the other end of the spectrum,

Olive baboon footprints (PR/FLPA)

that of a dwarf mongoose is only 2cm. Two deceptively proportioned carnivore prints are those of the Cape clawless otter and honey badger, both up to 8cm long. It would be possible to confuse primate and carnivore prints, but the former almost always resemble a human footprint in general shape, and have five clearly defined toes – baboon prints can measure up to 16cm from heel to tip, but most other monkey prints are 4–6cm long.

of their traditional medicinal applications explained to you. Especially in the early morning, the volume and variety of birdsong can be quite overwhelming, and a bush walk offers the opportunity to seek out mixed bird parties comprised of various inconspicuous sunbirds, warblers, bush-shrikes and other species.

Generally most active from mid-morning onwards, butterflies are often abundant near water and forest edges, while large webs made by colourful spiders dangle in the treetops, and creepy-crawlies such as dung beetles and millipedes creep and crawl along the ground. You'll probably want to look out for lizards and tortoises, and while snakes are unlikely to be observed (most would say fortunately), you may well see the odd series of S-shaped ripples created by their undulating method of locomotion on sandy soil.

Although walking is forbidden in most savanna reserves, it is permitted and even encouraged in many reserves where no dangerous wildlife is present. Good places for unguided walks with a possibility of wildlife sightings include Table Mountain National Park, uKhahlamba-Drakensberg, parts of iSimangaliso Wetland Park, and Augrabies Falls National Park.

Boat trips

Tourist boat on Lake St Lucia, KwaZulu Natal (AVZ)

Wildlife viewing from a boat makes a welcome change from the standard safari regime of two daily game drives, but in South Africa it is only an option at Lake St Lucia in the iSimangaliso Wetland Park, where you are likely to see plenty of hippos and birds, and possibly a few crocodiles, but little in the way of terrestrial wildlife. If you carry a long photographic lens, the constant rocking of a boat makes it too unstable to be a useful support: you'll need to handhold the camera and may have to sacrifice depth of field in order to maximise shutter speed and probable sharpness.

Bear in mind that the intensity of the sun is amplified when reflected by water, so you'll burn more quickly than on foot or in a vehicle. Wear a hat (ideally tied around your neck) and douse yourself liberally with sunscreen. Crocodiles pose no real threat unless your boat capsizes, in which case swim directly to the closest shore. There is always a risk of being drenched by a storm or by choppy waters, so carry all valuables and damageable goods in a waterproof bag.

Safari lodges can be as good as game drives for wildlife spotting. (AVZ)

Camps and lodges

After a long day driving in or between reserves, it is easy (and for many, desirable perhaps) to perceive time in your rest camp or lodge as downtime, and therefore take a quick nap or settle down at the poolside bar with a book and chilled drink. But for the dedicated enthusiast, lodge gardens often offer a welcome opportunity to seek out small wildlife on foot. Most camps are home to a range of lizards, frogs, hyraxes, squirrels and small predators, and can be relied upon to provide good birdwatching, especially in the early morning and late afternoon, when fruiting *Ficus* trees and flowering Aloe shrubs often attract species that are less easily seen from a fast-moving vehicle. In addition, many lodges are built alongside excellent natural viewpoints, from where you can scan the surrounding bush for passing wildlife, while others overlook rivers or lakes that attract a steady trickle of transient wildlife. Such aquatic viewpoints are especially worth your time to if they are spotlighted after dark, which is also when many camps are visited openly or surreptitiously by creatures such as scavenging hyenas, bushpigs, genets and other small predators.

Photography

Game drives, as opposed to walks, generally offer the best opportunity to photograph wildlife, because the vehicle doubles as a hide and as a stabilising device for your camera. Some drivers are more skilled at lining up vehicles than others, so some direction might be necessary. In most instances, you'll obtain the best result by approaching along a line that places you more or less directly between the animal and the sun, but which also avoids placing any distracting vegetation between subject and lens. It's worth trying to develop a feel for the right speed of approach: too fast and direct and you might scare off the animal, too slow or stop-start and your subject might sense it is being stalked. If the animal is getting twitchy, stop for a minute or two, and if it still doesn't settle, best to leave it in peace.

To improve the stability of a long lens (and increase the odds of a sharp result), use the car as a support, resting the camera on a beanbag or even some bunched-up clothing. Be aware, however, that the vibration of a running engine or any slight movement that affects the car while the shutter is open will almost certainly result in a blurred image.

Eating and drinking

Food

Almost all hotels, lodges and rest camps have their own restaurants, and on a guided tour inclusive of meals, that is where you will eat most of the time. Vegetarians and others with special dietary requirements should specify this to their tour operator in advance, and – bearing in mind the long chain of communications that links a desk in London or New York to a lodge in the remote African bush – are strongly advised to confirm (or ask their driver/guide to confirm) arrangements upon arrival at each hotel or lodge.

(SS)

Local cuisine

Most international cuisines are well represented in South Africa, but several dishes are more or less unique to the country. Traditional Cape Malay cooking, for instance, combines elements of Dutch dishes with those of the Malay slaves who were imported to the young Cape Colony. Cape curries are sweeter and milder than any Asian versions of the dish (or, for that matter, than the fiery Indian curries served in Durban), while *sosaties* are a variation on the Indonesian *satay* (kebab) marinated in a fruity Dutch *saus* (sauce). Other local specialities are a fruit-sweetened, baked mincemeat dish called *bobotie* and the lamb dish *waterblommetjiebredie* (water-flower stew).

Among local Africans, the staple dish is *mealiepap* or *sadza* (a stiff porridge made from maize meal) eaten with a plain bean or meat stew. Popular with almost all South Africans, a *braai* (barbecue) is a social event and male bonding ritual that usually involves cooking *boerewors* (spicy 'farmer's sausage'), steak, lamb chops and freshly picked corn on an open fire. *Potjiekos* is a meat and vegetable stew cooked slowly over a fire in the small black *potjie*, the pot for which it is named. *Biltong* consists of air-dried strips of salted and spiced beef or game meat and is reminiscent of American jerky.

In larger cities such as Cape Town, Johannesburg or Durban, where bookings are usually bed-and-breakfast only, you may have the choice of eating at a bespoke restaurant, either as a group or with your guide. Fortunately, there is no shortage of eateries catering to all tastes and budgets in these (and other) cities, with most global cuisines represented. Seafood is particularly recommended on the coast, while Durban excels when it comes to Indian restaurants, the latter usually offering a good vegetarian selection. If you want to explore beyond the selections listed in this book, ask your operator or hotel for local recommendations, and to arrange a taxi to drop and collect you.

Drinks

Ideally suited to the warm, dry conditions that prevail on safari, locally brewed lager beer is ubiquitous, with the most popular brands being Castle, Windhoek, Amstel and Black Label. Beers are served chilled in 330ml bottles or cans, and tend to be cheap to buy. Lighter versions such as Castle Light (4%) and Windhoek Light (2.5%) are also available. Draught beer is a relative scarcity, as are the darker bitters and ales favoured by many British visitors. Sodas such as Coke, Pepsi, Sprite and Fanta are widely available, and locally made pure fruit juices include

Cape wines

South Africa is justifiably renowned as one of the world's leading producers of wine and is ranked seventh in the world in terms of volume. While some critics claim that its top wines fail to match the very highest international standards, there's no arguing with the value for money or quality on offer at the more affordable end of the price spectrum. Most restaurants and hotels countrywide stock a good, and, by international standards, very affordable selection of everyday quaffers and more serious wines. Prices are generally cheapest close to source, so around Cape Town and the Western Cape, and highest in Gauteng and private game reserves catering mainly to the international market.

Historically, Cape viniculture dates back to 1659, when the colony's founder Jan van Riebeeck produced a small amount of wine – the quality of which goes unrecorded – from grapes he planted in the Company's Garden. Wine production increased under Simon van der Stel, Van Riebeecks's successor as Governor of the Cape, who founded the extant Constantia Estate in 1685. The colony's fledgling wine industry also spread inland to Stellenbosch, Franschhoek and Paarl, the site of historic vineyards such as Blaauwklippen, Boschendal and Vergelegen, and the quality reputedly improved under the tutelage of the French Huguenots. Indeed, the sweet 'Vin de Constance' produced at Constantia found favour with the likes of Charles Dickens and Napoleon Bonaparte, and is name-checked by the character Mrs Jennings in Jane Austen's *Sense and Sensibility*.

Today, numerous varietals are planted in South Africa. Cabernet Sauvignon, the most widely planted red, produces heavy wines that complement red meats. Herbier Shiraz and the smoother Merlot are also widely available, while Pinotage, a uniquely South African cultivar, is a fruity, purple wine that often represents excellent value. Of the whites, Sauvignon Blanc provides a crisp, zesty complement to Cape Malay dishes and curries, Chardonnay often goes well with fish and other seafood, while unfashionable Chenin Blanc is a diverse grape often used to produce good-value table wines.

the Liquifruit and Ceres ranges, both with at least a dozen flavours. Tap water is almost always fine to drink (the exception being at a few very remote bush lodges, in which case you'll be warned at reception) but sparkling and still mineral water are widely available.

Shopping

Gauteng, with its plethora of large, well-stocked shopping malls, attracts retail tourism from all over Africa, and other large cities such as Cape Town and Durban offer similar opportunities for buying Western-style goods if that's what you

Zulu hats are just one of the many local crafts that are available to buy in South Africa. (AVZ)

have in mind. Shops in smaller towns are less well stocked but should still have most things tourists are likely to require during the course of a holiday. By contrast, shopping opportunities are rather more limited in game reserves, and while many upmarket lodges have gift shops that stock things like batteries, electric adaptors and toiletries, it is advisable not to rely on such items being available outside of towns.

The opportunities for **craft shopping** are practically endless: handicraft shops and stalls can be found at many lodges and in most towns and other places where tourists congregate. A mind-boggling array of crafts from all over Africa are on sale at markets such as Cape Town's Greenmarket Square and Johannesburg's Bruma Lake and African Craft Market (Rosebank Mall). Shops invariably charge fixed prices, but bargaining is essential at markets. There are no fixed rules for bargaining, some people say that you should offer half the asking price and be prepared to settle at around two-thirds, but often it seems a lot more whimsical than such advice suggests.

Media and communications

Internet
Internet is widely available in South Africa, and while broadband speeds are generally slower than in Europe or the USA, this is constantly improving. Most hotels have Wi-Fi or a fixed internet connection point

VAT refunds

A Value Added Tax (VAT) of 14%, automatically included in most prices, can be reclaimed by foreign visitors within 90 days of purchase on goods that cost more than ZAR250. In order to do this, you'll need a tax invoice specifying the name and address both of the seller and of the buyer, as well as the seller's VAT registration number, and a description and the cost of the goods. Present this invoice, together with the goods, at the airport VAT Goods Inspection Desk prior to check-in on your departure from South Africa, and you should be refunded the VAT in full (minus an administration charge of 1.5%). See also ✆ www.taxrefunds.co.za.

in all their guest bedrooms. Others will have a business centre or a few computers at the disposal of the guests. In some cases this in-house service is free, but where it isn't, charges tend to be significantly higher than in public internet cafés, which can be found in most malls and other places where shops are concentrated. Alternatively, if your mobile phone has internet facilities and you intend to buy a local SIM card, ask the provider to change the network settings on your phone to pick up their service, and you'll be able to browse for next to nothing.

Be warned that public internet facilities may not exist in smaller towns, and access – even through a phone – may be problematic or erratic in game reserves. For this reason, it is advisable to catch up on any outstanding correspondence before you go on safari, and to warn anxious relatives used to 24-hour broadband not to panic if you are out of touch for the duration.

Telephones

Mobile (cell) phones are increasingly dominant in South Africa. The three main providers – MTN (✆ www.mtn.co.za), Vodacom (✆ www.vodacom. co.za) and Cell C (✆ www.cellc.co.za) – all operate on GSM digital, and will allow digital roaming if your phone is compatible. Alternatively, some international mobile phones will work in South Africa on a local SIM card, which is cheap to buy, easy to install, and offers you inexpensive SMS (text) messaging facilities as well as internet access (assuming your phone is compatible). All numbers starting 071 079 or 082 085 are mobile phones.

The land line service in South Africa is also very good, with the most common regional dialling codes being 011 (Johannesburg), 012 (Pretoria), 021 (Cape Town) and 031 (Durban). Public telephones are much cheaper than in hotels, and you can buy a prepaid phonecard from any post office or supermarket in denominations ranging from ZAR10 to 200. All domestic calls must be dialled as a full ten-digit number, starting with the regional dialling code, even from within the same region. From outside the country, dial (00)27 for South Africa, and then the rest of the number but drop the leading zero (so a Johannesburg number is just 11). To phone abroad from South Africa, dial 00 followed by the relevant country code, for example 1 for the USA or Canada 1, or 44 for the UK.

Media

South Africa has a high level of press freedom, despite government threats to impose a restrictive new Protection of Information Bill on the print media in 2011. The dominant player in the print media is the Independent News and Media Group (ᐃ www.iol.co.za), which produces daily the *Johannesburg Star*, *Cape Argus*, *Pretoria News* and *Natal Mercury*, as well as the national *Independent on Sunday*. Also recommended is the rather dry but refreshingly non-sensationalist *Business Day*, while the outspoken *Mail & Guardian*, published on Fridays, contains good arts coverage and entertainment listings, and has an excellent website (ᐃ www.mg.co.za). Another good source of online commentary news is the erudite *Daily Maverick* (ᐃ www.thedailymaverick.co.za).

The South African Broadcasting Corporation (SABC) broadcasts on three television channels, imaginatively called SABC 1, 2 and 3, which together with a private, free-to-air channel called e-TV contain a mix of local and international programmes, broadcast in a combination of English and other official languages, and interrupt programming with regular advertising. Most hotels subscribe to DSTV, a multi-channel service whose flagship station M-Net is supplemented by a bouquet including BBC, CNN, MTV, and several sports and movie channels. The SABC and various commercial and community radio stations broadcast in all 11 official languages.

Language

South Africa has 11 official languages, more than any other country in the world. English is spoken as a first or second language by most people involved in the tourism industry, and the other ten languages are Afrikaans (a Dutch derivative), IsiZulu, IsiXhosa, SeSotho, Sepedi (also known as North SeSotho), IsiNdebele, Tshivenda, Setswana, Xitsonga and siSwati.

Business

Business hours are broadly similar to those in Europe or North America. Shops, government offices and other formal businesses are generally open weekdays 09.00–17.00, and most shops are open until at least 13.00 on Saturdays. Many city shopping malls now stay open from 09.00–21.00 Monday to Saturday, with shorter opening hours on Sundays. Supermarkets are also usually open on Sundays, but cannot sell alcohol. Banks generally open 09.00–15.30 Monday to Friday and 08.30–11.00 Saturdays. Some Muslim-owned enterprises close for prayers between 12.00 and 13.00 on Fridays.

Car rental and domestic flights

Although this book is aimed primarily at people on organised tours, South Africa is particularly well suited to self-drive holidays and the usual car rental agencies are represented in all large cities, major international airports and many other tourist centres. Rental rates are good value by international standards, but be aware that driving is on the left (as in the UK rather than the USA or mainland Europe), a valid driving licence and credit card is required, and many agencies will not rent cars to under-25s. For further details, check the websites of companies such as Avis (☏ 086 1021 111; ⏧ www.avis.co.za); Budget (☏ 086 102 6622; ⏧ www.budget.co.za); Europcar (☏ 086 113 1000; ⏧ www.europcar.co.za); and Hertz (☏021 935 4800; ⏧ www.hertz.co.za).

South Africa is now well equipped with companies offering cheap domestic flights between the main centres such as Johannesburg, Cape Town, Durban and to a lesser extent Port Elizabeth, East London, George, Bloemfontein and Mbombela (Nelspruit). Airlines worth checking out are Kulula (⏧ www.kulula.com); Mango (⏧ www.flymango.co.za); 1time (⏧ www.1time.co.za); and a cheaper affiliate of SAA called SA Express (⏧www.flyexpress.aero). Book online with these airlines and well-priced hotel accommodation and car rental can be organised as part of the package.

Time

Southern African Time is two hours ahead of GMT/UTC and seven hours ahead of US Eastern Standard Time. There is no daylight saving.

South Africa Highlights

5 Johannesburg and the Northwest

Bustling, chaotic and unapologetically commerce-driven, Johannesburg – dubbed eGoli, Joburg or Jozi by locals – is the capital of Gauteng, the country's most progressive, urbanised and cash-intoxicated province. A seSotho name meaning 'Place of Gold', Gauteng as we know it exists purely because of the immense wealth that lies beneath its soil. Indeed, prior to the discovery of gold at Johannesburg in 1886, much of Gauteng was practically uninhabited farmland. Today the province supports 20% of South Africa's population and generates an astonishing 10% of the entire African GDP, all within a mere 18,178km^2 – less than 1.5% of the country's surface area. And while Johannesburg may not be as immediately appealing as Cape Town or Durban, it does offer plenty of sightseeing, from the UNESCO-certified Cradle of Humankind and the chilling Apartheid Museum to the lovely Pilanesberg and Madikwe Game Reserves in neighbouring Northwest Province.

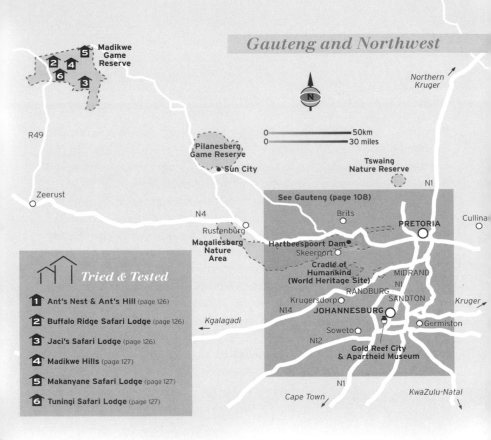

Madikwe
Game
Reserve

Northern
Kruger

R49

Pilanesberg
Game Reserve

Sun City

0 ————————— 50km
0 ————————— 30 miles

Tswaing
Nature Reserve

N1

Zeerust

See Gauteng (page 108)

N4

Brits

Cullina

PRETORIA

Rustenburg

Magaliesberg
Nature
Area

Hartbeespoort Dam

Skeerport

Cradle of
Humankind
(World Heritage Site)

MIDRAND

N1

RANDBURG

SANDTON

Kruger

Kgalagadi

Krugersdorp

N14   JOHANNESBURG

Soweto

N12

Germiston

Gold Reef City
& Apartheid Museum

N1

Cape Town

KwaZulu-Natal

Tried & Tested

1 Ant's Nest & Ant's Hill (page 126)

2 Buffalo Ridge Safari Lodge (page 126)

3 Jaci's Safari Lodge (page 126)

4 Madikwe Hills (page 127)

5 Makanyane Safari Lodge (page 127)

6 Tuningi Safari Lodge (page 127)

Gauteng

An economic powerhouse whose influence extends to most corners of sub-equatorial Africa, Gauteng is home to four of South Africa's most populous ten cities, including the provincial capital Johannesburg – southern Africa's largest city, with a

Pretoria, South Africa's capital city (FD/D)

population approaching four million – and the national capital Pretoria. Unsurprisingly, Gauteng is also the main regional centre of business travel, serviced by sub-equatorial Africa's busiest international airport, and it also forms an important funnel for incoming tourists, albeit by default as much as by design.

For all that, few people dedicate longer to Gauteng than a grudging one-night stand dictated by flight schedules and itineraries. This is a shame, because despite its high crime rate, Johannesburg, the provincial capital, is the vibrant social fulcrum of the country's most culturally integrated and forward-looking province. Furthermore, if you apply a modicum of common sense, Gauteng is probably no more threatening to tourists than most other African cities. Give it a chance and you'll find that it offers no shortage of stimulating museums and cultural experiences, ranging from three million-year-old prehistoric sites to contemporary theatres and music venues.

History

Fossils unearthed to the west of Johannesburg indicate that the region has been inhabited by hominids for more than four million years. The world's oldest *Homo erectus* fossil (1.4 million years old) was uncovered here, along with the earliest evidence of controlled fire usage (one million years ago). More recently, the Sotho and Tswana arrived from the north and established large stone settlements, many of which were evacuated in the early 19th-century Mfecane. In 1855, the city of Pretoria was established by the Voortrekker leader Marthinus Pretorius. Johannesburg was founded in 1886 following the discovery of what turned out to be the world's richest gold deposits, and by the turn of the 20th century it was the largest and wealthiest city in southern Africa.

Racial segregation has always existed in Johannesburg. As early as 1904, the non-White residents of Brickfields (present-day Newtown) were forcibly evicted to makeshift camps outside the municipal limits. Following its 1948 electoral victory, the National Party further enforced the apartheid model of residential segregation along racial lines, with 'townships' such as Soweto and Alexandra being reserved exclusively for Blacks, Eldorado Park and Westbury for Coloureds, and Lenasia for Indians. Several more integrated suburbs, most famously Sophiatown, were re-zoned for Whites and their existing residents forcibly removed to a suitable township.

Voortrekker at the base of the Paul Kruger statue, Pretoria (CZ)

Practicalities

All international and most domestic **flights** land at OR Tambo International Airport, which lies to the east of Johannesburg, 10 minutes' drive from Bruma, 30 minutes' drive from Sandton, and around an hour from Pretoria, dependent on traffic. On an organised tour your flight should be met by the ground operator, but failing that most hotels offer airport shuttles or transfers (indeed, if you are literally just stopping overnight in Johannesburg, several hotels located within a few kilometres of the airport offer free transfers). Otherwise, the options are a taxi cab, the cheaper Magic Bus shuttle (✆ www.magicbus.co.za), or the glittering new Gautrain (✆ www.gautrain.co.za), a high-speed rail service that connects the airport and Sandton, and should also run to the city centre, Rosebank and Pretoria by the time you read this. For further information, the Gauteng Tourism Authority airport desk is open 06.00–22.00 daily for advice.

Johannesburg and Pretoria have all the **tourist amenities** you'd expect of a world city. There are several banks at the airport with ATMs (where local currency can be drawn on a foreign card) and foreign exchange facilities. Hotels can also change foreign currency, though often at a poorer rate, and shopping

Accommodation

Exclusive
Michelangelo Towers Sandton ✆ www.michelangelotowers.co.za
Saxon Boutique Hotel Sandhurst ✆ www.thesaxon.com
Ten Bompas Hotel Sandton ✆ www.tenbompas.com

Upmarket
OR Tambo InterContinental At OR Tambo Airport ✆ www.ichotelsgroup.com
Peech Boutique Hotel Sandton ✆ www.thepeech.co.za
Rosebank Crowne Plaza Rosebank ✆ www.therosebank.co.za
Sheraton Pretoria Hotel Pretoria ✆ www.starwoodhotels.com

Moderate
Maropeng Hotel Cradle of Humankind ✆ www.maropeng.co.za
OR Tambo Garden Court Near OR Tambo Airport ✆ www.southernsun.com
Protea Hotel Balalaika Sandton ✆ www.balalaika.co.za
Protea Hotel Gold Reef City Gold Reef City ✆ www.goldreefcity.co.za
Protea Hotel Hatfield Pretoria ✆ www.proteahotels.com

malls such as Sandton City, Eastgate (Bruma), Rosebank Mall and Hatfield Mall (Pretoria) are packed with banks, supermarkets, boutique shops, eateries and cinemas. For craft shopping, the African Craft Market at Rosebank Mall, and Bruma Flea Market, are both exceptional, with wares from all over Africa on sale, usually at a negotiable price. Both cities have a cosmopolitan

Shops and restaurants along the Randburg waterfront, Johannesburg (SS)

dining out scene, and a few firm favourites are listed below. If you are venturing out to shop or eat, it is advisable to take a taxi, which can be arranged through any hotel reception desk. Hotels can also put you in touch with reliable local operators offering day tours to the Cradle of Humankind, Soweto and Pretoria.

Budget

Africa Centre Lodge Near OR Tambo Airport ⌂ www.africacentrelodge.co.za
Airport Backpackers Near OR Tambo Airport
⌂ www.airportbackpackers.co.za
Backpackers Ritz Dunkeld West ⌂ www.backpackers-ritz.com
Word of Mouth Backpackers Pretoria ⌂ www.wordofmouthbackpackers.com

Eating out

Cranks (Thai), Rosebank Mall ☎ 011 880 3442
⌂ www.themallofrosebank.co.za
DW Eleven-13 (Continental fusion), Dunkeld West Centre, Sandton
☎ 011 341 0663 ⌂ www.dw11-13.co.za
Gramadoelas (Cape & African), Market Theatre, Newtown ☎ 011 838 6960
⌂ www.gramadoelas.co.za
Le Canard (French & Continental), Rivonia Rd, Sandton ☎ 011 884 4597
⌂ www.lecanard.co.za
Moyo (pan-African), branches at Melrose Arch & Rosebank ☎ 011 664 1477
⌂ www.moyo.co.za

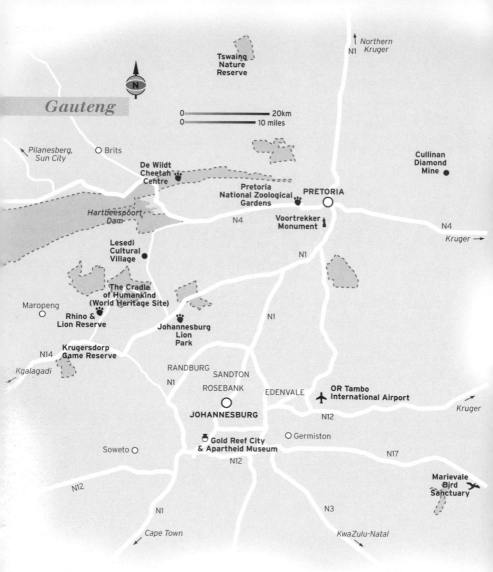

Since 1994, Gauteng has emerged as the country's most culturally diverse province, attracting job-seekers from all corners of South Africa, and beyond. There is no single dominant culture here – five different languages serve as a mother tongue to at least 10% of the provincial population – and a high level of post-apartheid upward mobility means that suburbs once reserved for Whites are now increasingly integrated. The inverse isn't quite as true: more than 25% of adults living in Africa's wealthiest urban conglomeration are unemployed, and fewer than 20% have a monthly income in excess of US$1,000. The townships and informal settlements established under apartheid remain almost exclusively Black, and generally very poor.

Gauteng highlights

Central Johannesburg

During the course of the 1990s, high crime rates persuaded most of Jozi's centrally located businesses and hotels to evacuate to the perceived safety of the suburbs such as Sandton, Rosebank and Bruma. Ever since, the city centre, bustling though it is by day, has worn a somewhat down-at-heel feel that transforms into an aura of complete abandonment after dark. Regular visitors to the city centre will tell you that crime is no longer the problem it once was – it, too, seems to have shuffled off to suburbia – but it would still be reckless to recommend that a first-time visitor explored central Joburg other than on an organised tour, which is easily arranged at any hotel.

Architecturally, central Johannesburg is of limited interest: in 'wow factor' terms, the few surviving early 20th-century buildings dutifully pointed out by tour guides are to, say, Westminster Cathedral, what a house sparrow is to a lion kill. By contrast, it's certainly worth catching

(PA/D)

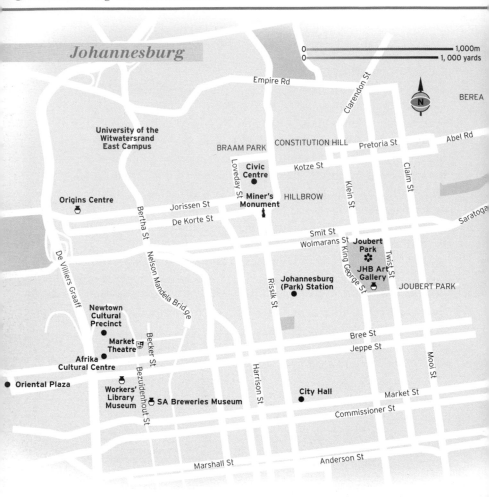

a high-speed elevator to the 50th floor of the **Carlton Centre**: this 223m-high relict of the 1970s economic boom still ranks as Africa's tallest building, and the expansive views across the city centre to distant mine dumps, slime dams and hills are stunning.

Otherwise, perhaps the most gratifying aspect of the Central Business District (CBD) today is how very African it feels – not unlike downtown Nairobi or Kampala – by comparison to the 'Whites-only' bastion it remained well into the 1980s. Nowhere is this transformation more evident than in the **Newtown Precinct** (⌖ www.newtown.co.za), formerly Brickfields, which was one of the city's earliest mixed-race suburbs. It supported some 7,000 labourers prior to 1904, when an outbreak of plague provided a pretext to evict its African, Indian and Coloured residents outside the city limits to what are now Alexandra and Soweto. Newlands emerged as a centre of artistic creativity and

Newtown landmarks

Market Theatre

📞 011 832 1641

🌐 www.markettheatre.co.za

The district's cultural hub since the 1970s, this historic building houses three theatres that specialise in modern South African dramas. The superb Gramadoelas Restaurant (see *Eating out*, page 107) is in the same building.

Museum Africa

📞 011 833 5624

🌐 www.museumafrica.org

🕐 09.00–17.00 Tue–Sun

(AVZ)

Also set within the former market building, this is well worth a couple of hours for its varied displays focussing mainly on the history of Johannesburg.

The Bassline

📞 011 838 9142 🌐 www.bassline.co.za

Superb music venue with live acts spanning everything from reggae and jazz to contemporary R&B and local sounds.

Mai-Mai Market

Cnr Berea and Anderson St 🕐 09.00–17.00 Mon–Fri

Not for the faint of heart, the market also known as Ezinyangeni (Place of Healers) comprises 150-plus stalls selling *muti* (traditional medicine) and the often macabre paraphernalia associated with traditional healers.

World of Beer

📞 011 836 4900 🌐 www.worldofbeer.co.za 🕐 10.00–17.00 Tue–Sat

Owned by the South African-founded, beer-producing multinational SAB-Miller, this place offers what are surprisingly engaging 90-minute tours that explore the history of brewing and culminate in a couple of cans of your favourite SAB lager.

anti-apartheid activism in the 1970s, when its old vegetable market was converted into the city's first non-racial theatre, and it has undergone intensive rehabilitation since the turn of the millennium (see box, page 111).

Connected to Newtown by the 284m Nelson Mandela Bridge, Braamfontein is home to the prestigious University of the Witwatersrand, or 'Wits' as it is more widely known. On the campus, the **Origins Centre** (✆ 011 717 4700 🖥 www.origins.org.za ⊕ 09.00–17.00 daily), a state-of-the-art museum opened by President Mbeki in 2006, forms a superb primer for the Cradle of Humankind to the west of the city. It houses a series of interactive displays covering the entire drama of human evolution alongside the world's largest collection of prehistoric rock art. Nearby **Constitutional Hill** (✆ 011 381 3100 🖥 www.constitutionhill.org.za ⊕ 09.00–16.30 daily) is now the site of the constitutional Court and a museum dedicated to its former incarnation as the infamous Old Fort Prison, where activists such as Nelson Mandela and Mahatma Gandhi were detained during the apartheid era.

(AVZ)

Gold Reef City
✆ 011 248 6800
🖥 www.goldreefcity.co.za
⊕ 09.00–18.00 daily

Johannesburg retains few genuine relics of its early days as a makeshift mining shantytown, but something of the formative gold rush era is preserved in a theme park called Gold Reef City, about 5km south of the city centre. The park stands above Crown Mines No 14 Shaft, which extends more than 3km underground and produced 1.4 million kilograms of gold between 1897 and its closure in 1971. Guided tours of the shaft involve a descent in a metal lift to about 220m below ground, while above ground, in the reconstructed Victorian mining town, you can watch molten gold being poured into ingot moulds and performances of the Isicathulo 'gumboot dance' associated with the migrant labourers who worked in the mines. It should be noted that for most visitors the park's main attraction is a selection of around two-dozen rides that range from the diverting to the genuinely terrifying – very popular with children.

Apartheid Museum

📞 011 309 4700

🌐 www.apartheidmuseum.org

🕐 10.00-17.00 Tue-Sun

Situated on the opposite side of the same car park as Gold Reef, and positioned at the other extreme on the 'fun-for-all-the-family' scale, the Apartheid Museum was officially opened by Nelson Mandela in 2002. The museum's motto is 'Today,

(AVZ)

apartheid is exactly where it belongs: in a museum', and it sets out its stall by randomly allocating all visitors with a 'White' or 'non-White' ticket that determines through which of the two segregated gates they must enter. Inside the museum there is an exhaustive selection of photographs, old newsreels and other imaginative displays documenting the rise and fall of apartheid, and the cruelty and barbarism with which it was enforced.

Soweto

The most infamous of the Black 'townships' associated with apartheid, Soweto is also the oldest such entity around Johannesburg, though its present name – rather prosaically, nothing more than an acronym of South West Townships – dates to 1963, when it was officially imposed on a cluster of loosely affiliated Black settlements to the southwest of the city centre. The setting for many pivotal events during the anti-apartheid struggle, Soweto has at some point been home to several of the country's most revered figures, including Nelson Mandela and Archbishop Desmond Tutu.

Pimville, originally called Klipspruit, is Soweto's oldest quarter. It was established in 1904 to accommodate, on a rental-only basis, Blacks who had been forcibly evicted from Brickfields (Indian and Coloured evictees were moved to Alexandra, where they were allowed to own property, a right that would be revoked in the apartheid era). **Orlando**, named after its first administrator, was established in the 1930s, and Johannesburg's first informal settlement, comprising some 20,000 squatters, was established by James Mpanza in the 1940s. The suburb of **Meadowlands** was created in 1959 to accommodate people forcibly evicted from Sophiatown.

Although it is no longer as unsafe to visit as it was during the apartheid era, Soweto is still best explored on one of the tours that are offered by

Soweto landmarks

Walter Sisulu Square

☎ 011 945 2200 ⌨ www.waltersisulusquare.co.za

Now a modern shopping mall in Kliptown, this was an empty field in June 1955 when some 3,000 representatives of various resistance organisations met here to draw up the Freedom Charter, the cornerstone of the present-day South African constitution.

Hector Pieterson Memorial & Museum

☎ 011 536 0611 ◷ 10.00-17.00 daily

It was the trigger-happy police response to a student protest against the enforced use of Afrikaans in schools that provoked the Soweto Uprising, a series of anti-apartheid clashes that claimed more than 500 young lives in 1976. This poignant memorial in Orlando West stands a few hundred metres from where its 13-year-old namesake was felled by the first wave of police fire during the initial protest on 16 July 1976.

Mandela House

☎ 011 936 7754 ⌨ www.mandelahouse.com ◷ 09.00-17.00 Mon-Fri, 09.30-16.30 Sat-Sun

The humble dwelling where Nelson Mandela lived with his family in the years preceding his imprisonment in 1962 has become a museum dedicated to the Mandela family.

Wandie's Place

☎ 011 982 2796 ⌨ www.wandies.co.za

Almost all Soweto tours include a lunch break at the one-time hole-in-the-wall shebeen (illegal bar) that was founded by Wandie Ndaba in 1981 and has developed into a delightfully unpretentious licensed restaurant serving buffets dominated by traditional African dishes.

FNB Stadium

Also known as Soccer City and the Calabash, this 95,000-seater ranks among the world's ten largest stadia. It hosted South Africa's 2-0 championship victory over Tunisia in the 1996 Africa Nations Cup, the 2010 FIFA World Cup final between Spain and The Netherlands, and one of Nelson Mandela's first speeches following his release from prison in 1990. It debuted as a concert venue when U2 performed here in February 2011.

Soweto is best explored on a township tour. (SS)

most hotels and operators in Johannesburg. These are typically guided by residents or former residents of Soweto, and they follow a route that not only avoids potential trouble spots, but will take in most of the landmark sites listed opposite.

Northern suburbs

To the north of the city centre, Johannesburg's smartest suburbs are for the most part bisected or flanked by Oxford Street, Rivonia Road and/or Jan Smuts Avenue, which run roughly parallel to each other for several kilometres. Some of these suburbs, for instance Houghton (home to Nelson Mandela), are strictly residential, while others, specifically Sandton and Rosebank, have emerged as important tourist focuses endowed with plentiful opportunities for retail therapy but limited opportunities for genuine sightseeing.

The more down to earth of these is **Rosebank**, which boasts a number of boutique hotels and is the site of a cluster of shopping malls, including the Rosebank Mall (www.themallofrosebank.co.za) and the funkier Zone (www.thezoneatrosebank.co.za). Between them, these malls must house a few dozen restaurants, along with a cinema complex, the excellent African Craft Market, and a mindboggling selection of shops. Other landmarks in and around Rosebank include the Johannesburg Zoo, nearby Zoo Lake, and the renowned Everard Read Gallery (www.everard-read.co.za) and Goodman Gallery (www.goodman-gallery.com).

Further north, prestigious **Sandton** probably has the most hotel beds of any suburb in Johannesburg, though most are at the pricier end of the scale. It is home to several malls including the immense Sandton City (🖰 www.sandtoncity.com), which opens out onto Nelson Mandela Square, overlooked by a towering bronze sculpture of its popular namesake. Both malls have a plethora of restaurants, chain stores and boutiques, as well as cinema complexes and restaurants to keep you amused on a rare rainy day.

Cradle of Humankind
📞 014 577 9000 🖰 www.maropeng.co.za ⏱ 09.00–15.00; combined tickets for Maropeng Visitors Centre & Sterkfontein Caves available until 13.00 only.

The paleontological treasure trove dubbed the Cradle of Humankind (COH) lies in western Gauteng, about 40km from central Johannesburg or Sandton. The drive out there can take anything from 30 minutes to longer than an hour, depending on traffic and where you start. The COH comprises an ancient Karstic landscape, the 2.5 billion-year-old dolomite bedrock of which started life as an ocean floor covered in blue-green algae, one of the earliest known life forms. The dolomite is rich in soluble and erosive calcium carbonate, which seeps into the fault lines and gradually transforms them into gaping limestone caverns and sinkholes in which living creatures are frequently trapped and their bones readily fossilised.

The main body of the COH, extending over 470km² and comprising 13 excavated paleontological sites, was inscribed as a UNESCO World Heritage Site in 1999, which was extended to include the Taung Skull

Fossil Site and Makapans Valley, both about 300km further northwest, in 2005. The most important excavations, which include Sterkfontein Caves, Swartkrans, Kromdraai and Drimolen, have collectively produced hundreds of specimens belonging to the three most widely recognised hominid genera: *Paranthropus*, *Australopithecus* and *Homo*. True, no single fossil unearthed here is of comparable antiquity to the oldest discoveries in Kenya and Ethiopia, but collectively they represent a uniquely complete record of the last 3–4 million years of human evolution.

The main focal point of tourism in the COH, officially opened by President Thabo Mbeki in 2005, is the **Maropeng Visitors Centre**, which lies along the D400 about 50km west of Johannesburg. Shaped like a giant tumulus (burial mound) and covered in grass, this award-winning, innovative and unusually child-friendly installation is a shoo-in as Gauteng's least stuffy museum. Self-guided tours, which take about two hours, start with an exciting boat ride through a subterranean waterway that takes you backwards in time, reproducing the volatile seismic conditions that shaped our planet's geology. This leads to the main hall, where a series of intelligent but accessible displays document the evolution of humankind – encompassing the birth of bipedalism, the controlled use of fire and the development of language – as well as addressing ecological challenges facing our species today.

The only one of the COH's palcontological sites open to the public is **Sterkfontein Caves**, which lies off the R563 about 10km from Maropeng. Exposed by lime-quarry blasting in the late 19th century, the caves comprise six cavernous chambers and an underground lake that's said to have healing powers. Under continuous excavation since 1966, this is the richest site in the world for early hominids, having yielded the partial fossil remains of more than 500 individuals. It was here, in 1936, that Dr Robert Broom discovered Mrs Ples, the 2.5 million-year-old *Australopithecus africanus* skull that provided the first fossil confirmation of Darwin's theory that humans evolved in Africa. Highly informative guided tours of the caves leave every hour on the hour, and joint tickets are available at Maropeng.

The Sterkfontein Caves give a fascinating insight into millions of years of human evolution. (AVZ)

Quick-fix wildlife venues

Several rather contrived wildlife sanctuaries and zoos lie within easy driving distance of central Johannesburg, and while none offers a holistic experience comparable to visiting a proper game reserve such as Kruger or Madikwe, all are useful fall-backs for those with limited time or travelling with easily bored children. The first three places listed below offer the opportunity to see lions and other large African mammals in drive-through enclosures; the latter two are straightforward zoos.

Johannesburg Lion Park ℂ 011 691 9905 ⏚ www.lion-park.com
🕐 08.00–17.00 daily
Rhino and Lion Reserve ℂ 011 957 0349 ⏚ www.rhinolion.co.za
🕐 08.00–15.45 daily
Krugersdorp Game Reserve ℂ 011 950 9900 🕐 08.00–17.00 daily
Johannesburg Zoo ℂ 011-646 2000 ⏚ www.jhbzoo.org.za
🕐 08.30–17.30 daily
Pretoria National Zoological Gardens ℂ 012 328 3265 ⏚ www.zoo.ac.za
🕐 08.00–17.00 daily

Pretoria

Established in 1855 and made capital of the Boer-ruled Zuid-Afrikaansche Republiek shortly thereafter, Pretoria is now part of Tshwane Metropolitan Municipality, which also includes a variety of satellite towns and former townships such as Atteridgeville, Centurion and Laudium. The political capital of South Africa since the union was forged in 1910, it lies a mere 50km north of Johannesburg, and is connected to it by an ever-solidifying ribbon of urban development, yet the two cities are wildly divergent in character. In economic and social terms, Pretoria is perennially overshadowed by its brash and flighty upstart sibling, while a long tenure as the directorate of apartheid has left it with a slight stigma of fuddy-duddy illiberalism.

It doesn't help that organised tours of Pretoria tend to focus on landmarks that hark back to the 'old' South Africa. Most famous among these, and visible from many points in the CBD, is the hilltop **Voortrekker Monument** (⏚ www.voortrekkermon.org.za), an isolated sentinel on the city's southern outskirts. At once dourly parochial and oddly affecting, this immense granite monolith was built in the 1940s as a 'monument that would stand a thousand years to describe the history and the meaning of the Great Trek to its descendants'.

These days, frankly, it feels more like a monument to the mounting Afrikaner nationalism and self-mythologising that led to the formal adoption of apartheid following the National Party electoral victory of 1948. Nevertheless, visited in a spirit of instruction, it does indeed pay powerful tribute to the intrepid Voortrekkers who opened up the South African interior to the outside world.

In most respects, however, Pretoria's stick-in-the-mud reputation seems unfair. Changing times have left their mark on such notorious 'Whites-only' preserves as the **Union Buildings**, whose architect Sir

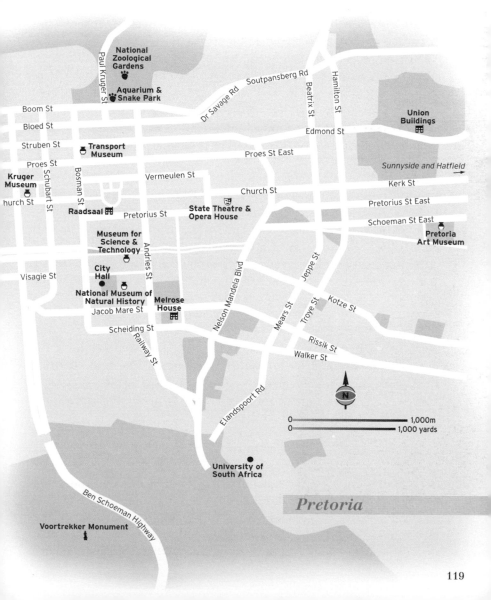

Herbert Baker thoughtfully allowed for 'a small, partly open council place where, without coming into the building, natives may feel the majesty of government'. This handsome, orange sandstone creation, perched dramatically on the crest of its lovely sloping gardens, is now remembered as the site of Nelson Mandela's presidential inauguration in 1994, and its bullet-proof windows have protected an ANC-dominated parliament ever since.

Pretoria's CBD, with its mishmash of 19th and early to mid-20th-century architecture, is intruded upon by a mere scattering of contemporary office blocks and shopping malls. It possesses a stately, almost old-world quality, and is particularly attractive in October when its famous jacarandas come into bloom. Within walking distance of the CBD, lived-in suburbs such as **Sunnyside** and **Hatfield** boast the sort of concentrated but easy going bar, restaurant and nightclub scene that crime and decentralisation have all but killed in Johannesburg. Here you'll find art galleries and gay bars, flea markets and Asian bazaars, backpacker hostels and boutique hotels.

Several historical sites in the CBD date back to the Zuid-Afrikaansche Republiek, among them the appropriately unpretentious **Kruger Museum** (⚲ www.ditsong.org.za), set in the small but immaculately restored house inhabited by President Paul Kruger and his wife between 1884 and 1901, and the pre-Union seat of government, the **Old Raadsaal** overlooking Church Square. Also on Church Street, the **State Theatre** (⚲ www.statetheatre.co.za) hosts regular drama, opera, ballet, and concert performances in its six auditoriums. To the southeast, **Melrose House** (⚲ www. melrosehouse.co.za) is a finely preserved, period-furnished Victorian mansion where the treaty ending the Anglo–Boer War was signed. Also highly worthwhile is the **National Museum of Natural History** (⚲ www.ditsong.org.za), which houses a diverse collection of fossils and prehistoric rock art.

Diamond mining has been carried out at Cullinan for over 100 years. (AVZ)

Cullinan Diamond Mine

☎ 012 734 2626 ⚲ www.cullinandiamonds.co.za
Situated 30km east of Pretoria along the R513, this small mining town is named after Sir Thomas Cullinan, who established the Premier Diamond Mine here in 1903. Two years later, the mine's surface manager

Frederick Wells stumbled upon the largest, rough-quality gem diamond ever found: the 3,106-carat Star of Africa (or Cullinan Diamond), which the Transvaal government in Pretoria bought as a birthday present for King Edward VII of England. It was later cut into nine major pieces – several of which are now on display in the Tower of London as part of the Crown Jewels – and 96 smaller ones. As with the Kimberley, a gaping hole marks the site of the original surface diggings, which closed in 1932 when it proved impossible to go any deeper. It re-opened as an underground mine in 1945 and has been operational ever since, though it was renamed Cullinan Diamond Mine in 2003 and sold by De Beers to Rio Tinto in 2007. Several 90-minute surface tours leave daily, and five-hour underground tours are also offered.

Tswaing Nature Reserve
℡ 012 945 5911 🖥 www.ditsong.org.za ⏰ 07.30–16.00 daily

Situated along the M35 only 30 minutes' drive north of Pretoria, this underrated 20km² reserve is centred on a 1.4km-wide, 200m-deep impact crater created around 200,000 years ago when a house-sized meteorite slammed to earth. The impact would have been beyond comprehension, releasing a blast of energy equivalent to 30 atom bombs, and obliterating all life within a radius of 35km. The setting is a lot more peaceful today; there is a small salt lake nestling on the crater floor, while the rim supports lush acacia woodland teeming with birds and supporting a fair amount of wildlife, including kudus and baboons. The three-hour hike that runs all the way around the crater is best tackled in the early morning, before the heat of the day kicks in.

The Tswaing Nature Reserve has explosive origins. (R/D)

Northwest Province

Running along the Botswana border to the east of Gauteng, the blandly named and thinly populated Northwest maintains perhaps the lowest profile of South Africa's nine provinces. Prior to 1994, much of it formed part of the nominally independent homeland of Bophuthatswana, and today roughly two-thirds of its three million inhabitants speak Tswana as a first language. Literacy and employment levels are among the lowest in the country, with the economic mainstay being mining – the world's largest platinum deposits are found near Rustenburg, and the province also has gold, uranium and diamonds – which generates more than half of the country's GDP.

None of Northwest's towns hold much appeal for visitors. The provincial capital Mahikeng (formerly Mafeking) was the site of the 217-day Anglo-Boer War siege that made a household name of Lord Baden-Powell, founder of the Boy Scout Movement. Much larger, with a population of 450,000, the city of Rustenberg is reputedly the country's fastest-growing urban centre, and will be a name familiar to many as it was England's training base for the 2010 FIFA World Cup. That aside, Northwest has a limited roll call of tourist attractions, with the ostentatious Sun City complex and the adjacent Pilanesberg Game Reserve topping the list, followed by the underrated Madikwe Game Reserve.

Northwest highlights

Sun City

℘ 014 557 1000 ⊕ www.suncity.co.za

Established in 1976 in what was then the homeland of Bophuthatswana, this legendary casino resort started life as a venue for forms of entertainment – for instance, gambling and topless revues – that were banned by the Calvinistic South African government of the day. Fortunately, it has moved on considerably since then and while the massive casino at its heart more or less justifies the 'Las Vegas in the bush' tag, a long list of more wholesome activities include two of the country's finest golf courses, both designed by Gary Player; a child-friendly, manmade inland beach called the Valley of Waves; four hotels, including the fantastically over-the-top Palace of the Lost City; and the 6,000-seater Sun City Super Bowl, which regularly hosts international musicians, WWE wrestling tournaments and beauty pageants. The complex can be great fun if you've cash to spare and you're in the mood for some unbridled hedonism, but for anybody seeking an idyllic African

Practicalities

The legendary casino resort of Sun City. (IF/D)

There are no longer any scheduled flights to **Sun City**, the main regional tourist focus, and while charters can be arranged it is easier to **drive**. This takes about two hours from OR Tambo Airport, Johannesburg or Sandton, or 90 minutes from Pretoria via the scenic Hartebeespoort Dam. Any hotel or tour operator in Gauteng can arrange a **road transfer** to Sun City or one of the lodges within or bordering Pilanesberg Game Reserve, all of which offer guided morning and afternoon game drives in open 4x4s. A rental car is also worth considering, especially with Pilanesberg being so well suited to self-drive safaris.

It's more like four hours' drive from Johannesburg to **Madikwe**, and since all lodges here offer all-inclusive packages and self-drive exploration is forbidden, the best option is to fly, either with Federal Air (⚒ www.fedair.com) or Madikwe Air (⚒ www.madikwecharter.com).

Sun City has excellent amenities – the complex hosts everything from ATMs, newsagents and pharmacies to cinemas and dozens of eateries – and there is a good Spar supermarket outside the main entrance. By contrast, public facilities in the Pilanesberg are limited to a couple of simple eateries and a shop at Manyane Camp, and there's nothing within Madikwe.

Accommodation

For full details of tour operator-recommended accommodation, see pages 126-7. Here follows a few further suggestions from the author.

Exclusive
Palace of the Lost City Sun City ⚒ www.suncity.co.za
Tshukudu Bush Lodge Pilanesberg ⚒ www.legacygroup.co.za

Upmarket
Bakubung Bush Lodge Pilanesberg ⚒ www.legacygroup.co.za
Cabanas Sun City ⚒ www.suncity.co.za
Kwa Maritane Bush Lodge Pilanesberg ⚒ www.legacygroup.co.za

Moderate, budget and camping
Bakgatla Resort Pilanesberg ⚒ www.goldenleopardresorts.co.za
Manyane Resort Pilanesberg ⚒ www.goldenleopardresorts.co.za

bush retreat, Sun City's main saving grace is the fact that it offers ready access to the neighbouring Pilanesberg Game Reserve.

Pilanesberg Game Reserve

☎ 014 555 1600 🖰 www.pilanesberg-game-reserve.co.za ⏱ Nov-Feb 05.30–19.00, Mar-Apr & Sep-Oct 06.00–18.30, May-Aug 06.30–18.00

Only two hours north of Johannesburg, this 550km², malaria-free reserve, nestled scenically within a collapsed volcanic crater, is the closest Big Five destination to Gauteng and one of the best places anywhere in the country for close-up encounters with white rhino and elephant. It was established in the late 1970s, on what was then low-yield farmland, as Bophuthatswana's premier national park, in a location chosen partly because of its proximity to glitzy Sun City. Resident wildlife such as leopard, brown hyena and kudu was supplemented by the likes of lion, buffalo, elephant, giraffe, white and black rhino, plains zebra, blue wildebeest and various antelope in a programme of reintroductions dubbed Operation Genesis. While some reintroduced species, such as cheetah and sable antelope, have struggled, the majority have flourished and game densities today compare favourably with the likes of the Kruger National Park.

Overall, Pilanesberg offers excellent game viewing, though large predator sightings are patchy by comparison to the Kruger and its associated private reserves. The reserve is particularly interesting to birdwatchers, with a total checklist of 350 bird species including several gems – among them crimson-breasted shrike, violet-eared waxbill, shaft-tailed whydah and pied babbler – that reflect a location transitional to the dry Kalahari biome of the west and the moister eastern *bushveld*. The rugged mountain landscape, sloping down the central Mankwe Dam in what used to be the base of a volcanic crater, is also very memorable and the most mountainous areas are the remote northwest and the southeast between Manyane Resort and Kwa Maritane Bush Camp. Another noteworthy aspect of Pilanesberg is that it is very well suited to an overnight self-drive safari out of Johannesburg, though

White rhinos, Pilanesberg Game Reserve (AVZ)

all the lodges and hotels in the vicinity arrange guided drives in an open 4x4, as well as night drives that offer a good chance of seeing nocturnal specials such as brown hyena, aardwolf, genet and leopard. All activities, along with recently introduced elephant-back safaris, can be arranged with a company called Gametrackers (✆ 014 552 5020 ⌨ www.gametrac.co.za) based at Manyane Resort.

Madikwe Game Reserve
✆ 018 350 9931 ⌨ www.madikwe-game-reserve.co.za; accessible to overnight visitors only

Sharing many ecological and historical attributes with nearby Pilanesberg, the more remote Madikwe Game Reserve is an even more recent creation that is rapidly gaining a reputation as South Africa's premier, malaria-free safari destination. Running along the Botswana border some two hours' drive north of Sun City, the reserve extends over 750km^2 of wooded plains flanked by the perennial Great Marico River along its eastern border, the rugged Rant van Tweedepoort Escarpment to the west, and the Dwarsberg Mountains to the south. Formerly unproductive farm- and ranchland, Madikwe was established as recently as 1991, as a result of a government study that recognised it could be utilised more profitably and offer greater benefits to local communities as a conservation area. During the 1990s, a total of 8,000 individual animals spanning 28 large mammal species were reintroduced, among them an elephant herd from the then drought-affected Gonarezhou National Park in southeast Zimbabwe.

Madikwe protects a similar range of species to the Pilanesberg, though birds associated with the western Kalahari biome are significantly more conspicuous (notably the pied babbler, which guides here dub the 'flying snowball', for reasons that become obvious when you first encounter one). The main difference is that Madikwe caters exclusively to the top end of the safari market. It hosts perhaps 30 exclusive bush camps, which offer a quality of accommodation and all-inclusive packages comparable with the private reserves bordering Kruger. The reserve can be explored only on organised game drives, which are conducted by knowledgeable guides in open 4x4s, and offer an excellent chance of sighting three of the Big Five – lion, elephant and rhino – while buffalo and leopard are also present, but scarcer, and common grazers include giraffe, plains zebra, greater kudu, springbok, red hartebeest and tsessebe. Madikwe is possibly the most reliable reserve in the country for enjoying encounters with the endangered African wild dog, and night drives frequently yield good sightings of the shy brown hyena and bizarre aardwolf.

Tried & Tested

Ant's Nest & Ant's Hill
⚲ www.waterberg.net

THE ZAMBEZI SAFARI
& TRAVEL CO. LTD

Ant's Nest and Ant's Hill are private bush homes in the magnificent malaria-free Waterberg. Specialising in a home-from-home experience, they can be booked exclusively or not. Enjoy fabulous horseriding safaris, guided bush walks or game drives on the privately owned reserve, and al-fresco wining and dining with a view. Flexibility is what they pride themselves on, individually tailoring stays for guests. Facilities include heated pools, gift shops and massages. Suitable for families, riders, honeymooners or just good friends travelling together.

Buffalo Ridge Safari Lodge
⚲ www.buffaloridgesafari.com

to**escape**to
w w w . t o e s c a p e t o . c o m

Buffalo Ridge stands out from other options in Madikwe by being a community-owned safari lodge that offers genuine five-star service. In choosing this lodge you will encounter a truly unique experience. Offering very private accommodation, Buffalo Ridge has eight individually decorated suites, each with expansive views across the Madikwe Reserve. The staff, known as the Balete, all own a part of the lodge and the pride with which it's run makes this place very special indeed.

Jaci's Safari Lodge
⚲ www.madikwe.com

THE ZAMBEZI SAFARI
& TRAVEL CO. LTD

Jaci's promises personal attention to detail from effervescent staff committed to ensuring you enjoy a superb safari. Safari Lodge has eight 'tents' and two exclusive suites, decorated with vibrant colour, earthy canvas, stone and shaggy thatch. Tree Lodge has breathtaking raised walkways and eight 'treehouses' amongst ancient riverine trees – the ultimate luxurious forest hideaway. There are daily game drives in Madikwe, conducted by knowledgeable and attentive guides. The fire-cooked meals under starlight are heavenly. Perfect for romantic safaris, weddings, and families.

Madikwe Hills
🖰 www.madikwehills.com

In a brilliant central location in the malaria-free Madikwe Game Reserve, the lodge has been ingeniously designed around rocky outcrops. High walkways link the suites to the spa, main pool and a waterhole and each of the ten unique suites are cleverly arranged around huge granite boulders. The lodge delivers on every level. The staff are extremely attentive – everyone knows your name. The food is exquisite, the spa treatments perfect after a morning safari and, most importantly, the guides are excellent.

Makanyane Safari Lodge
🖰 www.makanyane.com

BRIDGE & WICKERS
travel with experience

You always feel in the midst of the bush at Makanyane – on a game drive, a bush walk, from your bathtub or in one of the eight stunning suites with their floor-to-ceiling glass walls. Makanyane will indulge you with flexible activities, sublime meals and a bush spa, but remains focused on the wildlife – your guide will invite you to leave dinner to search for a nearby lion. We think a 'sleep-out' in the hide is one of the ultimate wilderness experiences.

Tuningi Safari Lodge
🖰 www.tuningi.com

RAINBOW
TOURS

Set in the malaria-free Madikwe Game Reserve, an easy drive or short flight from Johannesburg, five-star Tuningi does colonial afro-chic to perfection. The six rooms and family suites are capacious with huge bathrooms, air conditioning and large private decks complete with outdoor rock showers. Tuningi positively welcomes children of all ages and our guests rave about the special children's programme. There's a good chance of seeing the Big Five and also wild dog at this welcoming Fair Trade in Tourism-accredited lodge.

6 Kruger and the Northeast

Created from the Transvaal after the 1994 elections, Mpumalanga and Limpopo provinces border Swaziland and Mozambique to the east and Zimbabwe and Botswana to the north. They are among the country's most diverse provinces culturally: Swazi, Zulu, Tsonga, Ndebele and North Sotho each account for more than 10% of Mpumalanga's population, while Limpopo is dominated by North Sotho and to a lesser extent Tsonga and Venda. Both are relatively undeveloped and rural, but while the economy of Limpopo is almost exclusively agricultural, Mpumalanga – a siSwati word meaning 'Place of the Rising Sun' – also has a rapidly growing tourist industry. This is centred upon the Kruger National Park. Other key attractions are the exclusive private reserves that share open borders with the Kruger, and the scenic wonders of the Panorama Route, which incorporates the spectacular Mpumalanga Escarpment and Blyde River Canyon as well as the old mining town of Pilgrim's Rest.

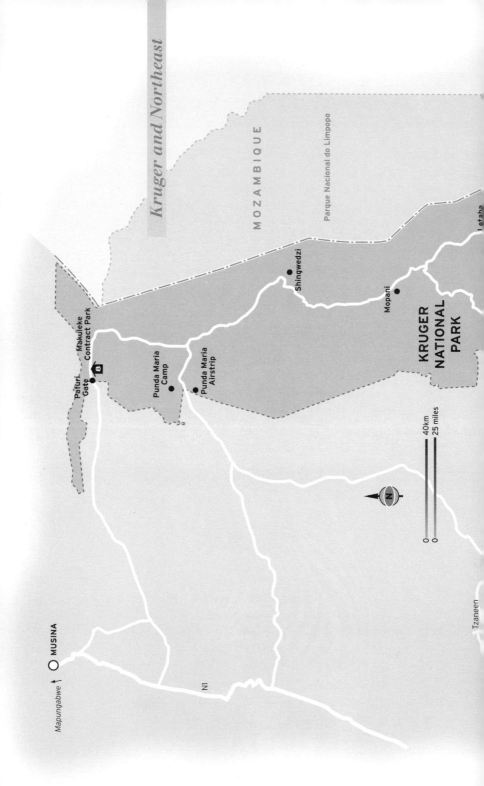

MOZAMBIQUE

Parque Nacional do Limpopo

Letaba

Shingwedzi

Mopani

KRUGER
NATIONAL
PARK

Pafuri
Gate

Makuleke
Contract Park

8

Punda Maria
Camp

Punda Maria
Airstrip

Mapungabwe

MUSINA

N1

Tzaneen

N

40km
25 miles

0
0

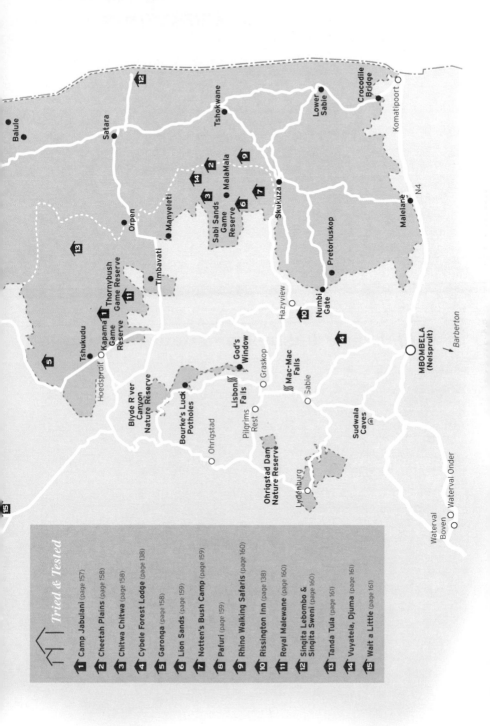

Balule

Satara

Tshokwane

Lower Sabie

Crocodile Bridge

Komatipoort

Orpen

Manyeleti

MalaMala

Sabi Sands Game Reserve

Skukuza

N4

Malelane

Thornybush Game Reserve

Timbavati

Pretoriuskop

Tshukudu

Hoedspruit

Kapama Game Reserve

Numbi Gate

Hazyview

Blyde River Canyon Nature Reserve

Bourke's Luck Potholes

Lisbon Falls

God's Window

Graskop

Mac-Mac Falls

MBOMBELA (Nelspruit)

Barberton

Pilgrims Rest

Sabie

Ohrigstad

Ohrigstad Dam Nature Reserve

Sudwala Caves

Lydenburg

Waterval Boven

Waterval Onder

131

Mbombela and the Panorama Route

The Kruger National Park and associated private reserves (covered later in this chapter) are emphatically the main tourist draws in Mpumalanga and Limpopo, but these provinces are not without other worthwhile attractions, many of which are associated with the tall, scenic escarpment that divides the breezy *highveld* grassland from the sweltering bush country of the lowveld. The main tourist sights in Mpumalanga, a loose circuit collectively referred to as the Panorama Route, include the old mining town of Pilgrim's Rest and the spectacular Blyde River Canyon. They can easily be explored as a one- or two-day add-on to a Kruger safari. Further north in Limpopo, the underrated Modjadji Cycad Reserve and Mapungubwe National Park provide contrasting insights into local traditions and history. Rather less appealing to tourists, Mbombela (formerly Nelspruit), provincial capital of Mpumalanga, is an important gateway to southern Kruger.

Mbombela and Panorama Route highlights

Mbombela

Originally known as Nelspruit, after the trio of Nel brothers who founded the town in 1905, the capital of Mpumalanga was officially renamed Mbombela (a siSwati word meaning 'crowded place') in 2009. It is one of the fastest-expanding cities in South Africa, with a population currently estimated at 250,000, and its outskirts have become visibly more industrialised since the 1990s. Set at an altitude of 650m, 330km east of Johannesburg, the town is surrounded by farmland and the fertile soil and hot climate are ideal for the production of tropical fruits, notably oranges, mangoes, bananas, avocados and macadamia nuts.

The town's sole tourist attraction, founded in 1969 on the confluence of the Nels and Crocodile rivers, is the 169-ha **Lowveld National Botanical Garden** (✆ 013 752 5531 ✆ www.sanbi.org ◐ 08.00–17.00 daily), which lies five minutes' drive along the R40 to White River. Of equal interest to ornithologists and botanists, the garden protects many typical lowveld species, while a highlight of the rainforest section is a vast collection of prehistoric cycads. Further afield, about 30km back along the N4 towards Gauteng, there are regular guided tours into the **Sudwala Caves** (✆ 013 733 4152 ✆ www.sudwalacaves. co.za ◐ 08.30–16.45 daily), where the cool, dank chambers are full of beautiful limestone formations. Also worth the 45km diversion south

The cemetery at Pilgrim's Rest is home to the fabled 'Robber's Grave'. (AVZ)

is the scenically located town of **Barberton**, founded in 1883 to exploit a short-lived gold rush. Details of the gold rush are explored in the local history museum on Crown Street, where staff can also point you to several well-preserved Victorian architectural relics or direct you to the long-abandoned Eureka mine workings 30 minutes out of town.

Pilgrim's Rest
☎ 013 768 1060 🖰 www.pilgrims-rest.co.za ⏰ most museums open: 09.00–16.00 daily
One of Mpumalanga's oldest settlements, Pilgrim's Rest mushroomed into life in 1873 when the prospector Alex 'Wheelbarrow' Patterson struck pay dirt in the form of what was then the largest deposit of alluvial gold ever discovered in southern Africa. Within years, the original makeshift camp of tents and shacks soon grew into a wealthy village of brick-and-tin houses and shops, and even produced its own newspaper. Pilgrim's Rest's initial heyday was short-lived, however, as most of the independent diggers moved on to nearby Barberton in 1883 when gold was discovered there, and on to Johannesburg five years

Practicalities

The main air gateway to **Mpumalanga** is Kruger-Mpumalanga International Airport (KMIA), which is connected to Gauteng's OR Tambo International Airport by several daily flights. There are also direct flights from Durban and Cape Town. Ideally positioned for exploring the southern Kruger or the Panorama Route, KMIA lies 25km north of Mbombela along the R40 to White River, and several car rental companies are represented there.

Most **organised tours** to Mpumalanga and south or central Kruger travel by road from Gauteng, following the N12 east from Johannesburg or OR Tambo, and connecting with the N4 to Mbombela (Nelspruit) at eMalahleni (Witbank).

Accommodation

For full details of tour operator-recommended accommodation, see page 138. Here follows a few further suggestions from the author.

Upmarket
Coach House Hotel & Spa Tzaneen ✿ www.coachhouse.co.za
Crocodile Country Inn Mbombela ✿ www.crocinn.co.za
Mount Sheba Forever Resort Near Pilgrim's Rest ✿ www.mountsheba.co.za
Sabie River Sun Main Sabie Rd ✿ www.southernsun.com

Moderate
Blyde River Canyon Lodge Blyde River Canyon
✿ www.blyderivercanyonlodge.com

later. Despite this, underground gold mining commenced at Pilgrim's Rest soon after the alluvial sources dried up, and remained in operation until 1971, when the village was sold to the government to be restored as a living museum evoking the gold rush era.

An easy diversion from the popular Panorama Route (see page 136), situated just 11km west of Graskop along the R533, Pilgrim's Rest has been a National Monument since 1986 and remains one of the most popular attractions in the region. Points of specific interest include the Anglican Church (built in 1884); the Methodist Church (1911); the Catholic Church (1928); the Old Police Station (1902); and the hilltop cemetery where all but one grave point in the same direction, the exception being the famous but anonymous 'Robber's Grave', which

The drive takes three to five hours, depending on your ultimate destination.

The more remote **Mapungubwe National Park** lies along the Botswana border about 70km west of Musina on the R572. It isn't too far out of your way if you are also visiting the far north of Kruger, which is most easily reached from Gauteng by following the N1 north 35km short of Musina, where the R525 leads east to Pafuri Gate.

Mbombela is a well-equipped city with innumerable shops, banks, restaurants, hotels and internet cafés. Other towns are smaller, but Sabie, Hoedspruit, Graskop and Lydenburg receive quite a bit of tourist traffic and have suitable **facilities**. Outside of the towns, you should be able to pick up mobile phone reception, but other facilities are very limited.

Hazyview Protea Hotel Hazyview ⌁ www.proteahotels.com
Magoebaskloof Hotel Tzaneen ⌁ www.magoebaskloof.co.za
Nelspruit Town Lodge Mbombela ⌁ www.citylodge.co.za
Royal Hotel Pilgrim's Rest ⌁ www.pilgrimsrest.org.za

Budget and camping
Big 5 Backpackers Hazyview ⌁ www.big5backpackers.co.za
Blyde Canyon Forever Resort Blyde River Canyon
⌁ www.foreverblydecanyon.co.za
Jock-Sabie Lodge Main Rd, Sabie ⌁ www.jock.co.za
Swadini Forever Resort Blyde River Canyon ⌁ www.foreverswadini.co.za

lies at a right angle to its neighbours and is marked with a cross and the legend that gives it its name. There are also several museums in the town, details of which can be obtained from the visitors centre close to the charming and historic Royal Hotel.

Blyde River Canyon Nature Reserve

Some 25km long and up to 1.4km deep, the red sandstone canyon carved by the Blyde River and protected within a 270km² nature reserve some 50km west of the Kruger National Park is one of the largest and most spectacular features of its type on earth. Most easily accessed from the R532, which runs above its western rim, the canyon is overlooked by several viewpoints, including the sensational Three Rondawels (see box, below), which lies almost alongside the main road. For those with time to explore, the canyon also offers much to keen walkers and wildlife lovers. The most rewarding of several day hikes in the area is the Kadishi Trail, which runs downhill from Blyde Canyon Forever Resort (at the main entrance gate) through a lush forest of tall evergreen trees, leafy cycads and ferns to the river via the Kadishi Falls, which run over some impressive stalactite-like tufa (calcium carbonate) formations.

Large mammals are relatively thin on the ground here – though the trees do support significant populations of vervet and Samango monkeys – but the reserve is a good place to seek out several localised or endemic birds. These include Knysna turaco, Narina trogon, cinnamon dove and other forest dwellers. Cliff nesters such as southern bald ibis, Cape vulture, Verreaux's (black) eagle, jackal buzzard and Taita falcon can also be seen, as well as Gurney's sugarbird and the malachite sunbird, both of which tend to be found around flowering aloes, proteas and red-hot pokers.

Scenic stops along the Panorama Route

The loosely defined Panorama Route, a very popular add-on to Kruger safaris, runs through a scenic area of viewpoints and waterfalls, most of which lie along or within a few kilometres of the R532 between Sabie and the Blyde River Canyon. It can easily be explored from Pilgrim's Rest or one of the resorts in the Blyde River Nature Reserve, as well as the small towns of Graskop or Sable. At a push, and with an early start, it can also be covered as a day trip if travelling between Gauteng and the Kruger. The route lies along the crest of the Mpumalanga Escarpment, a remote geological extension of the more southwesterly Drakensberg that rises sharply from the lowveld of the coastal plain (typically set at altitudes of below 500m) to several peaks that top the 2,000m mark. Much of the escarpment supports cultivation and plantation forest, but there are also significant tracts of indigenous forest, especially on steeper cliffs, as well as areas of indigenous grassland.

The following examples are just five of a number of scenic highlights along the Panorama Route:

Mac-Mac Falls
This 65m waterfall is named after a pair of Scots prospectors who camped here during the gold rush era. You can swim in the pool at the base of the falls, or continue by car for 2km to the start a 4km day trail to the little-visited Forest Falls.
(MO/D)

The breathtaking view over the Three Rondawels at Blyde River Canyon. (LK/D)

Lisbon Falls

The tallest single-drop waterfall in the region, the Lisbon Falls plunge in two streams over a 90m stone amphitheatre, the base of which is accessible via a steep footpath.

God's Window

The R532 near Graskop provides access to several locations offering views from the edge of the escarpment over the expansive *lowveld* and stretching all the way across the Kruger into Mozambique – more than 1,000m below. God's Window is arguably the finest viewpoint, though its impact depends on very clear weather.

Bourke's Luck Potholes

Situated at the southern end of the Blyde River Canyon, at the confluence with the Treur River, this series of cylindrical potholes created entirely by water erosion can be explored by means of a short network of paths and footbridges.

Three Rondawels

One of the most scenic spots anywhere in South Africa, this viewpoint gazes right across the wide Blyde River Canyon – the river itself a blue ribbon hundreds of metres below – to a striking trio of outcrops that recall traditional thatched rondawels (round houses).

Cybele Forest Lodge and Health Spa
🔗 www.cybele.co.za

This magical lodge is a great stop-off point if travelling to or from Kruger. Set in 300 acres of grounds, the main lodge is a charming old farmhouse with lovely views over the magnificent gardens. The cottages and suites accommodate up to 28 guests; all have walled gardens, many come with outside showers and the suites have beautiful private pools. The spa is one of the best around, offering a range of treatments to rejuvenate the body and restore the soul.

Rissington Inn
🔗 www.rissington.co.za

In a bush setting just outside Hazyview, the owner-run Rissington Inn is both an enchanting place to spend a first night in Africa and a homely base for exploring Kruger National Park, the Blyde River Canyon and the Panorama Route. We appreciate the unfailingly warm hospitality, the delicious meals, thoughtful wine list and 16 stylish and comfortable rooms and suites – and that owner Chris Harvie continues provide everything you need to enjoy the Lowveld at an affordable price.

White-throated bee-eater (R/D)

Kruger National Park

One of the world's oldest, largest and most iconic wildlife sanctuaries, the Kruger National Park vies with Cape Town as South Africa's top tourist destination. It clocks up well over a million domestic and international visitors annually. Comparable in size to Wales or the state of New Jersey, this vast expanse of African bush, about 25km east of Johannesburg, shares a 350km-long eastern border with Mozambique and a shorter northern one with Zimbabwe. Set in the lowveld below the escarpment, the park has an average elevation of around 300m, with the hilliest areas being the far southwest, around Pretoriuskop and Bergen-Dal, and the Lebombo Mountains that run along the Mozambican border. The climate is hot and seasonally humid, with summer daytime temperatures routinely topping the 30°C mark (frequently 40°C in the north) but the air dries out in winter, when nights can be very cold.

Kruger is unique among Africa's top safari destinations in several respects. For one, it is the most developed of the continent's major game reserves, and far and away the one most suited to affordable DIY safaris. There are 21 rest camps and a dozen concession lodges with a total sleeping capacity of around 5,000, concentrated mostly in the southern quarter. The main network of sealed roads ensures that it can be easily explored in an ordinary saloon car. Several other features make the Kruger unusually well suited to budget-conscious self-drivers: the relative affordability of the accommodation; the user-friendly online reservations system; the presence of grocery shops and restaurants in all the larger rest camps; and the excellent selection of Kruger-specific maps, guidebooks and other interpretive material that is available on site. Unsurprisingly, this has led to some purists lambasting the park as being too tame, but tar roads and a good website don't make the animals any less wild, and a 3,000km road network means that it is easy to escape the crowds.

History

The Kruger National Park started life in 1898 as the 4,600km^2 Sabi Game Reserve, which was established by President Paul Kruger of the South African Republic to protect the depleted wildlife herds between the Sabi and Crocodile rivers. At the time it included the part of present-day Kruger south of the Sabi River, as well as what is now the private Sabi Sands Game Reserve. In 1926, the Sabi and the more northerly Shingwedzi Game Reserve were amalgamated and gazetted as a national park, pre-dating the arrival of the first three tourist cars by just one year. The park was fenced in its entirety during 1959–60, partly to prevent the transmission of diseases between livestock and wildlife, and partly to curb poaching and demarcate the border with Mozambique.

Kruger attained its present-day area of 19,000km^2 in 1969 with the addition of the 240km^2 Pafuri Triangle, bounded by the Luvuvhu and Limpopo rivers along the northern boundary with Zimbabwe. In keeping with the apartheid ethos of the day, the Makuleke inhabitants of the Pafuri Triangle were forcibly relocated, an injustice rectified in the 1990s when a successful land claim restored the land to its former occupants. It now forms the Makuleke Contractual Park, which is managed as part of Kruger but hosts two private lodges on land leased from the community.

In the early 1990s, the park's area was further increased by removing fences between Kruger and neighbouring private conservancies such as Sabi Sands and Timbavati. In 2001, a memorandum of understanding was signed amalgamating Kruger with two other national parks – Gonarezhou in Zimbabwe and Limpopo in Mozambique – to form the 35,000 km^2 Great Limpopo Transfrontier Park. This cross-border park is still something of a work in progress, and while boundary fences have not been formally dropped they are no longer maintained, creating more and more gaps that allow elephants and other animals to follow ancient migration routes into Mozambique. Two other important post-millennial developments have been the creation of nine concessions that function much like private reserves within the park (see page 153), and the opening of the Giriyondo border post to allow direct road access into Mozambique's Limpopo National Park.

Wildlife

The main attraction of Kruger is of course its abundant wildlife, which includes significant populations of all the members of the eagerly sought Big Five, that is lion, leopard, elephant, buffalo and rhino. However, the tally of 147 mammal species – the largest of any African national park – includes plenty of other safari favourites, ranging from predators such as cheetah, African wild dog, spotted hyena and black-backed jackal to the herbivorous likes of hippo, zebra, giraffe, warthog, Chacma baboon and vervet monkey. A total of 21 antelope species are present, the most abundant being impala, though greater kudu, waterbuck, blue wildebeest and bushbuck are all common too.

Most first-time safari-goers are preoccupied with seeking out the Big Five and other charismatic large mammals, but Kruger also supports a fascinating and varied cast of smaller creatures. Among the more endearing small mammals are the banded mongooses that scurry through the bush in bands of up to 30 individuals, the rather cat-like

Kruger wildlife counts

Kruger is the only African reserve of comparable size whose Big Five populations are uniformly in good shape. Indeed, since the beginning of the 21st century the estimated elephant population has increased from 8,500 to 13,700, and buffalo numbers are up from around 22,000 to 37,000. Lion and leopard counts have remained stable at around 1,750 and 1,000 respectively.

Furthermore, Kruger now ranks as the world's most important rhino sanctuary, despite a recent outbreak of poaching that accounted for a loss of almost 150 individuals in 2010. The white rhino, once very rare in the park, now numbers around 12,000 (half the global total), while the estimated population of more than 600 'critically endangered' black rhino is probably the largest in any one conservation area.

As of mid-2010, populations of other more common and/or iconic large mammals were estimated as follows:

African wild dog	350	Kudu	8,000
Blue wildebeest	9,000	Mountain reedbuck	150
Bushbuck	>500	Nyala	>300
Cheetah	200	Sable antelope	300
Common reedbuck	300	Spotted hyena	2,000
Eland	300	Tsessebe	160
Giraffe	7,000	Warthog	2,500
Hippopotamus	3,000	Waterbuck	5,000
Impala	130,000	Zebra	20,000

(HK/D)

and beautifully marked genets and civets that emerge at dusk, and the hyraxes that perch on boulders like overgrown guinea pigs. The Nile crocodile is the most conspicuous of the park's 114 reptile species, and while its 34 amphibian species are seldom seen, the ethereal communal calls of the bubbling kassina and other tree-frogs often provide a haunting aural backdrop to dusk waterhole vigils. In addition, 49 fish species have been recorded, and a cast of many thousands of invertebrates includes the rather comical dung beetles that are often seen rolling balls of elephant dung along the road, and spectacular golden orb spiders perched in the centre of their giant webs.

The Kruger is revered among birdwatchers for its 517 bird species, but you don't need to be a twitcher to appreciate some of its more colourful and conspicuous avian residents. These include the spectacular lilac-breasted roller, often seen perching openly on isolated trees, and the stunning white-fronted bee-eater, joined in the southern summer by the equally colourful carmine and European bee-eaters. The park also provides refuge for several large birds that are now rare outside of protected areas, among them the eyelid-fluttering southern ground hornbill, the massive Kori bustard (the world's heaviest flying bird), the macabre marabou stork, and of course the ostrich. Raptors are very well represented too, among them the handsome bateleur, the hefty martial eagle, and the grim-looking lappet-faced vulture.

European roller (SB)

Many species are widely distributed throughout the Kruger, but others are restricted to particular elements in its rich mosaic of habitats, which encompass mixed acacia woodland in the southwest, rocky hills in the east, open savanna in the central region, and mopane woodland in the north. Oribi and sable antelope, for instance, are most common in the southwest, while Sharpe's grysbok and roan antelope favour the drier mopane woodland around Letaba. Rock hyraxes and klipspringer are frequently seen in the hilly country around Olifants, and blue wildebeest and zebra are seasonally abundant in the central grasslands, which also form the main

Vervet monkey (AVW/D)

prowling ground for the park's small population of cheetah. Aquatic habitats form an important niche in this generally dry environment, being strongly associated with the likes of hippo, crocodile, many dozens of species of water bird, and to a lesser extent waterbuck and elephant. The riparian woodland that follows the series of major rivers that flow eastward though the park *en route* to the Indian Ocean (from south to north, these are the Crocodile, Sabie, Olifants, Letaba, Shingwedzi, Luvuvhu and Limpopo rivers) is the main habitat for several striking bird species, ranging from purple-crested loerie and green pigeon to crowned eagle and crested guineafowl. The biodiversity peaks along the northerly Luvuvhu and Limpopo rivers, which are the main stronghold for the likes of Samango monkey and nyala antelope.

Kruger highlights

Southern Kruger

The busiest part of Kruger, with boundaries that approximate the original Sabi Game Reserve proclaimed in 1898, runs from the Sabie River south to the Crocodile and is serviced by several large rest camps, including village-like Skukuza. The popularity of this area is partly due to the exceptional game viewing – it certainly offers the best chance of seeing all the Big Five in a limited time – but is also because of its relative proximity to Gauteng. This makes it very convenient for stand-alone safaris out of Johannesburg or Pretoria, or for longer organised tours heading further south to Swaziland or KwaZulu-Natal.

Practicalities

For the southern rest camps, the Kruger-Mpumalanga International Airport or KMIA (see page 134) lies about 30km from Numbi gate, 40km from Phabeni gate and 70km from Malelane Gate. For central Kruger, regular charter **flights** run from Johannesburg to Hoedspruit's Eastgate Airport, 70km from Orpen Gate, and Phalaborwa's Kruger Park Gateway Airport, 3km from Phalaborwa Gate. Rental cars are available at all airports, ideally by prior arrangement, from the usual major rental firms. Alternatively, Private Connection Tours (☎ 011 316 1635 ⤤ www.pctours.co.za) can shuttle new arrivals at KMIA to Skukuza Rest Camp, where rental cars are also available.

If you are coming **by road** from Gauteng, follow the N12 to eMalahleni (Witbank) and N4 to Belfast. Then continue east along the N4 past Mbombela

Accommodation

Huts and chalets in the public rest camps mentioned below can be booked online at ⤤ www.sanparks.org. For full details of tour operator-recommended accommodation, see pages 157–61; a few further suggestions for concession lodges from the author can be found in the box on pages 148–9.

Ten top Kruger rest camps
Listed approximately from south to north.

Berg-en-Dal Close to Malelane Gate in the southeast, this likeable modern camp is a good first stop in Kruger, boasting superior accommodation, and hilly wooded grounds overlooking a dam, but it is on something of a limb in terms of game drives.

Skukuza Comprising 230 accommodation units and 80 camping sites, this sprawling camp is sometimes criticised for being too impersonal, but it boasts excellent facilities, a useful location for game drives, and a pretty setting overlooking the Sabie River.

Lower Sabie This riverside camp east of Skukuza is a favourite of many Kruger aficionados (this writer included) for its intimate atmosphere and wonderful setting, and as a peerless base for game drives.

Satara This is another large and rather impersonal camp, but it gets the nod for the plentiful wildlife – and top-notch cat viewing – on the surrounding plains.

for Malelane or Crocodile Bridge gates, or take the R540 and R536 via Mashishing (Lydenburg) for Numbi, Paul Kruger, Phabeni or Orpen gates. The drive takes around five hours.

Facilities in the parks are very good, but limited by comparison to most towns. They are centred on a network of fenced public rest camps, all of which offer affordable overnight accommodation in huts and chalets, but which vary in size from half a dozen to more than a hundred units. The larger rest camps are like little villages set in the wilderness: most have a grocery shop and restaurant, as well as a filling station, and there is a bank and ATM at Skukuza, and an ATM at Letaba. In addition, there is a mobile phone network at most camps (but not along the roads through the park) and Skukuza, Lower Sabie and Berg-en-Dal also have public internet facilities. Park rules and gate/camp opening times are printed on the entrance permit, and should be read carefully.

Tamboti An underrated gem that offers one of South Afruca's most affordable wilderness experiences, this self-catering tented camp located near Orpen Gate, 50km west of Satara, is set in lush riparian forest overlooking the seasonal Timbavati River.

Balule Comprising a mere six huts and 16 tent sites, this tiny electricity-free camp, fringing the southern floodplain of the Olifants River, offers an unforgettable and budget-friendly introduction to the raw African night.

Olifants Perched high on a cliff overlooking the Olifants River, this has the most thrilling location of any Kruger rest camp, as well as relatively modern accommodation units – and the wildlife viewing is usually pretty good.

Letaba Another favourite of many Kruger regulars, low-key Letaba has a wonderful bush feel, with plentiful birdlife around, including several 'northern specials', and some other wildlife passing through too.

Shingwedzi One of the park's undeniable gems, this unpretentious riverside camp is recommended to those who want to get right away from the crowds, and it is also a delightful spot for birders.

Punda Maria The small camp could be recommended purely for its proximity to the biodiverse Luvuvhu River, but is also among the most intimate camps, with a genuine wilderness atmosphere.

Extending about 90km from east to west, the far south is the widest part of the Kruger, and the hilliest, boasting several impressive rocky peaks of which the 891m Sithungwane near Pretoriuskop is the highest point in the park. The south receives a relatively high rainfall, averaging well above 500mm per annum, and supports a varied vegetation that is dominated by dense acacia scrub and mopane woodland in the west, open savanna in the east, and tall riparian woodland along the Sabie River. The main surfaced roads generally offer the best game viewing, but they also tend to get quite busy, so it is worth exploring some of the quieter dirt back roads.

The main centre of activity here, only five minutes' drive from Paul Kruger Gate, is Skukuza. The largest rest camp in Kruger, it also houses

Saddlebilled stork (SS)

the research and administrative headquarters, and has an excellent range of facilities. The camp boasts a memorable view over a stretch of the Sabie River regularly visited by thirsty wildlife, and large green grounds that teem with birds and small mammals. As for game-viewing opportunities, Skukuza lies at the junction of three of the park's most reliable roads: the H3 south to Malelane Gate, which is good for lion and white rhino; the H4–1 to Lower Sabie, where visitors can see buffalo, leopard, elephant and exceptional birdlife; and the H1–2 and H1–3 to Satara, for lion and cheetah.

The ever-popular Lower Sabie is a relatively small rest camp fringing the north bank of a dam on the Sabie River. Elephants are plentiful in the area, and Sunset Dam, a kilometre or two outside camp, is exceptional for storks, kingfishers and other water-associated birds. As with Skukuza, Lower Sabie stands at the junction of three excellent game-viewing roads. There is no better place to look for rhinos than the H4–2 and associated dirt roads running south towards Crocodile Bridge. The H10 north towards to Tshokwane Picnic Site passes several dams where hippo, lion, elephant and rhino are regular. The H4–1 to Skukuza, though often busy, often rewards with sightings of buffalo, lion and leopard, while a stop at the lushly wooded Nkhulu Picnic Site, set in riparian forest on the south bank of the Sabie River, often yields forest birds.

Of the other southern camps, Malelane and Crocodile Bridge are situated at entrance gates, making them useful first stops if you expect to arrive late in the day. A short drive east of Crocodile Bridge, a hippo pool and prehistoric rock painting site on the Crocodile River are well worth a look. Venerable Pretoriuskop, the park's oldest (and most old-fashioned) camp, lies in a tract of thick acacia woodland that tends to offer erratic game-viewing, though the dirt Voortrekker Road running east towards Afsaal Picnic Site is probably your best chance of seeing the localised black rhino, eland and sable antelope.

Central Kruger

Bounded by the Sabie River to the south and the Letaba to the north, the central Kruger is dominated by grassland and lightly wooded savanna, though there are also extensive tracts of mixed acacia woodland in the southwest and mopane woodland in the north. There is also some impressive riparian woodland along

Wildebeest (SB)

the banks of the seasonal Timbavati River, while the more northerly and perennial Olifants and Letaba rivers spill out onto wide floodplains lined with shady figs and jackalberries. Much of the region is flat and rather featureless, but the area around Olifants Camp is very hilly, as are the Lebombo Mountains along the Mozambican border.

Situated in the heart of these central plains is Satara, the park's second-largest rest camp. The rather bland layout of this camp and lack of any views make it feel a touch soulless, but there is no arguing

Top concession lodges

Some 15 private lodges now operate in the Kruger, set within nine individual tracts of bush – variable in size but typically at least 100km^2 – where exclusive traversing rights have been granted to a single concessionaire. These concession lodges function much like the private reserves bordering Kruger, each hosting between one and three exclusive small camps that offer guests an upmarket package inclusive of guided game drives in open 4x4s. Guiding standards are comparable to private reserves outside the park, but the concessions are typically much larger, the wildlife is less habituated to vehicles, and there is no cross-traversing. The net result is that while game viewing in the concessions tends to be more erratic, the overall experience is arguably more satisfying since there is a lot less tourist traffic, and guides focus less obsessively on chasing lion and other prime sightings based on radio alerts from other vehicles. If nothing else, the concessions are generally a lot cheaper than the private reserves.

For full details of tour operator-recommended concession lodges, see pages 157–61. Here follows a few further suggestions from the author.

(SB/Aa)

Shishangani Lodge, Camp Shawu and Camp Shinga
⌂ www.threecities.co.za
Rhinos are the speciality of this concession set in the extreme southeast bordering the Crocodile River, but it's also a good area for elephant and lion. Our pick of the three jointly managed lodges is the intimate Shawu Camp, set on the shore of a dam that attracts prolific wildlife.

Lukimbi Safari Lodge
⌂ www.lukimbi.com
Only 25km from Malelane Gate, this attractive stilted lodge has exclusive traversing rights across a 150km² tract of acacia woodland that supports plenty of lion, elephant and both types of rhino.

Hamilton's 1880 Camp
⌂ www.hamiltonstentedcamp.co.za
This Edwardian-style riverside camp is the pick of three in the Imbali Concession, which lies in the acacia woodland between Skukuza and Satara, an area renowned for its dense predator populations.

Singita Lebombo and Sweni
⌂ www.singita.co.za
Set in the rugged Lebombo foothills along the Mozambican border east of Satara, this ultra-stylish and very expensive lodge is the sort of place where you might find yourself hobnobbing with movie stars and other celebrities. Chic it may be, but the game viewing is excellent.

The Outpost
⌂ www.theoutpost.co.za
This clifftop creation in Makuleke Contractual Park is arguably the most gobsmacking lodge in the Greater Kruger, both for its innovative architecture and the stirring views across the Luvuvhu floodplain. As with Pafuri, however, the general game viewing doesn't match the setting.

Machampane Luxury Camp
⌂ www.dolimpopo.com
Not strictly a Kruger Concession, this camp lies in Limpopo National Park but is easily accessed from Letaba via the Giriyondo border post. The main activity here is guided walks, or 4x4 trails and canoeing safaris on the Olifants River can be enjoyed if organised in advance.

with its location at the crossroads of some superb game-viewing roads. This is the best part of the park for lion kills, which also often attract jackals and hyenas, and the open habitat is ideal for cheetah that can be seen within a 10km radius of camp. Nsemani Pan, 5km from camp along the H7 to Orpen Gate, frequently attracts rhinos, while the loop involving the H6 to Nwanetsi and S100 passes through plains that host large seasonal concentrations of wildebeest and zebra.

Two of Kruger's loveliest camps, Olifants and Letaba, lie to the north of Satara on the rivers for which they are named. Scenically, Olifants is utterly peerless, with its spectacular clifftop over a stretch of river that attracts abundant herds of elephant, giraffe and other game. Further north, Letaba, though less scenic, probably has the better wildlife viewing of the two. Either way, coming from anywhere to the south, the area around Olifants and Letaba feels very wild and untrammelled, thanks to the relatively low tourist traffic. That said, game viewing is less reliable than around Satara or Skukuza, certainly when it comes to rhinos or big cats, though elephants are abundant and several immense herds of buffalo inhabit the area.

Male impala (HK/D)

Northern Kruger

Almost half of the Kruger lies to the north of the Letaba River, yet this vast area supports a mere three public camps and the available bed space is exceeded by that of Skukuza alone. Unsurprisingly, then, northern Kruger sees few visitors by comparison to the south, and as such it is often touted as the park's 'best-kept secret', hosting a great many localised bird species – and a few mammals – absent from elsewhere in the park. Any such assertion requires qualification. Yes, the north possesses a mesmerising wilderness feel that will appeal greatly to experienced safari-goers, but be warned that the game viewing doesn't compare to the southern and central regions. In crude, Big Five terms, buffalo and elephant, though more abundant than in the south, are not any more visible here, while the likelihood of seeing a lion, leopard or rhino is slim indeed.

Coming from the south, the first of the northern camps you reach is Mopani, a relatively recent creation blessed with modern units and a winning location overlooking a dam. The camp is named after the rather monotonous dry mopane woodland that covers the surrounding plains, and while elephants are numerous, and the area comes with your best chance of spotting localised antelope such as roan and Sharpe's grysbok, it is probably the most poorly located of Kruger's camps for general game viewing.

By contrast, the smaller Shingwedzi Camp – perched on the south bank of the namesake river – has a real bush feel and offers some excellent game viewing, particularly along the dirt road that tracks the river for about 10km south of camp until it reaches the enigmatically named Kanniedood (literally 'Cannot Die') Dam. Elephant, buffalo and the handsome greater kudu are common in the area, and the spectacular birdlife includes several species of stork, heron and kingfisher, and the exquisite broad-billed roller.

The most northerly public rest camp in Kruger is Punda Maria, which lies on a wooded slope about 50km south of the Luvuvhu River, whose confluence with the Limpopo at Crooks Corner forms the tripartite border with Zimbabwe and Mozambique. The remote Pafuri game-viewing circuit on the southern banks of the Luvuvhu near the Zimbabwe border is one of the finest in the park, notable for its concentrations of elephant, buffalo and nyala antelope. Punda Maria is also the base for guided tours to the Thulamela Heritage Site, which protects the substantial hilltop ruins of a Zimbabwean-style, stone-wall royal village built in the 16th century.

The high biodiversity of this area is legendary among birdwatchers, who come here to seek out the likes of Pel's fishing owl, the racket-tailed roller and the triple-banded courser. However, in order to stand a realistic chance of seeing these rarities, or to explore remote, non-public sites such as the lush, fever-tree forest at Crooks Corner or the spectacular Lanner Gorge, you need to stay at one of the two private lodges set in the Makuleke Contractual Park (see pages 149 and 160)

Mapungubwe National Park

☎ 015 534 3545 🖰 www.sanparks.org 🕒 Sep–Mar 06.00–18.30, Apr–Aug 06.30–18.00

An interesting westerly excursion for those using the N1 to Musina to travel between Gauteng and the northern Kruger, this recently created national park was also inscribed as a UNESCO World Heritage Site in 2003. It is centred on Mapungubwe Hill, medieval capital of a wealthy trade empire that once supplied locally sourced gold, copper and ivory to the Swahili Coast of East Africa. At its 13th-century peak, prior to being abandoned, the city supported 5,000 people whose descendants probably went on to establish the more impressive stone ruins of Great Zimbabwe to the north. Guided tours of the archaeological site run every morning, and a museum, under construction in 2011, will soon display artefacts unearthed here. The most famous artefact to-date is a 12cm-long, gold-plated rhino sculpture discovered in 1933 that has been stowed away in a Pretoria museum ever since. Situated on the three-way border with Botswana and Zimbabwe, the park is serviced by a network of roads that offer great views over a stretch of the Limpopo River hemmed in by baobab-studded granitic hills. Wildlife likely to be seen includes elephant, kudu and klipspringer, though lion and leopard are also present.

Klipspringer (K/D)

Private reserves bordering Kruger

The western boundary of central Kruger, running for about 150km north from Paul Kruger Gate as far as Phalaborwa, is lined with a series of private reserves that dropped the fences with their larger neighbour in the 1990s, allowing for free movement of wildlife throughout their combined area. Paradoxically, while Kruger is the most populist African safari destination, these bordering private reserves include several of the continent's most prestigious game-viewing retreats, none more so than the southerly 'Sabi Sand' cluster that includes MalaMala and Londolozi.

Visiting a private reserve is a very different experience to a standard Kruger safari. Any given property will typically host between one and four camps, each one an intimate gem of safari chic where staff pamper clients with service levels in line with a luxury spa. Most camps offer overnight packages inclusive of guided game drives in open 4x4s, gourmet meals, and in some cases drinks. The high quality of the guiding and the opportunity to travel off-road ensures superior and more intensive game viewing than is normally the case in the Kruger proper. Indeed, two or three nights in any reputable private reserve comes with a near-guarantee of close-up viewings of all the Big Five.

The private reserves around Kruger offer a very good chance of close encounters with all of the Big Five. (AVZ)

Practicalities

There is no cheap way to visit most of the private reserves, they are closed to day visitors and it is forbidden to self-drive except between the gate and your camp. This means that even the most relatively affordable private reserve will require a significantly larger financial outlay than a self-drive or guided safari in the Kruger itself. If your budget can absorb it, however, **a three-night stay is highly recommended**, allowing sufficient time to see what you want to and to see it well. Failing that, tagging one night at a private reserve onto the end of a Kruger safari will greatly improve your chances of seeing lion and leopard properly – though be sure to time things so that you arrive at camp for the evening game drive included in the rack rate.

Details of reaching the private camps and lodges are broadly the same as for the Kruger (see page 144), though it is probably worth noting that a rental vehicle will sit idle from when you arrive at the lodge to when you leave, so it may be a costly luxury. For those **flying** into the region, your booking agent will be able to arrange a direct **road transfer** to the lodge from any nearby airport, or indeed from as far afield as Gauteng. Once at your lodge, all activities and food will be inclusive, but drinks may be extra. Not all lodges have internet access for clients or mobile phone coverage, so best either to assume that yours won't, or, if you will need to communicate with the outside world, to check the situation in advance.

For full details of tour operator-recommended **accommodation**, see pages 157–61. A few further suggestions from the author can be found in the reserve descriptions.

Sand River, Sabi Sands Reserve (AVZ)

Private reserves highlights

Sabi Sands and surrounds

In 1948, a cluster of about 20 private properties bounded by the Sabie River to the south, and bisected by the southeast-flowing Sand River, were amalgamated into a single 650km²-conservation management called the Sabi Sands Reserve. This area had formed part of the original Sabie Game Reserve, as it was proclaimed in 1898, but private properties were excluded from the national park when it was gazetted in 1926. The area has long been renowned for its superb game viewing, and though the three largest properties in the association – MalaMala, Londolozi and Singita – have all gone their own way in terms of game management since the millennium, the others still form part of the Sabi Sands (see ✆ www.sabisand.co.za for a full list of lodges and links to their individual websites), and the region is generally referred to by that name.

MalaMala (✆ www.malamala.com) is the largest individual private reserve in the original Sabi Sands, and it was the first to take paying tourists. It is also our definitive first choice, thanks to a management that places a firm emphasis on top-quality game viewing rather than trendy décor. The two small lodges on the property share exclusive traversing rights over a peerless 130km^2 of prime wildlife territory that includes a full 20km of Sand River frontage. Also highly recommended are **Londolozi** (✆ www.londolozi.com) and **Sabi Sabi** (✆ www.sabisabi. com), as they retain exclusive traversing rights on large properties, which generally create a more relaxed feel to game drives, and allow you to stay longer on a good sighting.

A disadvantage of any other property in Sabi Sands is that it will share traversing rights with at least one and in some cases half-a-dozen neighbours. This doesn't necessarily make for inferior game viewing, but it does tend to generate a more contrived feel to game drives, with guides communicating non-stop by radio, and there are strict rules limiting vehicle numbers often resulting in a long wait to join a sighting or being hurried off to make space for another lodge's clients. However, these lodges are generally cheaper than the premier properties listed above, though there are exceptions. The two main clusters of cross-traversing lodges are in the north and the west, and if keeping down

White rhinos (NS/D)

Hartebeest, Manyeleti Game Reserve (Y/D)

costs is a consideration it's worth noting that the northern lodges – in particular **Arathusa** (🦶 www.arathusa.co.za), **Elephant Plains** (🦶 www.elephantplains.co.za) and **Nkorho** (🦶 www.nkorho.com) – tend to be better value than those in the west.

Manyeleti Game Reserve

Immediately north of Sabi Sands is the 220km² Manyeleti Game Reserve, whose Shangaan name means 'Place of Stars', which was set aside in 1964 as the only game reserve in the country open to Black visitors. Today the reserve is managed by the Mnisi community, who were forcibly removed from the area when the national park was created, though the land claim they were awarded in 2002 was contested for several years, a controversy that was resolved only in 2010. It shares an unfenced 30km eastern border with the Kruger National Park and supports a similar selection of wildlife, though poaching and low tourist numbers mean that game viewing isn't quite up there with several of its neighbours. The only accommodation consists of two relatively affordable camps run by a concessionaire called Honeyguide (🦶 www.honeyguidecamp.com) and the costlier Tintswalo Safari Lodge (🦶 www.tintswalo.com).

Timbavati Private Nature Reserve

Named after the Timbavati River that flows close to its southern boundary before crossing into the Kruger at Orpen Gate, this 530km² private reserve has been managed by the non-profit Timbavati Association since 1962. The overall set-up is similar to Sabi Sands, with the advantage that the camps are far more spread out and tend to charge lower rates, though it isn't quite up there when it comes to leopard and rhino sightings. Timbavati is renowned for its white lions, whose unusual pigmentation is the product of a recessive gene that occasionally identifies itself in newly born cubs, none of which have survived into adulthood in recent years. Accommodation includes the exceptionally affordable Gomo Gomo Game Lodge (🖱 www.gomogomo.co.za), and the somewhat more upmarket Kings Camp (🖱 www.kingscamp.com) and Ngala Camp (🖱 www.andbeyondafrica.com).

Kapama Private Game Reserve

Unlike the other reserves mentioned above, the 130km² Kapama doesn't actually border the Kruger and is entirely fenced. As a result, it offers a more contrived experience than the likes of Sabi Sands or Timbavati, but all the Big Five are present within its confines and likely to be seen, with the significant exception of leopard, which are less habituated. The **Hoedspruit Endangered Species Centre** (☎ 015 793 1633 🖱 www.hesc.co.za ⏰ hourly tours 08.00–15.00 daily) is the only place where you are likely to see a king cheetah, whose semi-striped coat is caused by a rare recessive gene, and it is also home to the African wild dog and various bird species. The centre acts as a pick-up point for elephant-back safaris into Kapama, a truly wondrous opportunity that allows you to experience the bush from a giraffe's perspective. For details of the safaris, see 🖱 www.campjabulani.com. The Hoedspruit Centre and elephant-back safaris can both be enjoyed by day visitors, as well as those staying overnight.

Tried & Tested

Camp Jabulani
🖱 www.campjabulani.com

THE ZAMBEZI SAFARI & TRAVEL CO. LTD

Camp Jabulani is the epitome of style, luxury, gastronomic excellence and warm hospitality. The camp was started to sustain twelve orphaned and abandoned elephants and today offers guests the opportunity of a close encounter with these amazing animals. Its intimate environment is designed to blend seamlessly with the surrounding bush. Facilities include an open-air spa, lounge, dining area, and six exclusive suites. The Zindoga Villa will ideally suit the family traveller, smaller groups or those who seek complete privacy and exclusivity.

Cheetah Plains
🖥 www.cheetahplains.com

THE ZAMBEZI SAFARI
& TRAVEL CO. LTD

Cheetah Plains is situated in Sabi Sands, world renowned for its Big Five game viewing. The lodge exudes a distinct warmth and comfort, allowing you to feel right at home. The traditionally thatched accommodation blends seamlessly into the African bush. Each of the calming en-suite rooms features modern amenities including air conditioning, overhead fans, mosquito nets and telephones. Resident chef Henry de Villiers has designed an eclectic menu of delicious traditional South African flavours for the restaurant.

Chitwa Chitwa Game Lodge
🖥 www.chitwa.co.za

RAINBOW
TOURS

Everything about five-star Chitwa Chitwa shouts opulent luxury. Supersized suites with huge beds, lovely decks, private outside showers, plunge pools and original artworks will simply blow you away and you'll never want to leave! Overlooking a large lake that draws a constant stream of thirsty animals, this is Big-Five territory and most game drives see leopard. The food is sensational, washed down with wine you've chosen yourself from the cellar. For a top-end safari experience, Chitwa Chitwa is excellent value.

Garonga
🖥 www.garonga.com

THE ZAMBEZI SAFARI
& TRAVEL CO. LTD

Garonga is in a beautiful area of the Lowveld that offers excellent game viewing, including the Big Five (minus buffalo). The six luxury tents are unique, and the atmosphere is one of relaxation. The main area is open plan, overlooking a stunning view, and the rim-flow pool is designed like a waterhole. Activities on offer include a sleep out experience, a lunch picnic in a tree, and massage treatments. The food is delicious and complemented by a decadent variety of wines.

Lion Sands Private Reserve
📍 www.lionsands.com

A family-owned luxury reserve in a game-rich area of Sabi Sands. It's the only private reserve with access to the Sabie River – a big plus, with river tours offered in addition to game drives and bush walks. Three accommodation options in different locations include 1933 Lodge, a private exclusive-use luxury camp, and River

Lodge with 18 thatched, tranquil riverside rooms. But our favourite has to be Ivory Lodge with six private villas – one of the most luxurious lodges in South Africa.

Notten's Bush Camp
📍 http://nottens.com

RAINBOW TOURS

An old-established, family-run camp, Notten's eschews modern luxury, preferring the simple pleasures of authentic bush life. Furnished in traditional style, with antique mahogany and cane furniture, the seven enchanting rooms are lit by oil lamps. Hosted by the Notten family, descendants of the original owners, the camp

has conservation at its heart, and the personal attention and welcome helps set this lodge apart. The committed, long-serving staff are noted for their outstanding guiding and first-class cooking.

Pafuri
📍 www.pafuri.co.za

THE ZAMBEZI SAFARI & TRAVEL CO. LTD

Pafuri Camp lies in the wildest and most remote part of Kruger National Park. It houses a variety of vegetation, offers great game viewing and provides the best birding opportunities in the park. This region also boasts a wealth of folklore from early explorers and ancient civilisations. Pafuri Camp is well known for its

fever tree forests, beautiful gorges and Crooks' Corner – where the Limpopo and Luvuvhu rivers as well as three countries (Zimbabwe, South Africa and Mozambique) meet.

Rhino Post Walking Safaris
www.isibindiafrica.co.za/rhino-post

It's hard to beat the thrill of tracking elephant or rhino on foot. These exclusive walking safaris combine three very different Kruger camps. Rhino Post is the more luxurious 'base' camp with eight eco-friendly luxury suites. Plains Camp, with four luxury explorer-style tents, is a three-hour walk away. Finally, Plains Camp offers a true bush experience where you sleep out under the stars. Rhino Post are conservation aware and support local communities. A very well priced once in a lifetime experience.

Royal Malewane and Africa House
www.royalmalewane.com

toescapeto
www.toescapeto.com

The joys of a bygone era await you at Royal Malewane, situated on a private reserve within the greater Kruger area. Accommodating a maximum of 20 guests in the utmost colonial splendour, this is an exclusive getaway for those who value privacy, personalised service and superb game viewing. Eight free-standing private suites, with terrace, gazebo and spillway pool, rest in harmony with magnificent surroundings. Royal Malewane's expert guides and trackers ensure intimate game experiences and close sightings of the Big Five.

Singita Lebombo and Singita Sweni
www.singita.com

Aardvark
SAFARIS LTD

These two lodges are part of the Singita portfolio – known for sumptuous style and superb guiding – and they don't disappoint. Lebombo, with spectacular glass-walled suites that allow you to spot game by just stepping out of bed, and the intimate six-suite Sweni, on stilts by the Sweni River, are among the most spectacular lodges in Kruger. Their 33,000-acre private concession setting boasts one of the highest game concentrations in the park, including the Big Five and the 'Mountain Pride' of lions.

Tanda Tula
⚓ www.tandatula.com

This gorgeous tented camp is one of our Kruger favourites. In the heart of the Timbavati Private Nature Reserve, the 12 beautifully furnished tents are surrounded by lush bush, each with a private deck overlooking the riverbed and animal life beyond. The reserve is home to an incredible variety of game, including the Big Five, and the guides here are some of the best. Track wildlife in open Land Rovers or on foot for a truly unforgettable safari experience.

Vuyatela, Djuma Private Game Reserve ⚓ www.djuma.com

BRIDGE & WICKERS
travel with experience

Vuyatela is an intimate, five-star lodge in the game-rich northern Sabi Sands with eight secluded, luxury suites inspired by contemporary African vernacular architecture. Owned by ecologist Jurie Moolman, Vuyatela is distinguished by its extensive exclusive traversing area and its holistic approach to the ecosystem, reflected in the quality of the guiding and in the amazing aquarium and birdwatching tower. We love Djuma for its longstanding and genuine commitment to its local community - and incredible leopard sightings.

Wait a Little
⚓ www.africanhorsesafari.com

Aardvark
SAFARIS LTD

A riding safari through the African wilderness is one of the greatest pleasures there is in Africa and this is one of only a handful of places where you can see the Big Five close up from horseback. Gerti and Phillip Kusseler's beautifully schooled horses offer experienced riders thrilling animal encounters, from stalking elephant to galloping alongside plains game. Itineraries of varying lengths take small groups (maximum seven guests) through stunning wildlife habitats on the adventure of a lifetime.

Mpumalanga to KwaZulu-Natal via Swaziland

The most direct route between the Kruger National Park and KwaZulu-Natal passes through the Kingdom of Swaziland, Africa's only absolute monarchy, which is surrounded on three sides by South Africa. Indeed, Swaziland in some respects comes across as a peripheral tenth province of the regional powerhouse that engulfs it. Its currency, the lilangeni, is pegged to and interchangeable with the rand, and the towns are lined with chain stores, filling stations and fast-food franchises from across the border. Crossing between the two countries could scarcely be more straightforward, provided you have a passport to hand.

Boy drinking porridge from clay bowl, Mantenga Traditional Village (AVZ)

Swaziland is the land of the Swazi, a centralised kingdom forged during the regional shake-up initiated by Shaka Zulu. It became a British protectorate in the aftermath of the Anglo-Boer War, after which the Swazi king's title was downgraded to paramount chief. When it regained independence under King Sobhuza II in 1968, the country retained an autonomous identity rare in more culturally diverse states. In the 1970s, Sobhuza II scrapped a Westminster-based political system bequeathed by the British, in favour of one that placed absolute power in the monarch and outlawed meaningful opposition. This system remains in place under the incumbent King Mswati III, despite calls for a revised constitution that balances power between the monarch and a democratically elected parliament.

It is easy to cross between Mpumalanga and KwaZulu-Natal via Swaziland in one day, but it is worth lingering for at least one night in the kingdom. The mood of rural Swaziland has as many affinities with the Africa north of the Limpopo as it does South Africa. Cows and pedestrians wander blithely into the road, traditionally attired men cycle up the slopes alongside puffing minibuses and antiquated pick-up trucks, and a more singular identity starts

Milwane Nature Reserve (AVZ)

to emerge. Swaziland is one of the few modern African states whose borders approximate a pre-colonial polity, so that tribal and national identities amount to pretty much the same thing.

The main tourist focus is the **Ezulwini Valley**, the traditional power base of the royal family and home to the casinos that thrived under apartheid (when gambling was banned in the republic). More interesting to most international visitors are the excellent **Mantenga Traditional Village** (✆ www.sntc. org.sz), which offers cultural tours and musical performances, and the **Mlilwane Nature Reserve** (✆ www.biggameparks.org), a tract of revitalised farmland where wildlife can be seen on horseback or on foot. For more serious game viewing, **Hlane National Park** (✆ www.biggameparks.org) is home to a selection of antelope, who live alongside reintroduced lion, cheetah, elephant and white rhino.

Other highlights are **Malolotja Nature Reserve** (✆ www.sntc.org.sz), Swaziland's last true wilderness and a mountainous hiker's haven that supports regional endemics such as black wildebeest, blesbok, bald ibis, blue crane and Gurney's sugarbird. It is also the site of the world's oldest known mine, which dates back to 40,000 BC. For adrenaline junkies, rafting trips on the Grade I–IV rapids along the Great Usutu River, and the wobbly ascent of a domed batholithic protrusion called Sibebe Rock (the world's largest granite monolith) can be organised by Swazi Trails (✆ www.swazitrails.co.sz).

7 KwaZulu-Natal

This ecologically diverse province rises from the Indian Ocean coastline to the uKhahlamba-Drakensberg Mountains on its western border. Created when Natal was melded with the territorially interlocked homeland of KwaZulu in 1994, it is now the country's second most populous province, with 80% of its 10 million inhabitants being Zulu. It is the only province to recognise a monarch, King Goodwill Zwelithini, a descendant of King Shaka, founder of the Zulu Nation. Within South Africa, KwaZulu-Natal is known for the beach resorts that flank its southern coast either side of Durban. No less of a draw is its network of over 50 reserves, among them Hluhluwe-Imfolozi and Tembe Elephant Park. The province hosts two vast UNESCO World Heritage Sites: the uKhahlamba-Drakensberg Park, a hiker's paradise that follows the Lesotho border for 200km, and the iSimangaliso Wetland Park, which protects the long and untrammelled lake-studded coastline running north from the St Lucia Estuary.

Durban and the KwaZulu-Natal South Coast

The centrepiece of eThekweni Municipality, whose population of 3.5 million makes it the country's third largest, Durban is the most populous city on the east coast of Africa, and the continent's busiest port. It is a vibrant and interesting city – more manageable than Johannesburg, grittier than Cape Town, and with a large Indian population and sticky subtropical coastal climate that combine to give it a slightly Asiatic feel. It also supports a thriving seasonal tourist industry, thanks to the long, sandy swimming beach which follows the eastern verge of the Central Business District (CBD) south to the harbour.

Durban lies midway along the KwaZulu-Natal South Coast, a 200km stretch of subtropical beach nirvana stretching from the Tugela Mouth to the Eastern Cape border. This is South Africa's most conventional beach holiday destination, strung with palm-fringed expanses of broad white sand and popular seaside resorts such as Ballito, Umhlanga, Amanzimtoti, Umkomaas, Scottburgh, Port Shepstone, Margate and Ramsgate. Unlike Cape Town, however, the South Coast caters almost entirely to domestic holidaymakers from landlocked Gauteng, which means that it tends to get congested over school holidays and long weekends (especially around Christmas and Easter), but is very quiet at less popular times.

History

Known to the local Zulu as eThekwini (Place of the Sea), Durban lies on a bay that was first documented by the Portuguese navigator Vasco da Gama, who sailed past on Christmas Day 1497 whilst on a pioneering expedition to India. In keeping with the seasonal spirit, da Gama called the bay *Terra do Natal*, a name that has proved to be surprisingly resilient, considering that it would be more than three centuries before a permanent European settlement was established there. In 1824, a party of British traders led by Lieutenant Francis Farewell founded a trading post situated close to Durban's present-day City Hall and called it Port Natal. The settlement was renamed in 1835 after Sir Benjamin D'Urban (then the Governor of the British Cape Colony) but Natal remained the name of the associated British colony and later province of South Africa.

Durban acquired its first harbourmaster in 1839 but its development was impeded by a sandbar across the narrow harbour entrance that caused several dozen shipwrecks in the early decades. This problem

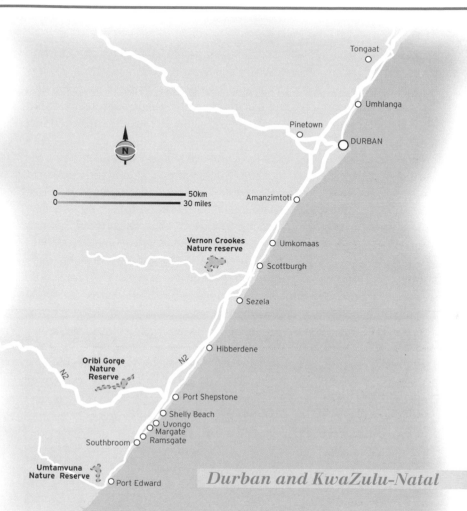

Durban and KwaZulu-Natal

was resolved in 1895, when 10 million tonnes of sand were dredged from the entrance, and the harbour now handles 4,000–5,000 sea-going ships annually. Culturally, Durban is strongly associated with the Zulu people who form the majority of the population, but it also supports about one million people of Indian descent (more, reputedly, than any city outside of India itself), who are descendants of indentured labourers shipped here in the 1860s to work on sugarcane plantations. Durban's Indian population – around 70% Hindu, 20% Muslim and 10% Christian – is an important component in the city's social fabric, and responsible for several of its best-known landmarks.

Durban highlights

The main tourist focus in Durban itself is the so-called **Golden Mile**, where the pedestrianised OR Tambo (formerly Marine) Parade divides the eastern end of the CBD Parade from the South and North beaches. Protected by shark nets and patrolled by lifeguards, both beaches are ideal for swimming, sunbathing and surfing, though South Beach can get very crowded in season, and is serviced by a string of (in some cases rather outmoded) high-rise hotels, affordable eateries and other tourist facilities. The top attraction is the child-friendly **uShaka Marine World** (☎ 031 328 8000 ⌂ www.ushakamarineworld.co.za ◑ 09.00–17.00 daily), which houses a superb aquarium (claimed to be largest in the southern hemisphere) alongside the Wet 'n' Wild Waterworld with its numerous water slides and rides. Other seafront attractions are a knee-high replica of the city called **Mini Town** (☎ 031 337 7892 ◑ 09.30–16.30 daily), the tranquil **Amphitheatre Gardens**, and the **Da Gama Clock**, erected to commemorate the quadricentennial of its namesake's 1497 Yule passing.

Hare Krishna Temple of Understanding (AVZ)

Landmarks associated with the city's large Indian population include the golden-domed **Juma Mosque**, which is the largest temple of its sort in southern Africa, and the less central **Alayam Hindu Temple** and marble **Hare Krishna Temple of Understanding**, where you'll find an excellent Indian vegetarian restaurant. Close to Juma Mosque, the colourful **Victoria Street Market** (☎ 031 306 4021) is a great place to stock up on Indian spices and

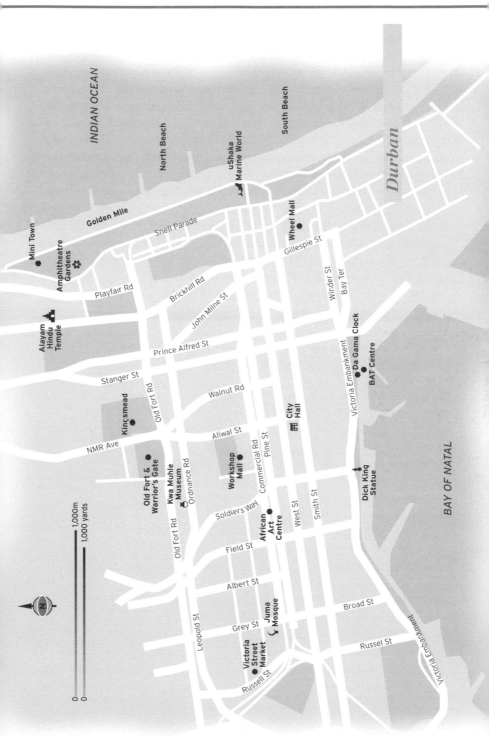

INDIAN OCEAN

North Beach

uShaka
Marine World

South Beach

Durban

Golden Mile

Mini Town

Amphitheatre
Gardens

Snell Parade

Wheel Mall

Gillespie St

Playfair Rd

Brickhill Rd

Wirder St

Bay Ter

Alayam
Hindu
Temple

John Milne St

Prince Alfred St

Da Gama Clock

BAT Centre

Stanger St

Old Fort Rd

Walnut Rd

Victoria Embankment

Kincsmead

City
Hall

NMR Ave

Aliwal St

Commercial Rd

Pine St

BAY OF NATAL

Old Fort &
Warrior's Gate

Kwa Muhle
Museum

Ordnance Rd

Workshop
Mall

Dick King
Statue

1,000m
1,000 yards

Old Fort Rd

Soldiers Way

West St

Smith St

N

Field St

African
Art
Centre

Albert St

Leopold St

Broad St

Grey St

Juma
Mosque

Victoria Embankment

Victoria
Street
Market

Russell St

Russel St

Practicalities

All flights land at King Shaka International Airport, which opened about 35km north of Durban in 2010, replacing the older international airport located south of the city centre. On an organised tour, your flight should be met by the ground operator, but metered taxis and the usual car rental agencies are available, and airport shuttles can be arranged at ✆ 086 661 1707 🖥 www.airportshuttle.co.za.

There are several banks with ATMs at the airport and around the city itself. Once settled in, taxis can be arranged through your hotel reception, which should also be able to put you in touch with agencies for day tours of the city and overnight tours further afield.

Durban has no shortage of good eateries, with Indian cuisine and seafood being particularly well represented. Prices are generally cheaper than Johannesburg or Cape Town. The options outlined below are all very central and are recommended.

Accommodation

Exclusive
Fairmont Zimbali Lodge Ballito (45km north of Durban)
🖥 www.fairmont.com
Oyster Box Umhlanga Rocks (20km north of Durban)
🖥 www.oysterbox.com
Selborne Hotel & Golf Estate Pennington (50km south of Durban)
🖥 www.selborne.com

Upmarket
Beverley Hills Sun Umhlanga Rocks (20km north of Durban)
🖥 www.southernsun.com
Dolphin Rock Guesthouse Ballito (45km north of Durban)
🖥 www.dolphinrock.co.za
Goble Palms Morningside, Durban 🖥 www.goblepalms.co.za
Royal Hotel Durban CBD 🖥 www.theroyal.co.za
Southern Sun Elangeni, Durban's Golden Mile 🖥 www.southernsun.com

Moderate
Beach Lodge Hotel Margate (100km south of Durban)
🖥 www.beachlodge.org.za

Durban waterfront (AVZ)

Oribi Gorge Hotel Oribi Gorge ⌂ www.oribigorge.co.za
Protea Hotel Karridene Illovo Beach (20km south of Durban)
⌂ www.karridene.co.za

Budget and camping
Beachcomber Bay Margate (100km south of Durban)
⌂ www.beachcomberbay.co.za
Oribi Gorge Rest Camp Oribi Gorge Nature Reserve
⌂ www.kznwildlife.com
Tekweni Backpackers Hostel Morningside, Durban
⌂ www.tekwenibackpackers.co.za

Eating out

Aangan (Indian, vegetarian) Denis Hurley St ☎ 031 307 1366
Beanbag Bohemia (pasta & sandwiches) Morningside ☎ 031 309 6019
New Café Fish (seafood) Victoria Embankment ☎ 031 305 5062
Oyster Bar (shellfish & sushi) Victoria Embankment ☎ 031 307 7883
Ulundi (Indian) Royal Hotel, Anton Lembede St ☎ 031 333 6000

silverwork, as well as local Zulu handicrafts. There are also local craft shops in the beachside **Wheel Mall** (✆ 031 332 4324) and downtown **Workshop Mall** (✆ 031 304 9894 🖰 www.theworkshop centre.co.za), while art enthusiasts might want to head to the

Durban City Hall houses a number of interesting museums. (HZ/D)

long-serving **African Art Centre** (✆ 031 312 394 🖰 www.afriart.org.za) in suburban Florida and the **Durban Art Gallery** (✆ 031 311 2264), situated in the City Hall and renowned for its collection of vintage Zulu handicrafts. The City Hall, which celebrated its centenary in 2010, is also the setting for the adequate **Natural Science Museum** (✆ 031 311 2256), while the nearby **Bergtheil Local History Museum** (✆ 031 203 7107), situated in the original Victorian courthouse, focuses on the city's early colonial days.

For a fix of greenery in the city centre, try the **Durban Botanical Garden** (✆ 031 202 5819 🖰 www.durbanbotanicgardens.org. za), with its fabulous collections of prehistoric cycads and rare orchids. Durban's most ecologically worthwhile conservation area, the **Beachwood Mangroves Nature Reserve** (✆ 083 293 3611 🖰 www. kznwildlife.com) offers a rare opportunity to see mangrove dwellers such as the brilliant mangrove kingfisher and quirky mudskipper fish from a wooden boardwalk, but is unfortunately accessible by appointment only. The neighbouring **Umgeni River Bird Park** (✆ 031 579 4600 🖰www.umgeniriverbirdpark.co.za) is a more gimmicky set-up, because most of the 1,000 birds protected are exotic to South Africa, but it's fun all the same, and great for children. To see indigenous birds, try the **Bluff Nature Reserve** (✆ 031 469 2807), where a pair of hides overlook a pan lined with reeds, or the **Kenneth Stainbank Nature Reserve** (✆ 031 469 2807), which is also home to various antelope and other small mammals.

South coast excursions

KwaZulu-Natal Sharks Board

☎ 031 566 0400 🖥 www.shark.co.za ⏰ 08.00–16.00
Mon–Fri, audiovisual shows 09.00 & 14.00 Tue–Thu ⁽ˢᴮ⁾
Situated in Umhlanga Rocks, 20 minutes' drive north
of Durban, this research centre has lifelike replicas of various sharks and rays,
while the audiovisual display emphasises the importance of these oft-maligned
creatures in the marine ecology.

Aliwal Shoal

☎ 039 973 2534 🖥 www.aliwalshoal.com
Situated 5km off the coast between Amanzimtoti and Umkomaas, this rocky
reef, named after a boat that sank here in 1849, offers great scuba diving in
a network of tunnels and caves teeming with fish. Ragged-tooth sharks are
common between August and November. Two wrecks – the *Nebo* (1884) and
Produce (1974) – lie off the reef's northern tip.

Oribi Gorge Nature Reserve

☎ 039 679 1644 🖥 www.kznwildlife.com
⏰ 06.30–19.30 daily
Situated 21km inland from Port Shepstone alongside the N2, the euphorbia-
studded canyon carved by the Mzimkulwana River is accessible by road and
can also be explored via walking trails. The birdlife is exceptional; other wildlife
includes bushbuck and Samango monkey, and white-water rafting and abseiling
are available outside the reserve.

Shelley Beach

☎ 082 877 3966 ✉ info@aquaplanet.co.za
Excellent snorkelling and diving opportunities are available offshore at
sites such as Potato Reef, Deep Salmon and Bo Boyi Reef. Protea Banks is
recommended for shark enthusiasts, with Zambezi, hammerhead, guitar, tiger
and ragged-tooth sharks all present.

Umtamvuna Nature Reserve

☎ 039 311 2383 ⏰ 06.30–17.30 daily
Protecting a forested gorge carved by the eponymous river on the Eastern
Cape border, this reserve offers some lovely coastal and forest hiking, and
it harbours various small antelope, along with a breeding colony of the
endangered Cape vulture.

Zululand

Unofficially but widely known as Zululand, the northern coastal belt of KwaZulu-Natal is perhaps the most emphatically African part of South Africa, characterised by lush subtropical vegetation, a moist, warm climate, and a low level of urbanisation. As its popular name implies, the region lay at the core of the Zulu Kingdom during its 19th-century peak. Today it is studded with historical sites related to that formative era, from the grave of Shaka Zulu to the site of the final decisive battle in the Anglo-Zulu War, while the living Zulu culture can be explored at several cultural lodges.

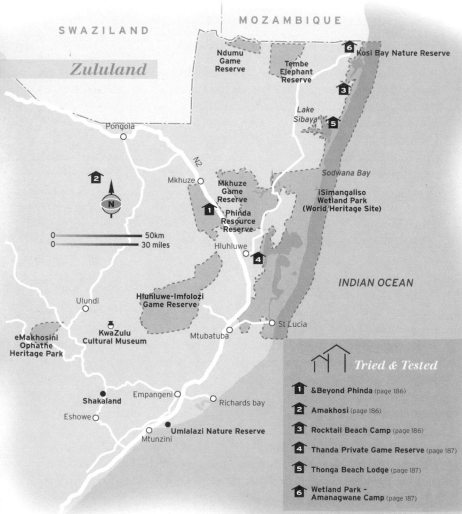

The rise and fall of the Zulu Empire

The Zulu were one of many small hereditary fiefdoms scattered around coastal KwaZulu-Natal prior to 1816, when an illegitimate prince called Shaka usurped the throne after killing his incumbent half-brother. A controversial African historical figure, Shaka grew up as a social outcast, his very name tinged with malicious irony (when his mother Nandi announced that she was pregnant by the chief, her claims were dismissed as an infection of ishaka, a beetle believed to suppress menstruation). Young Shaka also suffered from a rash of alleged impediments, ranging from a stutter to a deformed penis, which spurred his competitive instincts when it came to games and sports.

Even before he became chief, Shaka had risen to become a commander in King Dingiswayo's powerful Mthethwa army. In 1817, Dingiswayo was beheaded by the rival Ndwandwe army, and Shaka assumed *ipso facto* leadership of the Mthethwa. A year later, pioneering the innovative 'buffalo horn' formation he developed to trap enemies in battle, Shaka scored a decisive victory over the numerically stronger Ndwandwe, forcing them to retreat into present-day Swaziland. Shaka then turned his attention southward and westward, instigating an era of violent social turmoil and intertribal bloodshed remembered locally as the Mfecane or 'Crushing'.

Present-day KwaZulu-Natal was fully under Zulu rule by 1827, when Shaka's mother Nandi died – officially of dysentery, but allegedly due to a spear wound inflicted by Shaka during a heated argument. In the aftermath of Nandi's death, a grief-stricken Shaka initiated the massacre of 7,000 of his followers in one afternoon, then announced a year of national mourning during which it was forbidden to drink milk, grow crops or indulge in sexual intercourse. The self-indulgence of this policy, and its genocidal execution, left Shaka isolated and vulnerable. In September 1828 he was stabbed to death by a triumvirate of assassins including his half-brother and successor Dingane.

Under Dingane, the Zulu Kingdom faced fresh pressures in the form of a newly founded British settlement at Port Natal (Durban) and the arrival of the Boers from the southwest. A series of confrontations culminated in December 1838 with the Battle of Blood River, where 3,000 spear-wielding Zulus were mowed down by Boer guns, a defeat that shook the Zulu Empire to its core. As a result, Dingane's successor Mpande established diplomatic relations with Britain to secure Zulu sovereignty over the northern half of the kingdom. An uneasy truce reigned until January 1879, when Britain invaded Zululand. The first blow went to the Zulu army at Islandwana, but superior British firepower held sway thereafter. By December 1879, the Zulu royal kraal at Ondini had been razed, King Cetshwayo (who succeeded Mpande in 1873) was forced into hiding, and Zululand was effectively part of the British empire.

Zulu warriors (AVZ)

But while Zulu culture, both past and present, is an important facet of this compelling region, it is best known as the site of some of the country's finest wildlife and nature sanctuaries, from the vast lakes and wild coastline of the iSimangaliso Wetland Park to the superlative Big Five viewing of Hluhluwe-Imfolozi and various private reserves. The Zululand reserves are especially well known for their high densities of both white and black rhino, while other regional specials include the exquisite nyala antelope, the diminutive red duiker, the handsome Samango monkey, and a host of localised birds, of which the cumbersome-looking trumpeter hornbill is particularly conspicuous thanks to its loud and distressing mewling call.

Zululand highlights

iSimangaliso Wetland Park

☎ 035 590 1340 ⏚ www.kznwildlife.com

This UNESCO World Heritage Site, until recently known as the Greater St Lucia Wetlands, follows the magnificent and largely unspoilt north coast of KwaZulu-Natal for 200km between the mouth of the St Lucia Estuary and the Mozambican border. Five separate Ramsar Wetlands lie within iSimangaliso, which was amalgamated from about a dozen stand-alone reserves in the early 1990s. Today, it broadly splits into a southern portion centred on St Lucia Village and Estuary, and the more northerly Maputaland Coast.

iSimangaliso's rich diversity of habitats includes Africa's largest estuarine system, South Africa's largest freshwater lake, the world's most southerly coral reefs and tallest forested dunes (up to 170m high), and the fragile sand forest and savanna of the western shores and Mkhuze Game Reserve. This diversity is reflected by a higher count of vertebrate species than any other African conservation area: 129 terrestrial and aquatic mammals, 525 birds, 128 reptiles, 50 amphibians, and 991 marine and 48 freshwater fish. Nevertheless, iSimangaliso is not a conventional Big Five safari destination in the mould of Hluhluwe-Imfolozi, as much of the park is open to unguided exploration on foot, and while wildlife is abundant in parts, the stunning coastal scenery is at least as big an attraction as the game viewing.

Tourism to iSimangaliso is focussed on the peninsula-bound, jungle-swathed **St Lucia Village** and the eponymous freshwater estuary, which extends over 415km^2 when full, but – with an average depth of less than 1m – can come close to drying out during prolonged droughts. An abundance of wildlife can be seen in the village: hippos and crocs are resident in the adjacent estuary; the likes of porcupine, bushbuck and warthog pass through regularly; while charismatic birds such as African fish eagle, trumpeter hornbill and purple-crested turaco maintain a vociferous presence. There's also a popular crocodile farm, a wide sandy beach within walking distance, and regular launch trips onto the estuary.

Nyala drinking at a watering hole, Mkhuze Game Reserve (AVZ)

Popular organised excursions include seasonal whale-watching or turtle-tracking, snorkelling at Cape Vidal, and Hluhluwe-Imfolozi day safaris.

For general game viewing, the highlight of iSimangaliso is the 400km^2 **Mkhuze Game Reserve**, where resident populations of leopard, giraffe, impala, greater kudu, nyala, suni and warthog are boosted by reintroduced elephant, rhino, buffalo and cheetah. Mkhuze is a favourite of wildlife photographers who are attracted to the trio of hides overlooking its watering pans, and birdwatchers who can potentially tick off 420 species, among them several Zululand specials. The guided Fig Forest Walk near Nsumo Pan is a must for serious birdwatchers, and a Zulu cultural village within the reserve offers a glimpse of traditional lifestyles and crafts.

Practicalities

Most **organised tours** that visit Zululand do so *en route* between the Kruger National Park and Durban, a very long drive that is usually broken up by at least one overnight stay, often at Shakaland or at one of the lodges bordering Hluhluwe-Imfolozi. Otherwise, the closest airport for **stand-alone visits** is Durban's King Shaka International, which lies about two to three hours' drive from most sites of interest in south-central Zululand. There are also domestic **flights** to Richards Bay, a large but unappealing industrial port situated about 50km southwest of St Lucia as the crow flies, but they are far less regular and tend to be more expensive than flights to Durban. Most Durban-based tour operators offer one- to three-night trips to various sites in Zululand.

Accommodation

For full details of tour operator-recommended accommodation, see pages 185–7. Here follows a few further suggestions from the author.

Exclusive
Forest, Mountain, Vlei & Rock lodges Phinda Resource Reserve ⚲ www.andbeyondafrica.com
Kosi Forest Lodge Kosi Bay ⚲ www.isibindiafrica.co.za

Upmarket
Elephant Lake Hotel St Lucia Village ⚲ www.elephantlakestlucia.co.za
Hilltop Resort Hluhluwe-Imfolozi ⚲ www.kznwildlife.com

The more remote northern sector of iSimangaliso comprises a serpentine coastal strip of wide sandy beaches separated from a string of wetlands by a spectacular ribbon of tall, forested dunes. The most developed spot is **Sodwana Bay**, site of the world's southernmost coral reefs, notably **Seven Mile Reef**, a beautiful dive site with its overhangs and drop-offs 20m below the surface. Unfortunately, while Sodwana is justifiably legendary in diving circles, it is also the one place in iSimangaliso where fishermen are permitted to drive on the beach, and the rows of 4x4s lined up on the sand is an unedifying sight. North of Sodwana, **Lake Sibaya**, South Africa's largest natural freshwater body, backed by tall, forested dunes, is poorly developed for tourism, but it supports around 150 hippos and a wide diversity of aquatic birds.

Alternatively, the region is also well suited to **self-drive** visits (though a 4x4 is required for most places that lie north of Mkhuze Game Reserve and east of the N2) and several major car rental companies are represented at King Shaka International and Richard's Bay Airport. Some visitors to Phinda and other private reserves use direct charter flights.

There are few towns of substance north of Richard's Bay, but Eshowe, St Lucia Village, Hluhluwe, Mkuze and Ulundi all have at least one bank with an ATM, adequate supermarkets, and a small number of low-key restaurants. **Facilities** are more limited in the reserves, some of which have small shops and restaurants in their rest camps, but generally little else. Internet facilities are few and far between, and mobile phone networks are limited away from urban areas.

Shakaland Near Eshowe ⚲ www.shakaland.com
Simunye Zulu Lodge Near Eshowe ⚲ www.simunyelodge.co.za
Tembe Tented Lodge Tembe Elephant Park ⚲ www.tembe.co.za

Moderate
Mpila Resort Hluhluwe-Imfolozi ⚲ www.kznwildlife.com
Sodwana Bay Lodge Sodwana Bay ⚲ www.sodwanabaylodge.com
St Lucia Wetlands Guesthouse St Lucia Village ⚲ www.stluciawetlands.com

Budget
George Hotel Eshowe ⚲ www.eshoweaccommodation.com
Isinkwe Backpackers & Bush Camp ⚲ www.isinkwe.co.za
Sodwana Rest Camp Sodwana Bay ⚲ www.kznwildlife.com

Beach at Rocktail Bay, in the Maputaland Coast area of the iSimangaliso Wetland Park (AVZ)

Abutting the Mozambican border, **Kosi Bay** is a scenic wetland comprising eight lakes and a series of connecting channels that drain into the Indian Ocean through a sandy estuary. An unusual feature of Kosi Bay is the sanctioned use of the local Thonga people's complex fishing traps in the estuary mouth – a highly sustainable traditional form of natural resource management, since the estuarine fish are readily replenished from the open sea. For snorkelers, a rocky reef in the estuary mouth offers unusually calm conditions for those seeking out 150 marine fish species, including the bizarre devil's firefish. Samango monkey, Nile crocodile, hippo and a diversity of birds are likely to be seen on canoe trips through the channel.

Eshowe and the Valley of Kings

Situated a mere 25km inland of the N2, the small but pretty town of **Eshowe** lies amidst lushly forested hills that offer some respite from the midsummer coastal humidity. Bordering the town centre, the country's most accessible patch of mistbelt forest is protected in the **Dhlinza Forest Reserve**, home to the diminutive blue duiker, an interesting selection of forest birds, and a 125m aerial boardwalk that terminates at a tall tower offering grandstand views of the Indian Ocean.

The informative **Zululand Historical Museum** is housed in Fort Nongqai, built by the British in 1883.

Eshowe is the gateway to the historic heart of the former Zulu Empire, an area bisected by the R66 to Ulundi, former capital of the apartheid-era homeland of KwaZulu. The R66 provides access

Zulu maiden wearing traditional beads (AVZ)

The forested hills around Eshowe offer a cooler alternative to the midsummer humidity of the coast. (SS)

to several well-known lodges offering an institutionalised but nevertheless informative and enjoyable introduction to Zulu culture. Situated 15km north of Eshowe, the best known and most exciting of the lodges offering day tours is the showy but exuberant **Shakaland** (✆ 035 460 0912 🖱 www.shakaland.co.za), which was constructed as the set for the 1986 television series *Shaka Zulu*, on the site of one of King Shaka's original *kraals* (traditional cattle enclosures). Those with time for an overnight stay might want to look at the more low-key **Simunye Zulu Lodge**, built into a cliff overlooking the Mfule River (see *Accommodation*, page 179).

Nondescript **Ulundi** is distinguished mainly by its proximity to eMakhosini, the Zulu 'Valley of Kings' now protected in the 250km² **eMakhosini Ophathe Heritage Park** (✆ 035 870 5000 🖱 www.emakhosini.co.za). This park comprises a game reserve stocked with rhinos and other typical Zululand wildlife, along with cultural landmarks such as King Shaka's Grave, the reconstructed residence of King Dingane and the Hill of Execution where Piet Retief's trekker party were slaughtered. On the outskirts of Ulundi, the **KwaZulu Cultural Museum** (🖱 www.zulu-museum.co.za) is situated at Ondini, the partially reconstructed capital of King Cetshwayo, which was razed by British troops in 1879 in the last battle of the Anglo-Zulu War.

Hluhluwe-Imfolozi Game Reserve

Zululand's most important game reserve is Hluhluwe-Imfolozi, which extends over 960km² of rolling hills that formerly served as the royal

The Battlefields Route

The northern interior of KwaZulu-Natal was the site of most major battles in the 19th-century Zulu-Boer and Anglo-Zulu wars, and several of the most important clashes in the Anglo-Boer War of 1899–1902. The main sites are marked by memorials and/or museums, and several can be viewed along the so-called Battlefields Route, variations of which can be used to get between the Zululand coast and reserves, and the uKhahlamba-Drakensberg foothills. These routes converge on the small town of **Dundee**, site of the excellent **Talana Museum** (🕐 www.talana.co.za). The sites below are listed in chronological order.

Hill of Execution (February 1838)

Set in eMakhosini Ophathe Heritage Park (see page 181), this is where the Voortrekker party led by Piet Retief were slaughtered in front of their leader's eyes at the command of King Dingane. Retief's eyes, heart and liver were torn from his living body as muti (medicine) in an effort to ward off further European incursion.

Blood River (December 1838)

Two monuments commemorate this landmark battle in which a heavily armed troop of 468 Boers, their ox-wagons arranged in a circular laager, felled some 3,000 spear-wielding Zulu warriors and turned the Ncome River red with blood. The Blood River Monument, bronze cast in the apartheid era, comprises 64 life-size ox-wagons, while the Ncome Museum (🕐 www.ncomemuseum.co.za) recounts the conflict from the perspective of the defeated Zulus.

Isandlwana (January 1879)

The first major campaign of the Anglo-Zulu War was the most humiliating defeat ever suffered by Britain at the hands of an African foe. Some 20,000 Zulu warriors, armed only with spears, launched a surprise attack on 1,800 British troops encamped below Isandlwana Hill, and left behind fewer than 500 survivors.

Rorke's Drift (January 1879)

Immortalised in the 1964 film *Zulu* (starring Stanley Baker and Michael Caine), the defence of Rorke's Drift followed immediately after the Zulu victory at Isandlwana (see above). Of the 150 British troops who defended the mission against more than 3,000 Zulu warriors, 11 were awarded the Victoria Cross.

Ulundi (July 1879)

Situated a short way from the modern town of Ulundi (see page 181), the last decisive battle of the Anglo-Zulu War took place at King Cetshwayo's capital, which was razed in the process.

Spioenkop (January 1900)

Early in the Anglo-Boer War, the Boer victory atop Spioenkop Hill left 383 British soldiers dead and a further 1,300 wounded (as compared to Boer losses of 58 dead and 140 wounded). The dead were buried in trenches that can still be seen today, and a small museum has been built alongside. This unprecedented carnage in a remote corner of an African colony had such a deep impact on the English popular consciousness that three top football grounds had stands renamed in commemoration, most famously The Kop at Liverpool's Anfield. Curiously, three men present at the battle were destined to become national leaders: the Boer general Louis Botha, the rising English journalist Winston Churchill, and a part-time stretcher-bearer called Mohandas Gandhi.

Isandlwana Battlefield (FD/R)

hunting ground of King Shaka. The area was accorded official protection as long ago as 1895, albeit as the disjunct Hluhluwe Valley and Umfolozi Junction game sanctuaries, which were linked by a corridor reserve in the 1980s. These two original reserves played a crucial role in the conservation of both African rhino species and in particular the white rhino, which would most likely be extinct were it not for the Umfolozi population that bottlenecked at fewer than 20 individuals in 1916.

Hluhluwe-Imfolozi is the only provincial reserve in Zululand where all the Big Five are present, and game viewing here can be excellent, whether you self-drive or join the guided game drives that are offered by the reserve's rest camps, as well as by several private companies based outside. White rhino is especially visible, black rhino rather less so, and the reserve is also good for elephant, buffalo and to a lesser extent lion and leopard. Other prominent species include African wild dog, giraffe, zebra, impala, nyala, greater kudu, warthog and vervet monkey. The reserve offers excellent birding too, with a checklist of almost 400 species. For the more energetic, the Imfolozi sector has three self-guided foot trails, while guided two-hour game walks are conducted daily from both rest camps. From mid-March to mid-December, four-night wilderness trails are available, which lead through a 300km^2 area closed to vehicular traffic.

Female nyala (MT/D)

Zululand private reserves

The most prestigious wildlife destination in Zululand, the 170km^2 **Phinda Resource Reserve** (⊘ www.andbeyond africa.com) offers a wildlife experience comparable to the top private reserves bordering the Kruger National Park. All the so-called Big Five (except the more elusive leopard) are almost certain to be seen over a two- to three-night stay, but the biggest local speciality is cheetah, which tend to be very habituated, allowing for great close-up behavioural viewing. Ungulates include giraffe, zebra, greater kudu, impala and an estimated 4,000 head of nyala, and guided bird walks are good for Zululand specialities such as Neergard's sunbird, pink-throated twinspot and African broadbill.

Phinda Resource Reserve is an excellent place for seeing cheetah. (SS)

Not strictly speaking a private reserve, but effectively functioning as one, the 300km² **Tembe Elephant Park** (🔗 www.tembe.co.za) is part of the mooted Lubombo Transfrontier Conservation Area, which will eventually extend northward as far as the Maputo Special Reserve in Mozambique and reunite a cross-border population of at least 400 elephants. The elephants occur here naturally and include South Africa's three largest tuskers, but the rest of the Big Five have been reintroduced, and the birdlife is fantastic.

Other private reserves worth looking at, all offering a broadly similar experience, include **Zulu Nyala** (🔗 www.zulunyala.com), **Leopard Mountain** (🔗 www.leopardmountain.co.za) and **Thula Thula** (🔗 www. thulathula.com).

&Beyond Phinda
🐾 www.phinda.com

Teeming with wildlife, including the Big Five, &Beyond Phinda Private Game Reserve is home to six stunning safari lodges, each uniquely placed to take advantage of the distinct habitats found in this prime wilderness. From the gorgeous zen chalets of Forest Lodge to the romantic Vlei Lodge, it is hard to find finer accommodation in the region. For families or small groups, the Zuka Lodge and The Homestead, two luxurious and intimate villas, are a perfect home away from home.

Amakhosi
🐾 www.amakhosi.com

Amakhosi is a five-star lodge on the bank of the Mkuze River in the 'Big Five' Amazulu private game reserve, a beautiful mix of savannah, wetlands and mountain. We like the floor-to-ceiling windows in the eight suites, with views over the river. Experienced guides lead game drives and bush walks, and can satisfy passionate birders; but Amakahosi is distinguished by its seasonal 'frogging' and 'micro' safaris – which both demonstrate a profound understanding of the ecosystem and are a lot of fun.

Rocktail Beach Camp
🐾 www.wilderness-safaris.com

Top of our list for an unspoiled beach adventure, this 17-room camp provides world-class diving and snorkelling on a gloriously remote coastline. Set in a lush coastal forest the camp's ocean views are second to none. Summer guests can accompany researchers on night drives monitoring turtle nesting; other activities include birding, swimming, and forest and beach walks. Families are welcome, and divers can experience an underwater world heritage site with huge shoals of fish, dolphins and whales undisturbed by other visitors.

Thanda Private Game Reserve
⌁ www.thanda.com

An award-winning reserve with three accommodation options. Thanda Main Lodge has nine opulent bush villas, each with private pool. The exclusive Royal Suite is the epitome of luxury with five suites. Our favourite is Thanda Tented Camp. This small intimate camp, with colonial-style luxury safari tents and no children under 14, is perfect for honeymooners. This must be one of the only places where you can go on safari in the morning and dive in the Indian Ocean in the afternoon.

Thonga Beach Lodge
⌁ www.isibindiafrica.co.za/mabibi

Situated in a relatively undiscovered region of South Africa, Thonga Beach Lodge offers deserted beaches, and warm, crystal clear water with unparalleled snorkelling and diving. Nestled into the dunes with sweeping views of the Indian Ocean, the spacious suites provide complete privacy and are constructed to ensure minimal impact on the environment. Guests can relax beside the swimming pool or enjoy a delicious cocktail at the unique 'ocean' bar. For those needing a little pampering, there is also a rejuvenation centre.

Wetland Park Group - Amangwane Camp ⌁ www.thewetlandpark.co.za

RAINBOW TOURS

This is uncomplicated fun at its best. Stay in en-suite reed chalets with shower, stretcher beds and crisp linen, in a community-run campsite where you get a real insight into Thonga culture. Expert guides teach you to trap fish in traditional kraals, and kayak, canoe and snorkel in the pristine Kosi Bay lake system that runs into the Indian Ocean. Fresh seafood is a feature of the menu and the camp is huge hit with families and self-drivers all year round.

uKhahlamba-Drakensberg and the KwaZulu-Natal Midlands

Africa's largest protected montane wilderness, the 2,500km²
uKhahlamba-Drakensberg Park extends for a full 200km along the
border between KwaZulu-Natal and the cloud-scraping Kingdom of
Lesotho, where several dozen peaks top the 3,000m mark. The park is
known for its rich biodiversity and stunning prehistoric rock art, both
of which have combined to gain it recognition as one of only 27 'mixed'
natural and cultural sites included on the UNESCO World Heritage

Thukea River Gorge, Royal Natal National Park (AVZ)

list. While its official name combines the Zulu *uKhahlamba* (Barrier
of Spears) with an Afrikaans name meaning 'Dragon's Mountain' (the
jagged escarpment vaguely resembles an elongated saurian spine), such
is the singularity of this imperiously beautiful afro-montane landscape
that many simply refer to it as The Berg – 'The Mountain'.

Most people visit uKhahlamba-Drakensberg for the scenery or the
prodigious prehistoric rock art, both of which can be sampled on
numerous different day walks, but the park is also a hub of botanical
diversity, with 2,500 plant species identified. These include around 350
endemics, among them South Africa's only indigenous bamboo, and a
flowering protea whose natural range comprises less than 1ha of the
Royal Natal Park. Large wildlife is sparse, but the fearsome, dog-like

barking of Chacma baboons resounds through the gorges, and antelope present include common eland, bushbuck, mountain reedbuck, grey rhebok and grey duiker. Prominent among a 300-strong bird checklist are cliff-associated raptors such as Verreaux's eagle, the jackal buzzard, Cape vulture and lammergeyer, and 20 species whose range is restricted to South Africa, Lesotho and Swaziland.

The area referred to as the KwaZulu-Natal Midlands separates the foothills of the uKhahlamba-Drakensberg from the warmer coastal belt. The midlands is the site of the provincial capital Pietermaritzburg, which lies about 80km inland from Durban along the N3 to Johannesburg, and the area is known throughout South Africa for its rolling green scenery (reminiscent, some say, of parts of Britain, though this is basically

Practicalities

Although uKhahlamba-Drakensberg forms a cohesive ecological unit, the rugged topography divides it into a dozen or so different sectors, each effectively a self-contained destination with its own attractions and access roads. The most northerly and southerly sectors lie more than 150km distant as the crow flies, and much further apart by surfaced roads, so it makes sense to focus on one sector. As a guideline, Royal Natal ranks highly for scenic impact, Champagne Valley for overall tourist development, Giant's Castle and Kamberg for accessible rock art, and Sani Pass for birdwatching and 4x4 enthusiasts.

If you're not on an **organised tour, self-drive** is the most realistic option and you should expect it to take over three hours to cover the 350km from Gauteng to Royal Natal Park (in the north), or two hours from Durban to Himeville (near

Accommodation

For full details of tour operator-recommended accommodation, see pages 198-9. Here follows a few further suggestions from the author.

In addition to the hotels listed below, full details of moderate and budget rest camps and campsites operated by Ezemvelo KZN Wildlife at Giant's Castle, Royal Natal and Kamberg can be viewed at ⁰⁸ www.kznwildlife.com.

Upmarket
Cathedral Peak Hotel Cathedral Peak ⁰⁸ www.cathedralpeak.co.za
Drakensberg Sun Champagne Valley ⁰⁸ www.southernsun.com
Orion Mont-Aux-Sources Hotel Near Royal Natal ⁰⁸ www.oriongroup.co.za

because so much indigenous vegetation has been supplanted by exotics) and the Midlands Meander centred around the small town of Howick.

uKhahlamba-Drakensberg and the KwaZulu-Natal Midlands highlights

Royal Natal National Park
No single feature encapsulates the majesty of uKhahlamba-Drakensberg as fully as the Amphitheatre, a 5km wall of burnished sandstone that dominates the skyline of Royal Natal National Park and is particularly spectacular when blanketed in snow during winter. The Thukela Falls,

the base of Sani Pass). For ecological reasons, no hotels exist within the park proper, but Ezemvelo KZN Wildlife operates rest camps and campsites at several entrance gates, and there are private hotels in Champagne Valley and in the vicinity of Royal Natal, Cathedral Peak and Sani Pass. ATMs, supermarkets, fuel etc can be found in small towns such as Bergville, Winterton, Mooi River, Himeville and Underberg.

uKhahlamba-Drakensberg's non-nannyish management policy stands in user-friendly contrast to the strict regulations and hefty costs associated with most other iconic African mountains – simply pitch up at any entrance gate, hand over the nominal entrance fee, sign into the mountain register, and off you go. Hikers on the upper slopes frequently get trapped in stormy or misty conditions, and there are occasional fatalities, so do be careful and be prepared to turn back or stay put as weather conditions dictate.

Sani Pass Hotel Sani Pass ⚲ www.sanipasshotel.co.za

Moderate
Ardmore Guest Farm Champagne Valley ⚲ www.ardmore.co.za
Himeville Arms Hotel Near Sani Pass ⚲ www.himevillehotel.co.za
Howick Falls Hotel Howick ⚲ www.howickfallshotel.co.za
Protea Hotel Imperial Pietermaritzburg ⚲ www.proteahotels.com

Budget
Inkosana Lodge Champagne Valley ⚲ www.inkosana.co.za
Sani Top Chalet Sani Pass ⚲ www.sanitopchalet.co.za

which tumble down the Amphitheatre's face in five stages to register a total drop of 949m, are the goal of the popular Gorge Trail (see box, page 196). Overall, this is an inspirationally scenic park, offering walking opportunities to suit all levels of fitness, and also quite good rock art and wildlife.

Cathedral Peak and Didima
The striking, 3,005m Cathedral Peak, which towers above the main escarpment like a squat version of a cow horn (an image alluded to by its traditional name of Mponjwane), is an attainable goal for a tough full-day guided hike from the Cathedral Peak Hotel. Nearby, **Didima**

Rock art of the uKhahlamba-Drakensberg

One of world's most important alfresco art galleries, uKhahlamba-Drakensberg contains at least 500 painted caves and shelters, and a total of about 50,000 individual images, ranging from 3,000 to less than 200 years old. A rare 19th-century European description of one such panel – Giant's Castle's spectacular Main Cave – talks of 'hideous representations, each one more ugly than its neighbour'. Early settlers were no less contemptuous of the actual artists, who they referred to as Bushmen, and exterminated like vermin. Today, by contrast, the rock art of uKhahlamba-Drakensberg is recognised not only for its rich aesthetic merit, but also for its anthropological significance as the sole surviving legacy of the hunter-gatherer cultures that prospered in South Africa prior to European settlement.

Subjects painted by South Africa's earliest artists range from monochrome human figures and finely shaded polychrome elands to bizarre, half-human and half-animal creatures known as therianthropes. Once thought to be straightforward visual accounts of day-to-day life, the paintings are now recognised as being spiritual in nature, depicting the ritual trances experienced by shamans and reflecting their complex relationships with revered animals such as the eland. Therianthropes, for instance, represent the transformation of a person into a spirit, while the lines that often connect such figures to eland portraits represent the harnessing of the antelope's essence as a portal to the spirit world.

Rock art in Lower Mushroom Cave, Cathedral Peak (AVZ)

Rock Art Centre contains life-size reproductions of several actual rock art panels. The most accessible of the 17 rock art sites in the Didima Valley is Lower Mushroom Cave, only 45 minutes' walk from the hotel, which boasts a cartoonish scene of stick men contortedly evading a marauding leopard. The more remote Botha's Shelter and Eland Cave respectively contain 900 and 1,200 individual paintings.

Champagne Valley

uKhahlamba-Drakensberg's busiest tourist hub sprawls between the small town of Winterton and Monk's Cowl. Overlooked by a trio of distinctive high peaks – domed Champagne Castle, fang-like Monk's Cowl and free-standing Cathkin Peak – the valley houses a cluster of upmarket hotels, self-catering resorts and campsites, alongside facilities such as golf courses, stables, shopping malls and craft factories. Champagne Valley is perfect for those who want to bask in the splendid scenery without breaking a sweat, but it tends to be less popular with walkers and hikers.

The beautiful scenery and plentiful amenities of the Champagne Valley make it ideal for those looking for a lazy escape. (SS)

The rolling escarpment of the Giant's Castle Game Reserve (SS)

Giant's Castle Game Reserve

The 3,314m basaltic protrusion stands at the convergence of the northern and southern escarpments. Its Zulu name Phosihawu (Shield-thrower) alludes to the dark thunderclouds that spill over its peak, while the Sesotho name Thaba Ikonjwa (Mountain that Hates to be Pointed at) refers to a belief that storms are invoked whenever somebody mentions the mountain or points at it with a straight finger. The reserve below the peak is renowned for its rock art, in particular the superb Main Cave, only 30 minutes' walk from the rest camp. This is also a good place to see the stately eland antelope and other large mammals and raptors.

Kamberg

Named after a free-standing mountain that vaguely resembles a rooster's comb (*kam* in Afrikaans), the undulating slopes here support fair numbers of eland and mountain reedbuck, but are best known for Game Pass Shelter (see box, page 196), a rock art site dubbed the 'Rosetta Stone' in double reference to the nearby village of Rosetta and to its significance in helping scholars 'crack the code' of shamanistic symbolism that underlies the region's rock art.

Sani Pass

The only motorable track to breach the Barriers of Spears, rocky Sani Pass follows a series of switchbacks uphill to a remote Lesotho border post (passport required) set at a windswept altitude of 2,865m. Commercial 4x4 and quad bike trips culminate at the spectacularly sited Sani Top Chalets, which serve piping hot meals. Scenically spectacular, Sani Pass also offers access to the rarefied alpine zone, a treeless plateau of tussocked grass, mossy boulders and clumped heather that acquires an ethereal beauty in the soft light of dusk, and often features on birdwatching tours as the easiest place to see high-altitude specials such as Drakensberg rockjumper and mountain pipit.

Pietermaritzburg

Founded in 1838 as the capital of a Boer Republic called Natalia Boer, Pietermaritzburg was incorporated into the British Colony of Natal and chosen over Durban as its capital in 1843. It has been the provincial capital of Natal, and later KwaZulu-Natal, since union in 1910. With a population estimated at 500,000, the city has a rather small-town feel in comparison with Durban, and is visited by very few tourists. Nevertheless, the pedestrian-friendly Central Business District (CBD) contains several well-preserved Victorian buildings, both of which now form part of the **Voortrekker Msunduzi Museum** (✆ 033 394 6834 🖳 www.voortrekkermuseum .co.za ◷ 09.00–16.00 Mon–Fri, 09.00–13.00 Sat). Also worth a look are the redbrick **City Hall**, built in 1893, the **Railway Station** and the former Supreme Court, which now houses the exceptional **Tatham Art Gallery** (🖳 www. tatham.org.za).

City Hall, Pietermaritzburg
(AVZ)

Great day walks

Chain Ladder Trail, Witsieshoek

A feasible day hike from Royal Natal (start early), this is the easiest walk to the top of the escarpment. It includes a vertiginous ascent of two long chain ladders, and offers sensational views from the lip of the Thukela Falls as they crash over the Amphitheatre. Allow three hours in either direction and another hour's drive each way to the starting point at the Sentinel car park.

The Chain Ladder Trail is not recommended for sufferers of vertigo! (AVZ)

Gorge Trail, Royal Natal

This flattish trail, 8km (three hours) in either direction, follows a pretty riverine gorge to the base of the Amphitheatre and Thukela Falls. There are natural swimming pools *en route*.

Rainbow Gorge, Didima

Also following a riverine gorge, this 5km trail passes through pockets of riparian forest and leads to a narrow gorge containing suspended rocks, waterfalls and swimming pools. Five hours return.

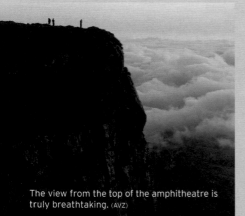

The view from the top of the amphitheatre is truly breathtaking. (AVZ)

Battle Cave, Injisuthi

An easy 10km (five-hour) trip, this guided trail near Champagne Valley leaves at 08.30 daily and leads to a spectacular rock art site comprising over 700 individual paintings.

Game Pass Shelter, Kamberg

A guided three-hour round hike, leaving thrice daily, this leads up to Game Pass Shelter, one of the country's most important and best-preserved rock art sites.

Howick

Situated about 30km northwest of Pietermaritzburg, this small town is the site of the 95m-high **Howick Falls**, which are known by the local Zulu as KwaNogqaza (Tall One), and can be observed from a viewing point right in the town centre. An important natural attraction north of town is the **Karkloof Nature Reserve**, which protects the country's largest remaining stand of mistbelt forest. Samango monkey, an endemic dwarf species, and a wealth of forest birds can be seen on the walking trail to the Karkloof Falls. The three-hour **Karkloof Canopy Tour** (✆ 033 330 3415 🖱 www.karkloofcanopytour.co.za) involves a series of eight steel cable slides suspended between a series of treetop platforms set up to 30m above the forest floor. A more contrived attraction, spread over a large area running from Howick to the uKhahlamba-Drakensberg foothills around Moor River, is the **Midlands Meander** (✆ 033 330 8195 🖱 www.midlandsmeander.co.za), which comprises a few dozen loosely affiliated cottage industries ranging from art and pottery studios to craft workshops and cheese producers.

The Howick Falls cascade from a height of 95m. (SS)

Cleopatra Mountain Farmhouse
🖰 www.cleomountain.com

In the foothills of the Drakensberg Mountains, Cleopatra Mountain Farmhouse is a foodies' paradise. It's the only place we know that advises against clients staying for more than three days because the food is so good and plentiful! All the ingredients are there for a complete treat: warm snug beds, peace, solitude and a spectacular view of the snow-capped mountains. The aromas of the kitchen, legendary throughout South Africa, will tempt you home from a mountain walk, horseride or fishing trip.

Fugitives Drift Lodge
🖰 www.fugitivesdrift.com

RAINBOW TOURS

Overlooking the heart of the Zulu Battlefields, Fugitives Drift is all about bringing history to life. Award-winning raconteurs, protégés of the late founder David Rattray, tell the story of Rorke's Drift and Isandlwana with such poignant delivery there's rarely a dry eye. The comfortable eight-bedroom lodge is full of original memorabilia and guests can explore the extensive reserve on horseback and on guided walks. This superb experience is completed with evening drinks on the terrace followed by delicious dinner.

Isandlwana Lodge
🖰 www.isandlwana.co.za

BRIDGE & WICKERS
travel with experience

Isandlwana stands where the Zulu commander stood in 1879. The 12 rooms, pool and main area overlook the plain where once he surveyed the battle's progress. Resident historian Rob Gerrard and his team are steeped in the history and capture the heroism and the tragedy of this bloody war from both sides. We like riding through open country and doing history on horseback; reliving the rout on the Fugitives walking trail; and the revelatory Qhudeni cultural tour.

Karkloof Spa
🏛 www.karkloofspa.com

Karkloof Spa is one of the premier spa destinations in the world. The spa boasts 17 treatment rooms attended by internationally experienced Thai therapists. With Kneipp pools, Rassoul, floatation, seven steam and sauna rooms, Jacuzzi and Roman baths, plus game drives, cycling, fishing and mountain biking, you are guaranteed an unparalleled sense of wellness and relaxation. The luxurious boutique lodge and 16 stylish villas offer views of abundant game, all enjoyed whilst dining on the freshest international cuisine, wines and beverages.

Montusi Mountain Lodge
🏛 www.montusi.co.za

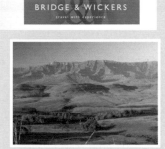

We recommend family-owned Montusi for the majestic views of the northern Drakensberg's Amphitheatre escarpment from each of its 14 comfortable garden suites; and for the delicious food, the enormous variety of trails and activities on offer and the genuine personal welcome. Over the past 11 years, the owners have planted indigenous trees and transformed what was a wattle-infested wasteland into a conservation area to which the wildlife and birds have returned.

Three Tree Hill
🏛 www.threetreehill.co.za

Overlooking the secluded malaria-free valley of Spioenkop Game Reserve in the foothills of the Drakensberg mountains, this small, owner-run luxury lodge invites relaxation with superb food and warm family hospitality. Large colonial-style verandahs, spacious rooms, and a secluded pool set amongst aloes and acacia trees infuse the experience with a tangible sense of history. Enjoy guided walks in the game reserve where rhino, giraffe, wildebeest, eland and other antelope species roam. Mountain biking, horseriding and battlefield tours are also offered.

8 Eastern Cape and the Garden Route

The long and lovely stretch of the southern coast belt that separates KwaZulu-Natal from the Cape Town area can be divided broadly into the Eastern Cape and the Garden Route. The first is somewhat sprawling, and much of it is relatively undeveloped for international tourism, but it boasts several varied highlights, ranging from the excellent elephant viewing at Addo to the blissfully unspoilt resorts and reserves of the so-called Wild Coast. Further west, the Garden Route is a more focussed area and more commonly included on tour itineraries, thanks in part to its relative proximity to Cape Town. The Garden Route, much of which is now protected in a scenic national park, is widely regarded to be the most beautiful part of the South African coast, notable for its rugged topography, wealth of indigenous forests and pretty lakes, and abundance of birds and other small wildlife.

Eastern Cape

In 1994 the Transkei and Ciskei, nominally independent Xhosa homelands created in 1963 and 1972 respectively, were re-incorporated into South Africa and merged with the eastern part of the old Cape Province to form the Eastern Cape. This large province protects a long stretch of Indian Ocean coastline, including the aptly named Wild Coast, the large port cities of Port Elizabeth and East London, and the surfing haven that is Jeffreys Bay. The provincial capital, oddly enough, is the small inland town of Bhisho, former capital of the Ciskei and rather nondescript if you discount the concentration of apartheid-era administrative buildings that huddle at its centre.

The Eastern Cape is less popular with international tourists than the flanking provinces of Western Cape and KwaZulu-Natal, in large part for logistical reasons as within the time frame of an ordinary tour it

makes sense to fly over most or all of the coast separating the Kruger or Durban from the Western Cape. But it has plenty going for it and the Wild Coast in particular is truly idyllic, being just remote and inaccessible enough to remain surprisingly unspoilt. Addo Elephant National Park and several nearby private reserves offer great malaria-free game viewing in relatively close proximity to the Garden Route or Cape Town, and for arts enthusiasts the annual National Arts Festival is held in Grahamstown every July and is a delightful mix of classical European and contemporary African influences.

Eastern Cape highlights

The Wild Coast

The scenic stretch of coastline bordered by KwaZulu-Natal to the northeast and the Kei River to the southwest, formerly part of the

Mkhambati Nature Reserve

MTHATHA

Port St Johns

Qunu

N2

Coffee Bay

50km
30 miles

Dwesa Nature Reserve

N6

Butterworth

tutterheim

Bisho

William's Town

Cintsa West

EAST LONDON

N2

INDIAN OCEAN

Tried & Tested

1 &Beyond Kwandwe (page 212)

2 Amakhala (page 212)

3 Camp Figtree (page 212)

4 Elephant House (page 213)

5 Gorah Elephant Camp (page 213)

6 Mount Camdeboo (page 216)

7 Shamwari (page 213)

Eastern Cape

Practicalities

The main entry points to the Eastern Cape are Port Elizabeth International Airport and East London Airport, both of which service the eponymous cities some 300km apart on the Indian Ocean coastline. The airports receive regular **flights** from Johannesburg, Cape Town and Durban, and host the usual car rental agencies. Within the constraints of an ordinary vacation, a common (and recommended) course of action is to fly from Durban or Johannesburg to Port Elizabeth, then continue overland to Cape Town via the coastal N2 and Garden Route (see page 218), a drive of almost 700km. Of the region's non-coastal attractions, Addo Elephant National Park and related private reserves are

Accommodation

For full details of tour operator-recommended accommodation, see pages 212-13 and 216. Here follows a few further suggestions from the author.

Upmarket
Hacklewood Hill Country House Port Elizabeth ⏚ www.hacklewood.co.za

Moderate
Brighton Lodge Port Elizabeth ⏚ www.brightonlodge.co.za
Buiten Verwagten Guesthouse Graaff-Reinet ⏚ www.buitenverwagten.co.za
Cock House Grahamstown ⏚ www.cockhouse.co.za
Halyards Hotel Port Alfred ⏚ www.riverhotels.co.za

Transkei, ranks among the most unspoilt tracts of ocean frontage in the country. It is also of interest as a preserve of traditional Xhosa culture – look out for traditionally dressed women smoking their trademark long-stemmed pipes – and as the birthplace of former presidents Nelson Mandela, Thabo Mbeki and many other ANC luminaries.

The main road through the region is the N2, which runs some 50km inland and is punctuated by the one-time Transkei capital **Mthatha** (formerly Umtata). This humdrum town is salvaged from total un-memorability by the **Nelson Mandela Museum** (☎ 047 532 5110 ⏚ www.nelsonmandelamuseum.org.za ⏰ 09.00–16.00), in the 19th-century Bhunga (Old Parliament) Building. Here, a series of displays follow Mandela's life story from his childhood in Qunu, 30km out of town, to his return to the same village after his retirement from frequently visited on an **organised round tour** from Port Elizabeth, or as part of a longer overland tour.

It is also possible to **drive** to the Eastern Cape from elsewhere in the country. The 675km stretch of the N2 between Durban and East London can be covered over a long day. Coming from Johannesburg, you could branch south from the N1 to Cape Town at Bloemfontein for the N6 to East London, or at Colesburg for the N10 to Port Elizabeth.

Within the region, East London, Port Elizabeth and other large towns such as Grahamstown and Mthatha have all the facilities you'd expect, but you may struggle to find ATMs or internet access at beach resorts, particularly along the Wild Coast.

Hemingway's Hotel East London ↰ www.southernsun.com
Hogsback Inn Hogsback ↰ www.hogsbackinn.co.za
Mountain Zebra National Park Rest Camp ↰ www.sanparks.org
Premier Hotel King David East London ↰ www.kingdavidhotel.co.za

Budget

Addo Elephant National Park Rest Camp ↰ www.sanparks.org
Away with the Fairies Hogsback ↰ www.awaywiththefairies.co.za
Buccaneers Cintsa (east of East London) ↰ www.cintsa.com
Cremorne Riverside Holiday Resort Port St Johns ↰ www.cremorne.co.za
Die Tuishuise Cradock ↰ www.tuishuise.co.za
Makana Resort Grahamstown ↰ www.makanaresort.co.za

politics. There's an annex of the museum in **Qunu** itself, where you can see Mandela's original three-hut maternal home, the remains of the stone church where he was baptised, and other relicts of his childhood.

From the N2, a sequence of *cul-de-sacs* lead down to the various resorts and reserves that dot the coast.

The Hole in the Wall was created by years of sea erosion. (AVZ)

Nongqawuse's vision

The Xhosa were the first South African Bantu-speakers to come into conflict with European settlers over their hunger for farmland. By the late 18th century, the Europeans had moved to the Great Fish River, the western border of Xhosa territory, and a series of skirmishes and full-scale battles took place in the early 19th century, often bloody but seldom resolving much. In 1857, however, a teenage Xhosa girl called Nongqawuse had an ancestral visitation that told her if the Xhosa killed all their cattle and burnt all their crops, the ancestral spirits would rise from their graves and drive the White intruders into the sea. Nongqawuse repeated her message to the famous diviner Mhlakaza and, after consultation with various chiefs, around 300,000–400,000 head of cattle were killed, and crops were burnt all over the region.

The ancestors never kept their side of the bargain. Instead, the area was gripped by a self-inflicted famine that left 30,000 people dead and caused almost as many to flee to the Cape Colony in search of work. It was a disaster from which Xhosa society never really recovered, as one by one the various Xhosa chieftaincies living east of the Great Fish River succumbed to colonial rule between 1879 and 1894. In the aftermath of the killing, Nongqawuse was arrested by the British authorities and imprisoned on Robben Island for several years prior to retiring to a farm near Port Alfred, where she died in 1898. The place where she received her vision is still known locally as Intlambo kaNongqawuse (Nongqawuse's Valley).

The largest of these resorts, situated 100km east of Mthatha on the R61, is **Port St Johns**, which is in a wonderful location at the mouth of the Mzimvubu River. There are several superb beaches nearby, and the somewhat arty vibe makes it very popular with backpackers but less attractive to mainstream tourists. About 60km further north, the 80km² **Mkhambati Nature Reserve** (℡ 043 705 4400 🏠 www.ecparks. co.za), protects a florally diverse stretch of coast noted for its riverine estuaries, waterfalls, birdlife and presence of large mammals such as eland and red hartebeest. South of Port St John, Coffee Bay is another idyllic but little-known beach resort only 8km on foot from the stunning, sea-eroded rock formation known as Hole in the Wall or EsiKhaleni (isiXhosa for 'Place of Noise').

East London
South Africa's only major river port, East London started life in 1847 as a British frontier fort on the west bank of the Buffalo. An active port since

1870, it is a strikingly industrialised town, and the economic fortunes of its population of 400,000 are strongly linked with those of the country's motor industry, which has long been based here. The agreeable seafront, **Latimer's Landing**, is reminiscent of Cape Town's Victoria & Alfred Waterfront, albeit on a more modest scale. **Eastern Beach** is good for swimming and **Nahoon Beach** is favoured by surfers. The **East London Aquarium** (📞 043 705 2637 🖥 www.elaquarium.co.za ⏱ 09.00–17.00 daily) houses 400 species of marine creature, from squids and sharks to penguins and seals. The central **East London Museum** (📞 043 743 0686 🖥 www.elmuseum.za.org ⏱ 09.30–16.00 Mon–Fri, 10.00–13.00 Sat–Sun), contains the very specimen of the 'living fossil' coelacanth that was discovered nearby in 1938 and astonished the ichthyologic world, because until then this bizarre fish had been presumed extinct for 65 million years!

Port Alfred

This pretty and often bypassed port, situated some 60km south of the N2 midway between Port Elizabeth and East London, straddles the mouth of the forest-fringed Kowie River. It was established in the early 1820s as a buffer town between the recently founded settlement at Port Elizabeth and the Xhosa territory to the east. It was later named after one of Queen Victoria's sons. Well-known for its **marina**, the modest town – population 20,000 – also has a good swimming and surfing

Port Alfred's famous marina (PCL/A)

beach, hemmed in by pretty dunes that provide a taster for the stunning scenery of the nearby **Alexandria Dunefields**, which can be explored along a hiking trail set within a newly added sector of the Addo Elephant National Park (see page 210). Another attraction is the **Kowie Canoe Trail** that leads inland to the **Waters Meeting Nature Reserve**, site of a horseshoe bend in the Kowie that resembles the shape of Africa when viewed from a nearby hill.

Grahamstown

Situated on the N2 some 50km inland from Port Alfred and midway between East London and Port Elizabeth, the university town of Grahamstown is best known as the host of the premier annual event on South Africa's arts calendar, the two-week **National Arts Festival** (⌘ www.nafest.co.za). Held in early July to coincide with campus holidays, this festival attracts a diverse bunch of performances, from Shakespearian plays and contemporary dramas to symphony orchestras and live African music. During this time the town is also alive with street artists and markets, but note that accommodation is at a premium so book well ahead.

At other times of year, the small town, named after its founder Colonel John Graham, is worth visiting for its tangible 1820 settler roots and lethargic, old-world charm. There are plenty of well-groomed Georgian and Victorian buildings in the town centre, while the **1820 Settlers Monument** on Gunfire Hill offers a view over some of the 40 churches alluded to in the nickname 'City of Saints'. Also of interest is the venerable **Albany Museum Complex** (✆ 046 622 2312 ⏰ 09.00–13.00 & 14.00–17.00 Mon–Fri, 09.00–13.00 Sat), which incorporates the Observatory Museum and its peculiar Camera Obscura, along with a local history museum where illuminating displays on rock art, Xhosa culture and settler history are supplemented by a somewhat misplaced Egyptian mummy.

1820 settlers

By the early 19th century most of the coastal belt west of present-day Port Elizabeth was settled by Boers, who had driven away, killed or taken as slaves the Khoikhoi who had traditionally lived in the area. More staunch resistance to foreign settlement was, however, provided by the militarised Xhosa on the opposite side of the Great Fish River. In 1820, the British colonial administration, hoping to create a new buffer zone between the existing Cape Colony and the Xhosa lands, moved a fresh wave of British settlers into the region. Most were innocents, lured away from home by the offer of a free passage to the colonies and a promise of ample land and good farming once there. It was a cynical move, as the authorities knew that farming conditions would be hard, especially as much of the free land in the area was actually the Xhosa's. Nevertheless, after initial hardships, the so-called 1820 Settlers thrived, and their legacy is an important part of the Eastern Cape's heritage, as evidence by the number of museums dedicated to their achievements.

Hogsback

Set at an altitude of 1,300m in the Amathole Mountains, 100km north of Grahamstown, is the quaint and remote village of Hogsback. It is known for both its beautiful forests and alternative eco-friendly vibe. Hogsback was where JRR Tolkein spent his childhood holidays, and the Bloemfontein-born writer reputedly used the enchanting landscape as inspiration for several scenic descriptions in *The Hobbit*. The lush, evergreen forest, peppered with fresh mountain streams, is wonderful for casual

The landscape around Hogsback may be recognisable to fans of *The Hobbit*. (KB/D)

rambling and for more serious hikes. Birders have the opportunity to see several localised forest species, among them Knysna loerie, emerald cuckoo, Knysna woodpecker and Cape parrot. The area also forms the most southerly haunt of the pretty Samango monkey, while the presence of deer-like bushbuck only enhances the rather English cast of the landscape.

Port Elizabeth

The largest city in the Eastern Cape, Port Elizabeth is the centrepiece of Nelson Mandela Bay, the country's sixth-largest municipality. It was founded by the 1820 Settlers on Algoa Bay (a corruption of the Portuguese *Bahia de Lagoa* – Bay of the Lagoon – as coined by Bartolomeu Dias in 1488) as part of a British plan to create an agricultural buffer zone between with the Xhosa territories to the northeast. As is the case with East London, Port Elizabeth – more normally referred to as PE – isn't an entirely convincing tourist hub. The beaches lack the scenic qualities of their less urbanised counterparts, while the city itself has less character than Cape Town or Durban. Still, the so-called 'Friendly City' is the main air gateway to the region, and there are certainly worse places to spend a night or two.

If you're after beach activity, **Kings Beach** is safe for swimming and is good for surfing, while the **Bayworld Complex** (✆ 041 584 0650 ⊕ www.bayworld.co.za ⊙ 09.00–16.30 daily) has an excellent aquarium and an adequate museum and snake park. Of some historical interest is the 5km **Donkin Heritage Trail**, which takes in 47 urban landmarks including the Victorian City Hall and Fort Frederick. The latter was constructed in 1799, two decades before the city was founded. A highly recommended excursion, if you're there over a weekend, public holiday or during school holidays is the **Apple Express** (✆ 041 583 4480 ⊕ www.apple-express.co.za), a half-day steam train trip that crosses the world's highest narrow-gauge bridge, built in 1906.

Addo Elephant National Park and surrounds

✆ 042 233 8600 ⊕ www.sanparks.org ⊙ 07.00–19.00 daily

The centrepiece of South Africa's premier, malaria-free game-viewing area, Addo Elephant National Park has come a long way since 1921 when it was set aside as a municipal reserve to protect the few shy but hardy individuals that constituted the continent's most southerly elephant population. The reserve was upgraded to national park status in 1931, when the region's last 11 elephants were herded into its confines, and was finally fenced in 1954 to prevent unwanted pachydermal raids into the surrounding farmland. Today, about 500 of the continent's most relaxed elephants roam the core 200km² park, which is one of the best places in Africa to witness elephant behaviour at close quarters. Leopard, buffalo, kudu and various smaller antelopes occur naturally in the area, while the recent reintroduction of black rhino, lion and spotted hyena has elevated Addo to the status of a full-on Big Five reserve. Furthermore, over recent years the park has been extended to cover almost ten times its original area (see box, page 214).

The main habitat of the national park is *spekboomveld*, a dense, tangled and thorny, 2–3m-high thicket dominated by a large succulent shrub called the *spekboom* (bacon tree). It is so-called as its thick waxy leaves reputedly taste like cured meat. The impenetrability of this habitat is probably what saved the region's last few elephants from the ivory traders who had hunted them to extinction in most parts of the country by the turn of the 20th century. The area also naturally supports large numbers of the handsome greater kudu, other antelope including eland, bushbuck and red hartebeest, and smaller mammals such as black-backed jackal, yellow mongoose and ground squirrel. The 188 bird species include endemics such as jackal buzzard, bokmakierie, southern tchagra, southern boubou, Cape weaver and Cape bulbul.

While Addo itself is ideal for self-drive visits, there is an excellent rest camp situated at the main entrance gate, and the surrounding area is home to several more exclusive private Big Five reserves where a beach holiday in Cape Town and/or the Garden Route can be rounded off with a short safari. The pick are Shamwari and Kwandwe Game Reserves, both of which are stocked with reintroduced elephant, rhino, lion, leopard, buffalo etc, and offer luxury all-inclusive game packages of a quality comparable to the best in Sabi Sands.

(AVZ)

&Beyond Kwandwe
🕐 www.kwandwereserve.com

Of the properties offering malaria-free safaris, few match both the game and luxurious accommodation found at &Beyond Kwandwe Private Game Reserve. Wildlife highlights include the Big Five, cheetah sightings and black rhino. On the accommodation front, Great Fish River Lodge sits on the river banks boasting uninterrupted wilderness views, Ecca Lodge is funky and intimate, overlooking a lush valley, Uplands Homestead a classic gracious sole-use farmstead, and Melton Manor's four bedrooms look out onto sweeping forest views.

Amakhala
🕐 www.amakhala.co.za

A Fair Trade in Tourism-accredited private game reserve protecting abundant wildlife and a variety of biomes, Amakhala was founded by five farming families descended from the original British settlers. The Bushman's River provides boat trips and canoeing, complementing game drives and bush walks. Leeuwenbosch is a lovely colonial house with an excellent children's programme. Woodbury Lodge is set in a ravine, which feels unchanged since the 1800s. Two romantic luxury lodges, Safari and Bush, offer the plunge pools and outdoor showers.

Camp Figtree
🕐 www.campfigtree.com

Situated an hour from Port Elizabeth and adjacent to the Addo Elephant National Park, Camp Figtree is a remote private lodge set on top of the stunning Zuurberg Mountain Range. It boasts jaw-dropping 360-degree views over the surrounding countryside and the plains towards the Indian Ocean. The lodge has been styled around its original 1920s traditional colonial building. The luxury suites are of a gracious old-world style, ensuring exclusivity and privacy. Safaris offer excellent sightings, including elephants, lion, rhino and kudu.

Elephant House
🖱 www.elephanthouse.co.za

Just 8km from the main entrance to Addo Elephant Park, Elephant House is an owner-run, thatched colonial farmhouse offering eight very comfortable rooms, sumptuous meals, genuine hospitality and lots of interesting things to do. We like the Addo game drives with the Elephant House expert guide and Clive Reed's tour of the Sundays River Valley, from the historic polo club, through the rich citrus plantations, to a garden and tavern in the Nomatamsanqa Township for a taste of rural township life.

Gorah Elephant Camp
🖱 www.hunterhotels.com/gorahelephantcamp

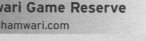

This luxurious tented camp is the only private lodge within Addo. Everything is to the highest standard – fine food, lavish accommodation, perfect service and excellent guiding. Each of the ten spacious, romantic tented suites have private decks with stunning views across the savannah. The two dining rooms and lounges are in the beautiful colonial manor house with its stately opulence. If you want luxury in Addo, it doesn't get any better than this. A stunning camp brilliant for elephant spotting.

Shamwari Game Reserve
🖱 www.shamwari.com

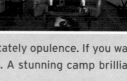

Home to the coveted Big Five and the crown jewel of private game reserves, Shamwari offers an unsurpassed nature experience. Situated in the malaria-free Eastern Cape, this privately owned 25,000ha of prime wildlife terrain has received numerous international awards. The reserve has seven unique lodges and boasts one of South Africa's most experienced wildlife teams, with a wildlife rehabilitation centre that guests can visit. At Shamwari, which means 'friend', guests and wildlife can live in harmony for a truly special experience.

Cape gannets (IB/FLPA)

Greater Addo

Like the Mountain Zebra and Bontebok national parks, Addo was created primarily to preserve one single endangered species. This was the case until 1997, when the government accepted a visionary proposal to allow the park to stretch from the arid Karoo to the coast east of Port Elizabeth. Progress over the subsequent decade has been heartening. Greater Addo Elephant National Park (GAENP) now embraces a contiguous 17,000km², from the peaks of the Zuurberg to the coastal dune fields west of Port Alfred. Future acquisitions of Karoo ranchland, together with the proclamation of an offshore marine zone, should eventually bring the total area to roughly 50,000km².

The ecological variety within GAENP exceeds that of any other African national park. Five of South Africa's seven terrestrial biomes are represented here, with habitats ranging from montane forest to coastal fynbos, from 100m-high dunes to the dry euphorbia-studded Karoo plains, as well as the tangled semi-succulent *spekboomveld* of Addo itself. And while elephants remain the big tourist draw, the marine sector offers fine whale-watching, while the offshore islands host a breeding colony of 100,000 Cape gannets, along with African penguin and Cape fur seal. Unfortunately, GAENP remains something of a work in progress. The offshore islands are currently inaccessible to tourists, while the former Zuurberg National Park and Woody Cape Nature Reserve can only realistically be explored on hiking trails. But, when plans to develop tourist access come to fruition, GAENP will quite possibly rank as the most diversely rewarding conservation area in southern Africa.

Graaff-Reinet

Pretty and neatly laid out, Graaff-Reinet is South Africa's fourth-oldest town, established as it was in 1786. It is enclosed within a U-shaped bend on the Sundays River, some 250km inland of Port Elizabeth. Ten years after its foundation, inspired by the revolutionary atmosphere in faraway France, the nascent town declared itself an independent republic, but it was soon co-opted back into the Cape Colony. Today it vies with Stellenbosch for having the country's strongest Cape Dutch architectural presence, with more than 200 buildings preserved as national monuments. Notable among these are the grandiose **Dutch Reformed Church** modelled on Salisbury Cathedral, the **Old Drostdy** (now a hotel), and **Reinet House**, a former parsonage built in 1811 and now a museum (✆ 049 892 3801 ☉ 09.00–12.00 Mon–Sun, 14.00–15.00 Mon–Fri). Also of interest is the **Obesa Nursery** (⌂ www. obesanursery.com), which hosts a superb collection of Karoo succulents including several endemic and endangered species.

The nearby 195km² **Camdeboo National Park** (formerly Karoo Nature Reserve; ✆ 049 892 3453 ⌂www.sanparks.org ☉ sunrise to sunset daily), incorporates a walking trail on the Van Ryneveld Dam as well as the towering domed rock formations in the stunning Valley of Desolation, 15km from the town centre. About 55km north of Graaff-Reinet, in the remote dorp of Nieu Bethesda, is the **Owl House** (✆ 049 841 1603 ☉ 09.00–17.00 daily), which is the former home of Helen Martins. This reclusive and eccentric artist decorated the interior of her dwelling with crushed glass murals, and populated the garden with a crushed concrete menagerie of owls and other creatures, before killing herself in 1976 by swallowing caustic soda.

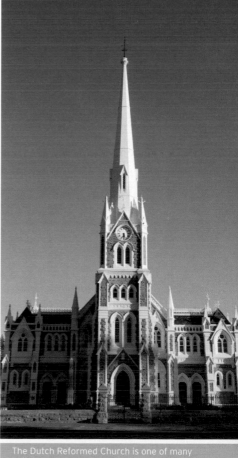

The Dutch Reformed Church is one of many buildings preserved as national monuments in Graaf Reinet. (AVZ)

Mount Camdeboo
⌂ www.mountcamdeboo.com

BRIDGE & WICKERS
travel with experience

On a seasonal river in a vast private game reserve, three historic homesteads provide modern comforts whilst respecting the architectural legacy of the settlers who made their homes in this valley. The bush they cleared has been restored and once again supports a wealth of wildlife. Even a safari cynic will be bowled over by the herds of plains game in a spectacular setting on the rich grasslands of the high plateau, with the mountains of the Karoo as the backdrop.

Cape mountain zebra (AVZ)

Mountain Zebra National Park
☎ 048 881 2427 ⌂ www.sanparks.org
⏱ Oct-Mar 07.00-19.00, Apr-Sep 07.00-18.00

This scenic 650km² park was established in 1937 to protect the endemic Cape mountain zebra, which almost suffered the same fate as the quagga. The quagga, a localised race of plains zebra that had a solid dark (as opposed to striped) hindquarters became extinct in 1883. Today, the park supports some 300 mountain zebras and significant populations of the endemic black wildebeest and blesbok, and is also the centre for a programme to re-breed the quagga from selected stripeless-reared plains zebras. Other wildlife includes buffalo, black rhino, cheetah, Cape fox, kudu and springbok, while the extensive bird checklist includes the endemic orange-breasted rockjumper and ground woodpecker. *En route* to the park, **Cradock**, on the N10 between Colesburg and Port Elizabeth, is an agreeable small town that was founded on the Great Fish River in 1813 and was the childhood home of Olive Schreiner (1855–1920), whose anti-racist novel *The Story of an African Farm* was published to considerable controversy in 1883. Her former family homestead is now **Olive Schreiner House** (📞 041 881 5251 ⊙ 08.00–12.45 & 14.00–16.30 Mon–Fri).

Jeffreys Bay

This otherwise rather nondescript seaside town, reputedly named after the whaler Captain Jeffreys and usually referred to as 'Jay Bay' by locals, stands out as South Africa's premier surfing destination. The town's **Blue Flag Beach** is the site of Supertubes, internationally rated as one of the world's top ten surfing spots, and hosts the International Billabong Pro surfing competition. For non-surfers, Jeffreys Bay has less to offer than the towns further west along the Garden Route, though it does have an interesting private **Shell Museum** (📞 042 293 1945 ⊕ www.jeffreysbay. com ⊙ 09.00–16.00 Mon–Sat) with a collection of hundreds of shells from all over the world. Definitely worth a diversion is the lighthouse and the unspoilt coastline protected within the nearby **Cape St Francis Nature Reserve** (📞 042 298 0073 ⊕ www.capestfrancis.co.za), where dolphins are frequently observed from the nature trails.

Jeffreys Bay is a top destination for surfers. (JSC/t/A)

The Garden Route

The short stretch of coast running west from the Storms River Mouth as far as Mossel Bay is commonly referred to as the Garden Route, thanks to a scenic abundance that encompasses unspoilt sandy beaches, deep blue lagoons, towering cliffs, quaint country towns, indigenous forests, freshwater lakes and fields of protea-rich fynbos. It's not an area to rush through, however, and visitors who drive straight through along the N2 might reasonably wonder how the name arose. Leave the N2 to get a different picture, and those with the time and inclination should explore the numerous walking trails that run through the Garden Route's protected forests, and along the coastal cliffs and beaches. While large terrestrial mammals are scarce, interesting fauna include forest antelope and monkeys, a wealth of butterflies and lizards, and striking avian endemics such as Knysna loerie, yellow-throated warbler and olive woodpecker. Seals, dolphins and even whales are commonly seen from the shore.

Garden Route highlights

Tsitsikamma (Garden Route National Park)

📞 044 302 5600 🌐 www.sanparks.org
🕐 07.00–19.00 daily

Gazetted as the Tsitsikamma Coastal National Park in 1964, this spectacular 80km stretch of coast at the eastern extreme of the Garden Route was amalgamated with the Knysna Lake National Area and Wilderness National Park in 2009 to form the 1,210km² Garden Route National Park. Tsitsikamma is a Khoisan phrase meaning 'place of abundant water', but this section of the park also supports one of the country's largest extant tracts of indigenous forest, as well as a series of breathtaking cliffs that rise 180m above the breakers below.

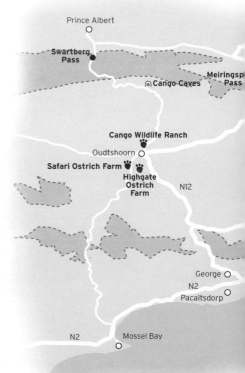

The most important tourist development here is **Storms River Mouth**, site of the only rest camp located within the park, but also open to day visitors. The thrilling suspension bridge across the river mouth, which re-opened in late 2010 following extensive renovations, is reached by a short, forested footpath notable for its birdlife. The steep footpath leads to a lookout point on the cliffs above the opposite bank. There are several other day walks to choose from, a favourite being the Waterfall Trail, a 6km return hike that follows the first stretch of the legendary five-day **Otter Trail** along the rocky, wave-battered shore west of the camp.

The newly renovated Storms River suspension bridge. (AVZ)

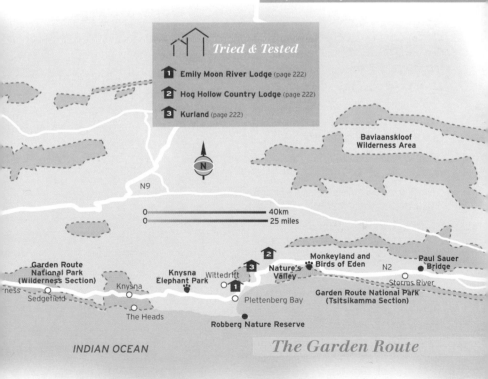

Tried & Tested

1 Emily Moon River Lodge (page 222)

2 Hog Hollow Country Lodge (page 222)

3 Kurland (page 222)

Baviaanskloof Wilderness Area

N9

0 — 40km
0 — 25 miles

Garden Route National Park (Wilderness Section)

ness

Sedgefield

Knysna

The Heads

Knysna Elephant Park   Wittedrift

Nature's Valley

Monkeyland and Birds of Eden

N2

Paul Sauer Bridge

Storms River

Garden Route National Park (Tsitsikamma Section)

Plettenberg Bay

Robberg Nature Reserve

INDIAN OCEAN   *The Garden Route*

Practicalities

(AVZ)

Although many **organised tours** pass through the Garden Route and usually stop overnight at one or two of its small towns whilst travelling between Port Elizabeth and Cape Town, the area is particularly suited to **self-drive** visits.

By air, the main port of entry is George Airport. It is found outside the town of the same name, and is connected to Cape Town and Johannesburg by regular scheduled **flights**. All the usual car rental agencies can be found there. Depending on the rest of your itinerary, it is also possible to drive to the Garden Route from Cape Town or Port Elizabeth in a few hours.

All towns in the area are very tourist-oriented, and you should have no problem locating **facilities** such as ATMs, internet cafés and supermarkets.

Accommodation

For full details of tour operator-recommended accommodation, see page 222. Here follows a few further suggestions from the author.

Upmarket
The Plettenberg Plettenberg Bay ⚓ www.plettenberg.com

Moderate
Bitou River Lodge Plettenberg Bay ⚓ www.bitou.co.za
Eden's Touch Knysna ⚓ www.edenstouch.co.za
Eight Bells Mountain Inn Near Oudtshoorn ⚓ www.eightbells.co.za
Moontide Wilderness ⚓ www.moontide.co.za
Protea Hotel Mossel Bay ⚓ www.proteahotels.com
Protea Hotel Outeniqua, George ⚓ www.proteahotels.com
Tsitsikamma Lodge Near Tsitsikamma ⚓ www.tsitsikammalodge.com

Budget
Knysna Backpackers Knysna ⚓ www.knysnabackpackers.co.za
Storms River Mouth Rest Camp Garden Route National Park ⚓ www.sanparks.org
Wilderness Rest Camp Garden Route National Park ⚓ www.sanparks.org

An altogether more serene landscape greets visitors to **Nature's Valley**, a small residential village separated from the eastern border of Tsitsikamma by a large calm lagoon. One of the prettiest and least developed spots on the Garden Route, Nature's Valley blends imperceptibly into the surrounding forest, and it's the epicentre of a 50km network of day trails that lead deep into the coastal forest, where ancient yellow-woods tower up to 50m. Some of the country's most easterly fynbos habitats are also found here. Even for non-hikers, the looping back road that connects the N2 to Nature's Valley passes through several patches of cool forest inhabited by a wealth of colourful birds, and antelope such as the shy red duiker and bushbuck.

Plettenberg Bay

Plettenberg Bay is an upmarket resort town with a good beach set on the aptly named Baia Formosa ('Beautiful Bay'). Well-equipped but rather characterless, it is very popular with South African families, though true outdoor lovers may prefer the wilder **Keurboomstrand** east of the town centre. Plett, as it's known locally, is only 6km from the **Robberg Nature Reserve** (☏ 044 533 2125 ⌂ www.cape nature.org.za ☉ Feb–Nov 07.00– 17.00, Dec–Jan 07.00–20.00), which protects the dramatically rocky Robberg (literally 'Seal Island') Peninsula. The reserve is circumnavigated by what is arguably the Garden Route's most scenic oceanic day trail, offering a good chance of seeing Cape fur seals, dolphins, humpback whales and the endemic African black

The scenic coastal path at Robberg Nature Reserve (AVZ)

oystercatcher. Altogether different in character is the **Keurbooms River Nature Reserve** (☏ 044 533 2125 ⌂ www.capenature.org.za ☉ 08.00–18.00 daily), which protects the forest-fringed river for which it was named, and can be explored on an overnight canoe trail.

Emily Moon River Lodge

🖱 www.emilymoon.co.za

A real gem, located in a quiet secluded location on the Bitou River yet only 4km from Plettenberg Bay. With an ambience of luxury and style whilst still being warm and welcoming the lodge has eight spacious private suites looking out over the river, wetlands and distant mountains. The lodge also has a fantastic restaurant and we love their sundowners and fire pit. Perfect for anyone looking for a quiet spot on the Garden Route in a small, stylish hotel.

Hog Hollow Country Lodge

🖱 www.hog-hollow.com

We think this scenic four-star retreat is as good as it gets on the Garden Route, and so do our customers. The owners' vision has created a Fair Trade accredited, family-friendly lodge that wins every time on hospitality, style, service and food. Sixteen attractive and well spaced out suites, and a three-bedroom private villa, mix funky African art with contemporary European style, all with breathtaking views. The central location in the Tsitsikamma Forest is ideal for exploring the local Plettenberg attractions.

Kurland

🖱 www.kurland.co.za

With just 12 suites, this luxurious hotel in the heart of the Garden Route is a gem. Set in a beautiful, vast private estate, it's a particularly good destination for families with excellent facilities for children. Activities include riding, cycling and quadbiking and there's easy access to the nearby beaches of Plettengerg and the forests and trails in the Tsitsikamma Mountains. The spa is a wonderful spot to relax and experienced nannies can look after children while parents take time out.

Family outings on the Garden Route

Monkeyland

☎ 044 534 8906 🖰 www.monkeyland.co.za
🕐 08.00–17.00 daily

Created as a refuge for monkeys rescued from captivity, this private sanctuary near the turn-off to Nature's Valley is home to more than a dozen primate species, including some lemurs from Madagascar. It offers guided tours every hour on the hour.

(AVZ)

Knysna Elephant Park

☎ 044 532 7732 🖰 www.knysnaelephantpark.co.za 🕐 08.30–16.30 daily

Home to a small herd of domestic elephants translocated from elsewhere in South Africa, this place 10km west of Plettenberg Bay is a reliable hit with children, who take delight in touching or feeding a bona fide tusker.

Safari Ostrich Farm

☎ 044 272 7311 🖰 www.safariostrich.co.za 🕐 08.00–17.00 daily

Situated along the Mossel Bay Road on the outskirts of Oudtshoorn, this popular ostrich farm has a fantastically ostentatious old homestead, and offers a variety of activities including the opportunity to ride on the back of the world's largest bird.

Cango Wildlife Ranch

☎ 044 272 5593 🖰 www.cango.co.za 🕐 08.00–17.00 daily

This ranch on the outskirts of Oudtshoorn, though very popular with youngsters who can touch hand-reared cheetahs and see a variety of big cats from around the world as well as a selection of indigenous snakes, has a more serious purpose as an endangered wildlife breeding centre.

The violet turaco is one of the many species of bird found at Birds of Eden. (AVZ)

Birds of Eden

☎ 044 534 8906 🖰 www.birdsofeden.co.za
🕐 08.00–17.00 daily

Situated alongside Monkeyland (see above), this consists of a 2ha free-flight aviary – reputedly the world's largest – traversed by a 1km walkway and suspension bridge.

(SN/D)

Knysna

The most characterful town along the Garden Route, Knysna, 25km west of Plettenberg Bay, is named after a large eponymous lagoon whose seaward entrance is hemmed in by a pair of sheer rock faces known as the Knysna Heads. The port has been in use since the late 18th century when the surrounding indigenous forests were first exploited for their yellow-wood and other hardwood timbers, and a permanent European settlement was established here in 1825. The dominant figure in the early development of Knysna was a landowner called George Rex, who controversially claimed to be the illegitimate son of King George III of England.

Modern Knysna landmarks include the **Holy Trinity Church**, which looks like it belongs in a sleepy English village, and **Mitchell's Brewery** (✆ 044 382 4685 www.mitchellsbrewery.com ☉ guided tours 10.30 & 15.00 Mon–Fri), one of the few small ale brewers in South Africa. The town is well-known for the oysters that are cultivated in the lagoon and can be sampled at several quayside eateries, and it has plenty of shopping opportunities. The rather quaint atmosphere is counterbalanced by a thriving alternative scene, the annual highpoint of which is the five-day gay and lesbian carnival, the **Pink Loerie Mardi Gras** (www. pinkloerie.com) held every April or May.

Keen walkers have plenty to occupy them in and around Knysna. A recommended formal excursion is to the privately owned **Featherbed Nature Reserve** (✆ 044 382 1693 www.featherbed.co.za ☉ 4-hour tours which include lunch leave Knysna at 10.00, 11.30 & 12.30), which lies on the western Knysna Head and supports the likes of blue duiker and the endangered Knysna sea horse. A more demanding but recommended self-guided coastal hike, set in the Harkerville State Forest (now part of the Garden Route National Park ☎ 044 532 7770 🖰 www.sanparks. org), is the circular 9km **Kranshoek Trail**, which covers an exceptional variety of habitats in a relatively short distance, including indigenous forest, a rocky seashore dotted with rock pools, and patches of coastal fynbos where proteas attract the endemic Cape sugarbird and orange-breasted sunbird.

Wilderness

This pleasant and relatively upmarket resort village, sandwiched between a pretty beach and even prettier lagoon, lies adjacent to the Wilderness sector of the Garden Route National Park (☎ 044 877 0046 🖰 www.sanparks.org ○ 08.00–17.00 daily), which protects a network of freshwater lakes and connecting streams fed by the Touws River. It's a birdwatcher's paradise, easily explored along a network of walking trails (each named for one of the park's six kingfisher species) of which the **Half-Collared Kingfisher Trail** is highly recommended. The trail passes through the riparian forest flanking the Touws River to reach an attractive waterfall. The same route can be followed in a canoe, and these are available for hire at the main rest camp.

The area around Wilderness is a prime place for birdwatching. (SS)

George

The largest town on the Garden Route and the site of the most important airport between Port Elizabeth and Cape Town, George's setting at the base of the Outeniqua Mountains is striking. Founded in 1811, it is of some historical interest with landmarks such as the **Old Drostdy**, built in 1812; the **Slave Tree**, reputedly the largest oak in the Southern Hemisphere; and a trio of 19th-century **churches**. Overall, though, it

Garden Route adventures

Bungee jumps

📞 044 697 7001

🌐 www.faceadrenalin.com

Face Adrenalin has operations at both ends of the Garden Route. The 215m Bloukrans Bridge jump above Storms River is the world's highest, and there's the Gourits Bridge jump near Mossel Bay.

(AVZ)

Blackwater tubing

📞 042 281 1757 🌐 www.blackwatertubing.net

This ultimate *kloofing* (canyoning) experience starts with a descent into the otherwise inaccessible Storm River Gorge by rope ladder. This is then followed by a scenic and exhilarating ride downriver to the suspension bridge at its mouth.

Seal Island

📞 044 690 3101 🌐 www.mosselbay.co.za

Boat excursions leave Mossel Bay hourly from 09.00–16.00 to view this island breeding colony of Cape fur seals.

Shark dives

📞 044 691 3796

🌐 www.whitesharkafrica.com

Shark Africa operates daily cage dives from Mossel Bay to view great white sharks in their natural habitat.

Cango Adventure Tour

📞 044 272 7410

🌐 www.cango-caves.co.za ⏱ 09.00–16.00 daily

The 90-minute guided tour into Cango Caves involves squeezing and clambering through crevices and is unsuitable for claustrophobics or the significantly overweight.

(AVZ)

Dutch Reformed Church, George (SCB/A)

is too large and developed to have an appeal comparable to Knysna or Plett, especially as it lies 12km inland from the sea. Worth a look, however, is **Pacaltsdorp Mission**, which is about 10km south of town and was founded in 1813 at the request of a Khoikhoi leader, Kaptein Dikkop. Its Norman-style church has a battlemented tower that offers great views over the surrounding area.

Mossel Bay

The most westerly town on the Garden Route, Mossel Bay is where Bartolomeu Dias became the first European to set foot on South African soil on 3 February 1488. Three years later, the stranded Portuguese navigator Pedro d'Ataidea left an account of his misfortunes addressed to João da Nova in an old shoe suspended from a milkwood tree in Mossel Bay, initiating a tradition that led to the same tree being used as South Africa's first 'post office' for decades thereafter. However, the area remained unsettled by Europeans until 1787, when a fortified granary was constructed close to the old Post Office Tree.

Today the town doubles as a popular but arguably rather charmless holiday resort, and is best known as a base for caged shark dives and visits to Seal Island (see box, page 226). Mossel Bay has become an unlikely industrial centre, exploiting the natural gas off the coast. It does, however, host the best museum along the Garden Route in the form of the **Bartolomeu Dias Complex** (℡ 044 691 1067 ⏏ www.diasmuseum. co.za ⏲ 09.00–16.45 Mon–Fri, 09.00–15.45 Sat–Sun), which is housed in the above-mentioned granary. There is a full-scale replica of one of Dias's boats, along with a boot-shaped letterbox hanging from the giant milkwood first used as a post office in 1501.

Oudtshoorn

Situated 60km inland fromf Mossel Bay and George, Oudtshoorn is set in the comparatively arid Little Karoo, an area starkly different in character from the coastal resorts of the Garden Route. Despite this, Oudtshoorn has some major tourist attractions nearby, including the Cango Caves and a scattering of operational ostrich farms founded in the late 19th century. Back then, Oudtshoorn was the booming centre of a lucrative trade in ostrich feathers, which were used to decorate hats in Europe. The town enjoyed two heydays, the first between 1875 and 1885, after which it experienced a slump due to overproduction, and the other between the end of the Anglo-Boer War and the start of World War I, when a number of 'feather palaces' were built.

There is some moderately interesting sightseeing in the town itself. Top of the list, on the corner of Voortrekker and Baron Van Reede Street, is the **CP Nel Museum** (℡ 044 272 7306 ⏏ www.cpnelmuseum.co.za

There are several ostrich farms around Oudtshoorn, allowing you the chance to meet these strange birds up close. (AVZ)

08.00–17.00 Mon–Fri, 09.00–13.00 Sat), which has good displays on local history and the ostrich trade. The nearby **Le Roux Townhouse**, built in 1908 by the ostrich baron Johannes le Roux, is one of the most impressive of the town's 'feather palaces', and is still filled with period fittings and furnishings. Although fashions have changed, the industry must still be fairly lucrative as ostrich farming remains widely practised in the area. By-products such as ostrich meat and eggs are readily available and several ostrich farms, including **Safari** (see box, page 223), **Highgate** (℃ 044 272 7115 www.highgate. co.za) and **Cango** (℃ 044

Waterfall on the Meiringspoort Pass (AVZ)

272 4623 www.cangoostrich.co.za) also double as tourist attractions, offering the opportunity to learn about, pet, ride and even eat these bizarre, outsized birds.

The scenic **Swartberg** (Black Mountains) north of Oudtshoorn are rich in travel possibilities. Foremost among these, at the southern base of the mountains some 35km out of town, are the world-renowned **Cango Caves** (℃ 044 272 7410 www.cango-caves.co.za 09.00–16.00 daily), where regular guided one-hour tours lead visitors deep underground through a sequence of well-lit labyrinthine tunnels and chambers decorated with all manner of unusual limestone formations. For self-drivers, a wonderful day trip is the round drive traversing the Swartberg using the wildly attractive Meiringspoort Pass in one direction and the equally scenic but unsurfaced Swartberg Pass in the other. If you follow this route the old-world country town of **Prince Albert Hamlet**, set at the southern tip of the Great Karoo, makes for an interesting lunch stop.

9 The Western Cape

South Africa's most visited province, the Western Cape is dominated by the incomparable Cape Town, the country's oldest settlement, set beneath the slopes of majestic Table Mountain, and one of the most scenically and culturally rewarding cities in the world. Cape Town is the gateway to a region rich with other highlights, including the Cape Peninsula, whose serene beaches lie below a mountainous spine that terminates 60km south of the city centre at the sheer cliffs of Cape Point. The Western Cape also boasts some of the world's finest wine estates, concentrated in the Constantia Valley and around the Boland towns of Stellenbosch, Franschhoek and Paarl. There's some thrilling marine Wildlife viewing here too, from the seal and penguin colonies of the Cape Peninsula to the whale-watching at the seaside resort of Hermanus. The region also forms the epicentre of the world's smallest and most botanically diverse floral kingdom, with a wealth of endemic species.

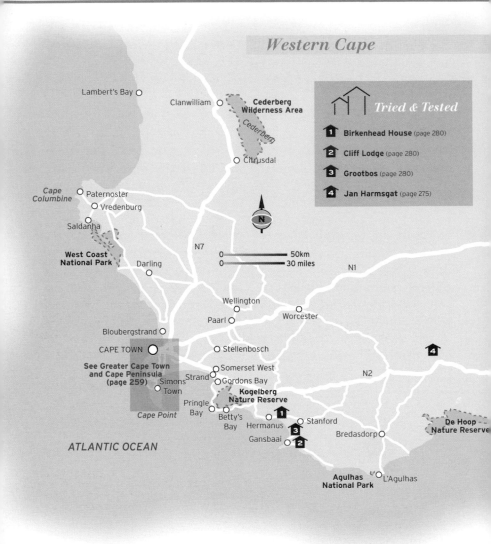

Western Cape

Lambert's Bay ○

Clanwilliam ○

Cederberg Wilderness Area

Cederberg

○ Citrusdal

Cape Columbine ○ Paternoster

○ Vredenburg

Saldanha ○

West Coast National Park

Darling ○

N7

0 ———— 50km
0 ———— 30 miles

N1

Wellington ○

Paarl ○   Worcester ○

Bloubergstrand ○

CAPE TOWN ○

See Greater Cape Town and Cape Peninsula (page 259)

○ Stellenbosch

○ Somerset West

Strand ○ Gordons Bay

Simons Town ○

Kogelberg Nature Reserve

Pringle Bay ○

Cape Point

Betty's Bay   Hermanus

Gansbaai ○

○ Stanford

Bredasdorp ○

De Hoop Nature Reserve

N2

ATLANTIC OCEAN

Agulhas National Park   ○ L'Agulhas

Tried & Tested

1 **Birkenhead House** (page 280)

2 **Cliff Lodge** (page 280)

3 **Grootbos** (page 280)

4 **Jan Harmsgat** (page 275)

History

The discovery of 1.4 million-year-old Acheulean stone-age tools on the Cape Peninsula dates human habitation back at least that long. San hunter-gatherers arrived 30,000 years ago, to be joined by Khoikhoi pastoralists some 2,000 years back. In 1488, a Portuguese expedition led by Bartolomeu Dias was blown around Cape Point in conditions that led to his dubbing it *Cabo das Tormentas* (Cape of Storms). Ironically, it is better known today as the Cape of Good Hope, a name bequeathed on it from afar by the delighted King John of Portugal, who correctly perceived his subject's rounding of the Cape as the key breakthrough in the quest for a maritime trade route to India.

In 1652, the Dutch East India Company (Vereenigde Oost-Indische Compagnie, VOC) appointed Jan van Riebeeck to establish a refreshment station at Table Bay. Within a century, Cape Town consisted of more than 1,000 dwellings and was home to settlers from all over Europe, although slaves – both local and those imported from Asia – outnumbered free citizens. Several other towns in the Western Cape date to the early Dutch colonial era, among them Stellenbosch (1679) and Simon's Town (1687), both founded by and named after Simon van der Stel, who was Van Riebeeck's successor as Governor of the Cape.

The British occupation of 1795 heralded an era of relative liberality, leading to the emancipation of slaves in 1834 and the consequent indignant Great Trek inland of around 12,000 slave-owning settlers. The pivotal figure in late-19th-century Cape Town was Cecil John Rhodes, a British settler who became Prime Minister of the Cape after making his fortune in the diamond fields of Kimberley. He was largely responsible for the outbreak of the Anglo-Boer of 1899–1902, which led to British colonisation of the gold-rich Transvaal and the creation of the Union of South Africa in 1910.

Cape Town's recent history has been influenced by its unique demographic. Roughly half of the Western Cape's population comprises of so-called Coloureds (mixed-race descendants of early settlers and their slaves), and almost 75% speak Afrikaans or English as a first language. In the pre-apartheid era, Coloureds enjoyed more civil rights than their Black compatriots, but these were mostly revoked in the 1950s and 1960s as apartheid entered its darkest era and racially integrated suburbs such as District Six were re-zoned as 'White'. The Cape Flats immediately to the east of Cape Town were the setting for several pivotal events in the struggle, notably the 1960 Sharpeville Massacre of 69 peaceful protestors by police, and the formation of the United Democratic Front (UDF) – effectively the domestic representative of the banned ANC – on Mitchell's Plain in 1983.

Statue of Cecil John Rhodes, a key figure in the history of Cape Town. (AVZ)

CECIL JOHN RHODES

255

Offshore, Robben Island is where prominent political prisoners such as Nelson Mandela were held in the apartheid era, and Cape Town City Hall is where Mandela made his first speech after his release in 1990. Nevertheless, in the 1994 election the Western Cape was one of only two provinces lost by the ANC, and the only one where the National Party retained power. Today, the province is the sole chink in the ANC's political homogeny, with the Democratic Alliance, led by Helen Zille, the former Mayor of Cape Town, currently holding 22 of the 42 provincial parliamentary seats.

Cape Town

Castle of Good Hope (AVZ)

It may not be as populous as Johannesburg, nor does it exude the same fevered air of economic activity, but Cape Town stands alone as the country's loveliest city and its most important tourist hub. Indeed, few towns anywhere in the world offer a portfolio of natural and cultural attractions comparable to the so-called Mother City. The City Bowl boasts an utterly breathtaking setting, enclosed by the lofty heights of Table Mountain to the south, the dramatic outcrops known as Lion's Head and Signal Hill to the west, and the choppy waters of the Atlantic Ocean to the north. Furthermore, it is endowed with some fine colonial architecture, more than a dozen worthwhile museums reflecting every facet of its complex multicultural history, the culinary and retail delights of the scenic Victoria & Alfred Waterfront, and the innumerable boutiques and night spots that line funky Long Street. Worth several days in its own right, the city also provides an excellent base for day trips to sites as diverse as Table Mountain, the Alcatraz-like confines of Robben Island (where Nelson Mandela was incarcerated for almost two decades), the peaceful Kirstenbosch Botanical Garden, historic wine estates such as Groot Constantia, and the stirring, wave-battered cliff-scapes of Cape Point.

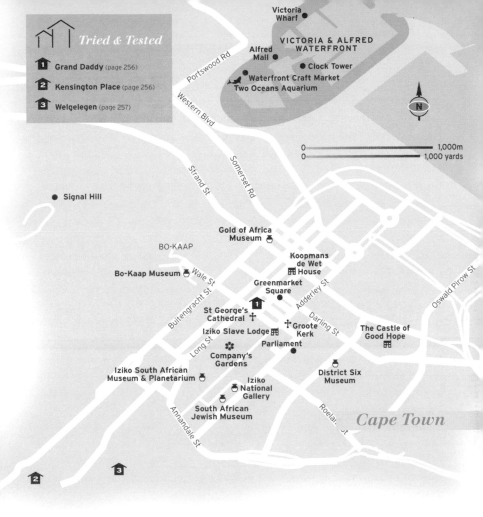

Tried & Tested

1 Grand Daddy (page 256)

2 Kensington Place (page 256)

3 Welgelegen (page 257)

VICTORIA & ALFRED
WATERFRONT

Victoria
Wharf

Alfred
Mall

Clock Tower

Waterfront Craft Market

Two Oceans Aquarium

Portswood Rd

Western Blvd

Somerset Rd

Strand St

0   1,000m
0   1,000 yards

N

Signal Hill

Gold of Africa
Museum

BO-KAAP

Koopmans
de Wet
House

Bo-Kaap Museum

Wale St

Greenmarket
Square

Buitengracht St

Adderley St

Oswald Pirow St

St George's
Cathedral

Iziko Slave Lodge

Groote
Kerk

Darling St

The Castle of
Good Hope

Long St

Parliament

Company's
Gardens

District Six
Museum

Iziko South African
Museum & Planetarium

Iziko
National
Gallery

Annandale St

South African
Jewish Museum

Roelar...

Cape Town

2

3

Cape Town highlights

Castle of Good Hope

Buitenkant St ☏ 021 787 1260 🖰 www.castleofgoodhope.co.za ⏱ 09.00–16.00
daily; free guided tours are offered at 11.00, 12.00 & 14.00

This pentagonal fort, constructed between 1666 and 1679 with slate
quarried on Robben Island and sandstone from Lion's Head, is the oldest
working building in South Africa. The seat of Dutch colonial government
for longer than a century, the castle has long outlived its original
naval protection role, largely due to successive land reclamations that
stranded it about 1km from the seafront. However, it does still serve
as the military headquarters of the Western Cape. Interesting external
features include the *Leeuhek* (Lion's Gate), an 18th-century sentry
portal topped by two stylised leonine sculptures, and a yellow stone
bell tower adorned with the VOC symbol. An outstanding feature of the

Practicalities

Cape Town is served by an ever-increasing number of international **flights**, as well as by several dozen daily flights from Gauteng, and domestic flights from all other major centres in South Africa. Flights land at Cape Town International Airport (🖰 www.acsa.co.za), which lies on the Cape Flats about 20km east of the city centre, and is connected to it by the N2 highway. On an organised tour your flight should be met by the ground operator, but failing that many hotels in Cape Town and elsewhere on the peninsula offer free or inexpensive airport shuttles or transfers. Otherwise, the options are a taxi cab, or a cheaper shuttle such as Randy's Tours (📞 021 934 8367 🖰 www.randystours.com) or the Backpacker Bus (📞 021 439 7600 🖰 www.backpackerbus.co.za). For further information, Cape Town Tourism has a desk in the international arrivals hall.

Cape Town is the one city in South Africa that lends itself to casual exploration using **public transport**. A very popular option, aimed directly at tourists, is the Cape Town Explorer (📞 021 511 6000 🖰 www.citysightseeing.co.za), a hop-on hop-off, open-top double-decker bus service that leaves the V&A Waterfront at 45-minute intervals from 09.30 to 15.00 daily. It stops at several places of interest within the city centre, including all the major museums, the Table Mountain Cableway, Camps Bay, Sea Point and Kirstenbosch Botanical Garden. Also worth considering is the Metrorail train service (📞 080 065 6463 🖰 www.capemetrorail.co.za), which connects the central railway station on Adderley Street to the southern suburbs. Golden Arrow (📞 0800 656463 🖰 www.gabs.co.za) runs bus services within the city as well as around the peninsula.

Accommodation

For full details of tour operator-recommended accommodation, see pages 255–7. Here follows a few further suggestions from the author. For details of recommended places to eat see pages 238–9.

Exclusive
Bay Hotel Camps Bay 🖰 www.thebayhotel.co.za
Cape Grace Hotel V&A Waterfront 🖰 www.capegrace.com
Mount Nelson Hotel City Bowl 🖰 www.mountnelson.co.za

Upmarket
Andros Boutique Hotel Southern suburbs 🖰 www.andros.co.za
Cellars-Hohenort Southern suburbs 🖰 www.cellars-hohenort.com
Victoria & Alfred Hotel V&A Waterfront 🖰 www.vahotel.co.za

Use taxis after dark; they can be arranged through the reception of any hotel, or contact Rikki's Intercity (☎ 086 174 5547 🖱 www.rikkis.co.za), which operates to most parts of the City Bowl and beyond. Your hotel can also put you in touch with a reliable local operator offering day trips to the Cape Peninsula, Hermanus, the Winelands and elsewhere.

(AVZ)

Cape Town has all the **amenities** you'd expect of the country's leading urban tourist destination. There are foreign exchange facilities at the airport, as well as several ATMs where local currency can be drawn on a foreign credit card. Shopping malls such as the V&A Waterfront are packed with banks, supermarkets, boutique shops, eateries and cinemas.

For craft shopping try the V&A Waterfront, Long Street, Greenmarket Square African Craft Market at Rosebank Mall, or Bruma Flea Market. Cape Town has a world-class dining out scene, with hundreds of good restaurants to choose from. A shortlist of favourites is included below.

Winchester Mansions Hotel Sea Point 🖱 www.winchester.co.za

Moderate
Cape Town Hollow Boutique Hotel City Bowl 🖱 www.capetownhollow.co.za
Derwent House Boutique Hotel City Bowl 🖱 www.derwenthouse.co.za
Grand Daddy Long St 🖱 www.granddaddy.co.za
Peninsula All Suites Hotel Sea Point 🖱 www.peninsula.co.za

Budget
Ashanti Gardens Lodge Green Point 🖱 www.ashanti.co.za
Breakwater Lodge V&A Waterfront 🖱 www.breakwaterlodge.co.za
Daddy Long Legs Art Hotel Long St 🖱 www.daddylonglegs.co.za
Long Street Backpackers Long St 🖱 www.longstreetbackpackers.co.za
Vicky's B&B Khayelitsha 🖱 www.vickysbedandbreakfast.com

Eating out

The choices are practically endless, with almost all global cuisines represented along with some fine fusion restaurants and the ubiquitous seafood. The following shortlist represents some of our longer-serving personal favourites:

Belthazar Restaurant & Wine Bar (excellent steak & seafood; peerless wine list) V&A Waterfront ✆ 021 421 3753 🖥 www.belthazar.co.za
Biesmiellah (unpretentious Cape Malay eatery in the Bo-Kaap) Cnr Wale & Pentz St ✆ 021 423 0850
Bukhara (North Indian) 33 Church St ✆ 021 424 0000 🖥 www.bukhara.com
Chef Pon's Asian Kitchen (inexpensive pan-Asian) 12 Mill St ✆ 021 465 5846
🖥 www.chefponsasiankitchen.co.za
Emily's (fusion & Cape cuisine) V&A Waterfront ✆ 021 421 1133

interior is the Kat Portico, an ornate covered balcony sculpted by Anton Anreith that leads to the William Fehr Collection, colonial-era artworks which provide a fascinating insight into the lifestyle and attitudes of the early settlers. There is also a military museum, and a grim torture chamber, where racks, thumbscrews and other instruments were used to enforce the Dutch law that required a criminal to confess prior to being sentenced.

The best time to visit is shortly before 10.00 or 12.00 on a weekday, when the key ceremony is followed ten minutes later by the firing of the Signal Cannon. Immediately outside the fort is the late Victorian City Hall; Nelson Mandela made his first public speech from the balcony here following his release from prison on 11 February 1990.

District Six Museum

25A Buitenkant St ✆ 021 466 7200 🖥 www.districtsix.co.za ⏰ 09.00-13.30 Mon, 09.00-16.00 Tue-Sat

The most engaging and moving of Cape Town's impressive assembly of museums, this award-winning heritage centre, established in 1994, is housed in the Buitenkant

(SS)

Gold Restaurant (pan-African set menu accompanied by vibrant drumming & dancing) 96 Strand St ☎ 021 421 4653 🖰 www.goldrestaurant.co.za
Green Dolphin (good seafood & great live jazz every night) V&A Waterfront ☎ 021 421 7471
Mama Africa (traditional Cape & game dishes) 178 Long St ☎ 021 426 1017; 🖰 www.mamaafricarest.net

Selection of traditional African dishes (AVZ)

Savoy Cabbage (fine dining with emphasis on fusion & game meat) 101 Hout St ☎ 021 424 2626 🖰 www.savoycabbage.co.za
Toni's (affordable Mozambican/Portuguese) 88 Kloof St ☎ 021 423 6717 🖰 www.tonis.co.za

Methodist Church. A former wine shop, it was sanctified in 1883 and then forced to close in 1988 due to its anti-apartheid associations. The museum is named after District Six, a municipal suburb that was established in 1867 on the slopes below Devil's Peak, immediately to the southwest of the Castle of Good Hope. The suburb housed a cosmopolitan community of freed slaves, Malaysian immigrants and Coloureds who worked in the nearby city centre or port. A century later, in 1966, the apartheid government re-zoned the vibrant suburb as a 'Whites-only' area, bulldozed every last home, and forcibly relocated its 60,000 residents to the outlying Cape Flats. Today, the community-funded museum draws on taped recollections, donated possessions and evocative photographs supplied by former residents to celebrate everyday life as it once was in this rare multi-racial suburb, and to mourn its destruction at the hands of the apartheid government. Allow at least two hours to feel the full impact, or better still phone ahead to arrange a guided tour.

The Company's Garden

Queen Victoria St ☎ 021 400 3912 ☀ 09.00–17.00 daily

An ideal place to start a walking tour, the Company's Garden lies at the historic heart of Cape Town. It is overlooked by Table Mountain, and forms the most important oasis of greenery in the city centre. Originally an agricultural concern, it was established by Jan van Riebeeck just weeks after his arrival at the Cape in 1652 to provide fresh produce for Dutch ships *en route* to and from India. By the 18th century the farmland

Landmarks around the Company's Garden

The Company's Garden is enclosed by several venerable buildings, and it would be easy to spend half a day exploring the immediate vicinity's museums, galleries, etc.

Delville Wood Memorial Garden

Featuring pigeon-splattered statues by Anton van Wouw and Anton Turner, the monument near the southern end of the garden commemorates the 2,300 South African casualties of the World War I Battle of Delville Wood, France.

Iziko South African Museum

25 Queen Victoria St ✆ 021 481 3800 ⊕ www.iziko.org.za ⊙ 10.00–17.00 daily

Situated at the southern end of the garden since 1897, this is mainly a natural history museum and is best known for its massive mounted whale skeletons. It also houses a superb collection of rock art and other artefacts relating to the so-called San or Bushmen.

Iziko Planetarium

✆ 021 481 3900 ⊕ www.iziko.org.za

Adjacent to the museum, this dome-roofed, child-friendly institution hosts a constantly changing programme of shows and displays about the sparkling South African night sky.

Iziko National Gallery

Paddock Av ✆ 021 467 4660 ⊕ www.iziko.org.za ⊙ 10.00–17.00 Tue–Sun

On the east side of the garden, this is the leading art museum in southern Africa. It was founded in 1871 and houses a permanent collection of contemporary African and classic European canvases, often supplemented by exciting, themed temporary exhibits.

South African Jewish Museum

88 Hatfield St ✆ 021 465 1546 ⊕ www.sajewishmuseum.co.za ⊙ 10.00–17.00 Sun–Thu, 10.00–14.00 Fri

Next to the National Gallery, this modern building charts the history of Cape Town's substantial Jewish community. It incorporates South Africa's oldest synagogue, built in 1862, and the Great Synagogue built in 1904. Its 2000 inauguration was attended by Nelson Mandela.

Cape Town Holocaust Centre

☎ 021 462 5553 🖥 www.ctholocaust.co.za ⏰ 10.00–17.00 Sun–Thu, 10.00–13.00 Fri

In the same compound as the Jewish Museum, this chilling centre contextualises racism in South Africa and the European holocaust during World War II.

Iziko Slave Lodge

Cnr Adderley & Wale St ☎ 021 460 8242 🖥 www.iziko.org.za ⏰ 10.00–17.00 Mon–Sat

Constructed in 1679, Cape Town's second-oldest building, set at the north end of the garden, once provided crowded and unsanitary shelter to hundreds of slaves sourced from Asia and Madagascar. Following abolition in 1834, it served as a post office, library, Supreme Court and even brothel. It is now a sobering multimedia museum documenting the history of slavery on the Cape and elsewhere.

Keiskamma Altar piece, Iziko Slave Lodge (AVZ)

St George's Anglican Cathedral

Wale St ☎ 021 424 7360 🖥 www.stgeorgescathedral.com ⏰ 08.30–16.30 Mon–Fri

Diagonally opposite the Slave Lodge, this elegant sandstone cathedral, designed by Sir Herbert Baker, was a key centre of political protest during the 1980s under Archbishop Desmond Tutu. A modest display close to the main entrance evokes the church's role in the struggle, while the courtyard labyrinth is a replica of the 13th century one at Chartres Cathedral in France.

Groote Kerk

Church Sq ☎ 021 461 7044 🖥 www.grootekerk.co.za ⏰ 10.00–14.00 Mon–Fri

Situated around the corner from the Slave Lodge, Cape Town's oldest Dutch Reformed edifice is the somewhat unadorned Groote Kerk (Big Church) built in 1704. It is of interest mainly for the pulpit sculpture by Anton Anreith dating back to 1789.

Houses of Parliament

Parliament St ☎ 021 403 2262 🖥 www.parliament.gov.za ⏰ guided tours by advance arrangement only

Backing onto the Company's Garden but best viewed from Parliament Street, this ostentatious Victorian artefact has been a seat of parliament since it was built in 1864. It houses an interesting collection of artworks and maps.

had been transformed into an 18ha zoological and botanical garden that earned its keep by growing bulbs and other produce for export to Europe. Today, the park-like garden's primary role is aesthetic, it is a popular lunchtime retreat for city workers, and is attended by cooing flocks of feral pigeons, honking Egyptian geese and a delightfully tame population of grey squirrels introduced from North America. The garden is dotted with historic statues, and is graced by South Africa's oldest cultivated tree (a pear planted circa 1652), the country's largest tree-aloe (standing 18m high), a rose garden dating to 1929, and the popular **Gardens Tea Room**, where you can grab an inexpensive lunch or drink. Several of Cape Town's most important museums and buildings enclose the garden (see box pages 240–1).

Long Street is the heart of Cape Town's alternative scene. (SS)

Long Street

Running uphill from the waterfront to the foot of Table Mountain, a block west of the Company's Garden, Long Street is the longest and hippest thoroughfare in Cape Town. Its susceptibility to changing fortunes and fashions is reflected in the engagingly curious mismatch of architecture styles, which range from Turkish-style baths and the country's second-oldest mosque to ornate Victorian relicts and curvaceous hangovers from the early 20th-century Art Deco boom. The grungy centre of Cape Town's thriving backpacker and alternative scenes, Soho-esque Long Street houses a cosmopolitan selection of excellent but inexpensive eateries, numerous live music venues and all-night bars, gay clubs, and the city's largest concentration of quirky shops selling anything from vintage clothes and collectable books to crafts and CDs from all over Africa. Exploring

Six specialist Long Street shops

Clarke's Books
211 Long St ☎ 021 423 5739 🖥 www.clarkesbooks.co.za
The city's top second-hand bookshop, now more than 50 years old, has plenty to amuse casual browsers as well as serious Africana collectors.

Mali South Clothing
90 Long St ☎ 021 426 1519 🖥 www.malisouthclothing.co.za
West African cloths tailored by innovative Malian designer Maiga Abdoulaye to form a range of colourful clothing suited to men and women of all ages.

Pan-African Market
76 Long St ☎ 021 426 4478
Spanning three chaotic, stall-packed floors, this is a great place to dig around for inexpensive knick-knacks from all over Africa.

Tribal Trends
72-4 Long St ☎ 021 423 8008 ✉ sales@tribaltends.co.za
This owner-managed store, though not cheap, is practically a work of art in itself, displaying with genuine flair the finest selection of quality African crafts, artworks and antiques we've ever seen.

(AVZ)

African Women's Trading Market
112 Long St ☎ 021 424 5356
🖥 www.africanheritage.co.za
A fun range of affordable jewellery made entirely from natural African materials.

African Music Store
134 Long St ☎ 021 426 0857
The enthusiastic staff at South Africa's top specialist African music shop can point you to worthwhile CDs of vintage and contemporary sounds from all corners of the continent.

Long Street, and its more genteel southern extension, Kloof Street, is more about following your nose than any prescribed itinerary but a few shopping highlights are listed in the box on page 243.

Greenmarket Square and surrounds

Surrounded by historic buildings, street cafés and smarter eateries, this cobbled square in the heart of old Cape Town has been in existence since 1696 when it was known as Burgher Watch Square. It served as a slave market from 1710 until the era of abolition, after which it was converted into a vegetable market before becoming a car park in the 1950s. In the post-apartheid era the square has been revitalised and is now a bustling pan-African craft and clothing market, where vendors often speak as much French or Swahili as they do English. It also attracts a lively cast of mime artists, jugglers, musicians and other street performers.

Among the buildings overlooking Greenmarket Square is the **Old Townhouse**, which was built in 1755 and boasts a handsome, triple-arched portico and belfry. The City Hall until 1905, it now houses the **Michaelis Collection** (✆ 021 481 3933 ✈ www.iziko.org.za ◐ 10.00–17.00 Mon–Fri, 10.00–16.00 Sat), a world-renowned cache of 16th–18th-century paintings by Dutch and Flemish masters donated by Sir Max Michaelis in 1914. A couple of blocks away, **Koopmans-De Wet House** (35 Strand St ✆ 021 481 3935 ✈ www.iziko.org.za ◐ 10.00–17.00 Mon–Fri) is an elegant, neo-classical, 18th-century double-storey townhouse, maintained and decorated in period style and named after its last private owner Marie Koopmans-De Wet, who donated it to the city after her death

There is no end of crafts available at the lively Greenmarket Square. (AVZ)

in 1906. On the same road, located in an old townhouse built in 1788, is the **Gold of Africa Museum** (96 Strand St ✆ 021 405 1540 ✈ www.goldofafrica.com ◐ 09.30–17.00 Mon–Sat), which was established by the Anglo-Gold mining company to display a peerless collection of gold artefacts from Mali, Senegal, Ghana, Zimbabwe and elsewhere in Africa.

Bo-Kaap

Running up the foothills of Signal Hill immediately to the west of the city centre, the Bo-Kaap (Upper Cape) is the spiritual home of the Cape Malay community, whose colourfully painted but otherwise

unpretentious houses, many dating to the mid-18th century, form the largest concentration of historic buildings in Cape Town. The history of this fascinating suburb is explored in the small **Bo-Kaap Museum** (71 Wale St ℓ 021 481 3939 ⏣ www.iziko.co.za ☉ 10.00–17.00 Mon–Sat), which is set in a beautifully restored homestead built in the 1760s and includes a collection of typical household items, as well as displays charting the Cape Malay experience from its roots in enslavement and oppression under apartheid.

Several historic mosques are dotted around this predominantly Muslim quarter and the **Auwal Mosque** in Dorp Street is the oldest in South Africa. It was founded in 1798 by the influential religious leader Tuan Guru, whose is buried at the Baru Karamat (Shrine) at the top of Longmarket Street. The **Nurul Islam Mosque** off Buitengracht Street is the city's third oldest, founded in 1844, while the **Borhan Mosque** on Chiappini Street had the first minaret in Cape Town.

Victoria & Alfred Waterfront

ℓ 021 408 7600 ⏣ www.waterfront.co.za ☉ shops open 09.00–18.00 or until 21.00, restaurants mostly until after 22.00

Ranked the most-visited tourist attraction in South Africa, the V&A Waterfront is one of the country's best and largest malls. It is a partially open-air complex offering a choice of 60 eateries, hundreds of shops and innumerable leisure activities. Named after Queen Victoria and her son Duke Alfred of Saxe-Coburg and Gotha, it is also a working harbour of historic note, developed at the turn of the 20th century to accommodate the increased shipping requirements associated with the mining boom

Waterfront icons

The waterfront's historic clock tower (AVZ)

Clock tower

This Gothic-style octagonal landmark, which is reached via a swing bridge that opens to accommodate passing boats, dates from 1882 and sits alongside the modern tourist information office.

Two Oceans Aquarium

📞 021 418 3823 🖰 www.aquarium.co.za

🕑 09.30–18.00 daily

This fine, three-storey aquarium houses 3,000 marine creatures, ranging from anemones and octopus to sharks and turtles. The River Meander with its colourful tree frogs, strutting penguins and black oystercatchers is a highlight, as is the kelp forest inhabited by hundreds of colourful fish.

Waterfront Craft Market and Wellness Centre

This is reputedly South Africa's largest indoor market, a densely packed concentration of more than 100 micro-ventures specialising mostly in local crafts or alternative health treatments.

Musica Megastore

📞 021 425 6300 🖰 www.musica.co.za

Probably the largest CD and DVD shop in the country, this double-storey warehouse doesn't quite match the African Music Store on Long Street (see page 243) for its selection of African music, but it's a close second.

Nobel Square

Life-sized statues of South Africa's four Nobel Peace Prize winners – Luthuli,

inland and the Anglo-Boer War. The harbour became very rundown in the dying years of apartheid and its subsequent redevelopment as a premier tourist attraction is emblematic of Cape Town's modern resurgence. Several of the buildings have been converted from 19th-century warehouses. It wouldn't be difficult to while away a day exploring the waterfront and its immediate surroundings; a selection of its most worthwhile stops are listed in the box above.

Tutu, de Klerk and Mandela – stand alongside a more enigmatic Makonde-esque sculpture incorporating several key anti-apartheid figures.

Alfred Mall

This converted Edwardian warehouse is lined with alfresco bars and cafés from where patrons can enjoy views across the harbour to Table Mountain, and often see Cape fur seals. In the evening, stop at the Green Dolphin to enjoy live jazz.

Victoria Wharf Shopping Mall

Almost every major South African chain store is represented in this covered mall within a mall, which also hosts several clothes boutiques, numerous cafés and the multi-screen Art Nouveau 'art cinema'.

Vaughan Johnson's Wine & Cigar Shop

☏ 021 419 2121

With famously knowledgeable staff and the option of shipping to anywhere in the world, this long-serving emporium is a great place to sample and stock up on Cape wines.

A boat ride is a great way to see the wildlife living in Table Bay. (AVZ)

Ferryman's Tavern and Mitchell's Bar

Facing Market Square, this pair of easy-going pubs have graced the V&A Waterfront since 1989. They remain great places for chilled sundowners or a cheap pub meal.

Sunset Cruises

Offered by several operators in front of Victoria Wharf or Alfred Mall, cruises around Table Bay often result in encounters with dolphins or seals that are frolicking below the outline of Table Mountain.

Robben Island

☏ 021 419 1300 🖰 www.robbenisland.org.za 🕐 tours depart hourly 09.00–15.00 daily

The largest island in Table Bay, named after the colony of *robben* (seals) that lived there in van Riebeeck's day, Robben Island lies 12km offshore from the city centre and is clearly visible from the summit of Table Mountain or Signal Hill. A UNESCO World Heritage Site, it is often referred to as South Africa's answer to Alcatraz, having been a place of incarceration since 1658, when a rebellious local trader called Autshumatom was exiled here by the Dutch administration. By the 1760s the island held 70 prisoners, many of them prominent Muslim leaders as evidenced by the existence of a shrine to the Islamic cleric Tuan Guru, and it doubled as a leper colony between 1846 and 1930. More recently, Robben Island achieved notoriety in the apartheid era as a maximum security prison used to hold political leaders such as Robert Sobukwe, Nelson Mandela, Walter Sisulu, Govan Mbeki and Jacob Zuma.

Prison cell at Robben Island (AVZ)

The last prisoner left the island in 1996 and it is now a museum that can only be visited on one of the (rather pricey) guided four-hour tours that leave from V&A Waterfront's Nelson Mandela Gateway several times a day. The gateway itself houses multimedia displays about the island's history and the anti-apartheid struggle, while the 30-minute boat ride there and back often results in dolphin sightings. Once on the island, a guided bus tour runs between several of its most important landmarks, including the lonely dwelling where PAC leader Robert Sobukwe was held in solitary confinement for a decade, and the quarry where Mandela and other prisoners endured years of hard labour in blinding conditions created by bright sunlight reflected on limestone. Finally, tours of the disused Maximum Security Prison Block, conducted by former political prisoners, include a visit to the tiny cell where Mandela lived for 18 years.

Table Mountain Cableway

Tafelberg Rd ☎ 021 424 8181 🕐 www.tablemountain.net 🕑 08.30–18.00, or 22.00 in midsummer, weather permitting

Table Mountain, a flat, sandstone plateau that rises from Table Bay to an altitude of 1,086m, was South Africa's most iconic natural feature long before Cape Town was established, and a landmark known to mariners from around the world. Today, the striking outline of the mountain dominates the southern city skyline, whether it basks in golden sunlight, or is swathed in the misty shroud known as the tablecloth. The 'table top' is most easily reached by the cableway that opened south of the city centre in 1929 and carried its 20-millionth passenger to the summit in 2010.

Offering exhilarating views of both the bay and the massif as it rotates 360° during the ascent, the cableway is best prioritised for as early as possible in your visit, as wind, rain or mist frequently force it to close for several days running. Once at the top, the rewards are innumerable – stunning views in every direction capture the geological drama of the Cape Peninsula, and the plateau is also an important refuge for proteas and other fynbos vegetation, as well as wildlife ranging from rock hyrax and baboons to several endemic birds. The Dizzy Dassie, set in an old sandstone building near the Upper Cableway Station, is a great spot for a high-altitude meal or drink, and adventurous visitors can arrange to

(SS)

abseil the cliffs overlooking Camps Bay at a few minutes' notice. A free, and less weather-dependent, alternative to the cableway is the lesser-known climb or drive up **Signal Hill**, a particularly rewarding excursion at dusk when there are superb views southeast across the City Bowl to Table Mountain, and northeast over the V&A waterfront and new Cape Town Stadium to Robben Island.

Six standout beaches

An enormous number of beaches are scattered on and around the Cape Peninsula, but the following warrant special mention for various reasons:

Bikini Beach

Arguably the finest swimming beach in the vicinity of Cape Town, Strand's Bikini Beach lies in the northeast corner of False Bay below the Helderberg Mountains and has good facilities for families.

Sandy Bay (SS)

Bloubergstrand

Nowhere is Table Mountain – the nominal 'Blouberg' (Blue Mountain) – seen to better advantage than from this long, pretty beach. It can be reached by following the R27 along the west coast 10km north of central Cape Town.

Camps Bay

The first choice for fashionistas is this wide, sandy beach set below the spectacular Twelve Apostles formation, so come and be seen in one of the row of lively cafés, restaurants and bars. The chilly water is often compensated for by the low wind, as compared to False Bay.

Muizenberg

People don't come here for the scenery but for the safe swimming, fine surfing and varied facilities, all of which make it a firm family favourite. It's accessible by train from the city centre.

Sandy Bay

The closest thing in the Cape to an official nudist hangout, this secluded beach near Llandudno also hosts a low-key gay scene. The chilly water makes it better suited to sunbathing than to swimming.

Seaforth

Within walking distance of Simon's Town, in the direction of Boulders, this relatively uncrowded beach is overlooked by gigantic rocks and a great seafront restaurant, and there is the added bonus of occasional stray penguins waddling past.

The Atlantic coastline to Camps Bay

West of the city centre, a series of contiguous suburbs run along the narrow strip of sloping but habitable seafront strung below the steeper upper slopes of Signal Hill and Lion's Head. Coming from the direction of the V&A Waterfront the first of these suburbs is **Green Point**, where the dominant feature is the Green Point Common. An area of protected parkland, it houses Cape Town Stadium, which was custom-built for the 2010 FIFA World Cup and hosted eight games in the tournament. At the northern tip of the common is the red-and-white Green Point Lighthouse; built in 1824 it is the oldest lighthouse in South Africa. Inland from here the suburb is architecturally notable for the terraced 19th-century houses that cling to the lower slopes of Signal Hill, overlooking Main Street, which runs roughly parallel to the coast before the neighbouring and rather insalubrious suburb of **Sea Point** starts.

The view to Camps Bay on the walk down from Lions Head. (SS)

The trio of narrow suburbs running along the Atlantic Coast south of Sea Point boast some of the most expensive real estate anywhere in South Africa. **Bantry Bay** and **Clifton** are both primarily residential, though the latter is known for its quartet of wind-free coves – referred to somewhat prosaically as First to Fourth Beach – and is generally packed when conditions are even vaguely conducive to swimming. Finally, the most southerly and trendy of Cape Town's Atlantic seaboard suburbs is the delectable **Camps Bay**, its idyllic beach set within view of the staggering rock formation known as the Twelve Apostles, and lined with an excellent selection of bustling hotels, cafés, bars and restaurants. In common with other Atlantic resorts, the water at Camps Bay is often dauntingly cold but the beaches are otherwise very relaxed, and there's a large tidal pool where you can usually swim safely in rougher weather.

Kirstenbosch and the southeast suburbs

The scenically positioned 528-ha **Kirstenbosch National Botanical Garden** (Rhodes Dr ℡ 021 799 8783 ☝ www.sanbi.org ☉ Apr–Aug 08.00–18.00, Sep–Mar 08.00–19.00) is the most worthwhile and popular tourist attraction among the affluent suburbs that run downhill from the east side of Table Mountain to the Cape Flats. Formally established in 1913, the garden had previously been the private property of Cecil

The extravagant Rhodes Memorial (AVZ)

John Rhodes, who bequeathed it to the nation upon his death in 1902, and it contains a hedge of indigenous wild almonds planted by Jan van Riebeeck in 1660. A network of well-marked trails runs through the garden, where thematic beds of indigenous flora – most notably a lush cycad garden, a fascinating collection of well signposted 'useful plants', and a conservatory containing a tree-sized *kokerboom* and other succulent species typical of the arid Kalahari and Namaqualand – give way to a natural cover of heath-like fynbos at higher altitudes. The starting point of a popular walking route up Table Mountain, Kirstenbosch also contains a statue garden showcasing contemporary sculptures by local artists, and there is a good gift shop and restaurant.

Situated in the southern suburbs below Devil's Peak is the **Rhodes Memorial** (Residence Rd ℂ 021 689 9151 ⊕ www.rhodesmemorial. co.za), fronted by Doric columns and a flight of 49 steps, with inscriptions penned by Sir Rudyard Kipling. It was built in 1912 to commemorate the life of Cecil John Rhodes, the one-time Prime Minister of the Cape and founder of the Rhodesias (Zimbabwe and Zambia). Architecturally overblown it undoubtedly is, but the view, across the Cape Flats to the distant Helderberg and Hottentots Holland Mountains, is fantastic. In the nearby suburb of Rosebank, the absorbing but relatively unpublicised **Irma Stern Museum** (Cecil Rd, ℂ 021 685 5686 ⊕ www.irmastern.co.za ⊕ 10.00–17.00 Tue–Sat) displays a selection of portraits by the eponymous artist – whose modernistic rendition of African subjects provoked considerable controversy during her lifetime – alongside a collection of ethnic artefacts accumulated on her extensive African travels.

Constantia Valley

The birthplace of Cape wine, this scenic valley lies in the shadow of the Constantia Mountains some 10km south of the city centre. Governor Simon van der Stel established a large estate here in 1685 and planted the first vines, but international renown came under the 18th- to 19th-century stewardship of the Cloete family, whose Vin de Constance, a dessert wine that was beloved of Napoleon Bonaparte, is name-checked in the works of Charles Dickens and Jane Austen. In 1796, the British naval officer Robert Percival asserted that 'every stranger who arrives at the Cape ... makes a point of visiting the village of Constantia and those famous wine plantations', and indeed, the likes of William Burchell, Anthony Trollope and King Edward VIII all visited the estate at some point.

The most important estate is still **Groot Constantia**, which was bought by the Cape Government in 1885 and is now run by a trust. Here, the **Iziko Groot Constantia Manor House Museum** (☏ 021 795 5140 ⚓ www.iziko.org.za ◷ 10.00–17.00 daily) comprises two buildings: the original 1680s homestead built by van der Stel and later expanded to become an elegantly sprawling manor house notable for its handsome front gables and sculpted niche, and the Cloete Cellar, famed for its triangular gable and now housing a collection of antique wine storage and drinking vessels. Otherwise, Groot Constantia remains a functional estate responsible for several fine contemporary wines, which can be sampled in the tasting room or in the superb Jonkershuis Restaurant,

Groot Constantia has been producing fine wines for over 100 years. (AVZ)

Guga S'Thebe Arts & Cultural Centre, Langa, Cape Flats (AVZ)

set in a converted outbuilding that dates from van der Stel's time. Three other fine historic Constantia wine estates welcome visitors to their restaurants and tasting rooms; these are **Steenberg** (☎ 021 713 2211 🖰 www.steenberg-vineyards.co.za), **Klein Constantia** (☎ 021 794 5188 🖰 www.kleinconstantia.com) and **Buitenverwachting** (☎ 021 794 3522 🖰 www.buitenverwachting.co.za).

The Cape Flats

In contrast to the city centre and wealthy suburbs abutting Table Mountain, the flat sandy plains that stretch eastward along the northern shore of False Bay are bleak of prospect and almost totally lacking in agricultural potential. As such, this scrubby and flood-prone area remained practically uninhabited until the 1920s, despite its relative proximity to the city centre. In 1927, however, Cape Town's 'Black' township, Langa, was established on the Cape Flats to accommodate an influx of migrant Xhosa labourers from the present-day Eastern Cape. A trend was established, and the apartheid era saw the Cape Flats emerge as a dumping ground for tens of thousands of Capetonians who were forcibly relocated from their former homes in newly re-zoned 'Whites Only' areas, to townships such as Mitchell's Plain and the sprawling shacklands of Khayelitsha and Gugulethu, which naturally enough became a hotbed of anti-apartheid activism, particularly in the 1980s.

A visit to the Cape Flats is essential for anybody who wants to see beyond the Cape Town of glossy tour brochures. However, poverty and crime levels remain high despite significant development since 1994, and while the area is safe enough to visit it is advisable to do so as part of an organised tour or with a local guide (either can be arranged through any local tour operator or hotel). A tour will almost certainly include a stop in **Langa**, now a relatively smart township whose points of interest include the **Sharpeville Massacre Memorial**, unveiled on 20 March 2010 to commemorate the 50th anniversary of this tragic event, and the vibrant **Guga S'Thebe Arts & Cultural Centre**.

In Gugulethu, the **Gugulethu Seven Monument** is dedicated to a group of seven young men who were framed and then shot dead by police in 1986. A visit to **Khayelitsha**, the country's second-largest township after Soweto, normally starts at **Lookout Hill**, which provides an overview of the township from atop a sand dune, then continues to the **Khayelitsha Craft Market**, an NGO-supported co-operative that trains formerly unemployed women to make crafts for the tourist market. Outside Khayelitsha, on the N2 near Somerset West, is the **Lwandle Migrant Labour Museum** (☎ 021 845 6119 ✆ www.lwandle.com ☼ 09.30–16.00 Mon–Fri), a former hostel for migrant labourers that has been preserved as a reminder of living conditions under apartheid.

Tried & Tested

Cape Grace
✆ www.capegrace.com

Location, location, location! Set right on the Waterfront, this elegant five-star hotel is an outright Rainbow Tours favourite. Cape Grace has become a byword for phenomenal service. It's one of the top-rated hotels in the world, yet everyone feels at home here. Heritage Environmental Management accredited, it manages to be both family-friendly and romantic, with 120 rooms, suites and penthouses to choose from, and top-class amenities including library, pool, spa, whisky bar and a renowned restaurant serving modern cuisine.

Four Rosmead
✆ www.fourrosmead.com

This four-star, French-inspired, boutique guesthouse on the slopes of Table Mountain is within walking distance of Greenmarket Square, the parliament buildings and Company Gardens. We love the modern classic style interiors, adorned with paintings by well-known South African artists. Each of the eight en-suite bedrooms is individually decorated and there are exceptional views across Cape Town and Table Bay. The solar-heated pool, spa and landscaped gardens make this a haven for recuperation between city excursions.

Grand Daddy
🖰 www.granddaddy.co.za

THE ZAMBEZI SAFARI
& TRAVEL CO. LTD

Plush and playful, the legendary, luxurious Grand Daddy hotel - centrally located on Long street, the vibrant hub of Cape Town - is an award-winning project that mirrors the talent, style and flavour of the city. The hotel is famous for its Airstream Rooftop Trailer Park, featuring seven shiny silver airstream trailers
– a novel adventure indeed! Flamboyant, yet elegant and friendly, Grand Daddy offers a gorgeous, opulent interior. Choose one of 26 rooms (including two spacious suites).... or even one of the trailers.

Kensington Place
🖰 www.kensingtonplace.co.za

IMAGINE
AFRICA

Stylish, elegant and in a stunning location this boutique hotel is bound to be a favourite. The eight chic rooms are all different and boast marble bathrooms and exquisite fabrics with the city, harbour and surrounding mountains all visible from the private terrace of each room. But what really puts it beyond the reach
of other hotels is the personal service. Feedback is always wonderful about the friendly and professional team. Nothing is too much trouble.

The Cascades on 52
🖰 www.lescascades.co.za

IMAGINE
AFRICA

The Cascades on 52 is all about stylish contemporary design mixed with fantastic service and wonderful views of the Atlantic. Feedback is outstanding with lots of repeat clients. The six elegant modern rooms, including two suites, each have floor to ceiling windows with panoramic sea views across
Bantry Bay. The main reception area has a large open guest lounge and outside, oversized umbrellas and a row of comfy, modern sun loungers invite for immediate relaxation by the pool.

The Last Word Long Beach
🐚 www.thelastword.co.za

The Last Word Long Beach is right on the beach in the picturesque lobster-fishing village of Kommetjie, just 30 minutes from Cape Town. It is an unspoilt paradise in which to walk, ride horses, surf or simply laze in the sun. From the inviting pool or your private deck you can watch whales frolic a hundred metres offshore. The five-star, intimate hotel has six ultra luxurious rooms with stylish, comfortable interiors, private patios and sea views!

The Last Word Sea Five
🐚 www.thelastword.co.za

The Last Word Sea Five is ideally situated in central Camps Bay. Capitalising on an outstanding location, just 300m from South Africa's most glamorous beach, this intimate hotel offers six exclusive en-suite rooms with clear, sweeping mountain and sea views. Every room has been individually styled with a stunning blend of spaciousness and refined luxury. It boasts the harmony of a garden redolent with mandarin, lemon, lavender and rosemary or the sociability of a large blue pool and welcoming bar.

Welgelegen Guest House
🐚 www.welgelegen.co.za

For a great base from which to explore the delights of Cape Town, look no further than Welgelegen. We love this owner-run luxurious 13 room guesthouse spread over two beautifully renovated period properties at the foot of Table Mountain and just minutes away from Cape Town's greatest attractions. Relax by the courtyard pool or stroll down nearby Kloof Street with its vibrant restaurants and bars; drive 15 minutes and you're at the botanical gardens or glorious beach. Perfect!

The Cape Peninsula

Extending for some 60km south of Cape Town to the wave-battered cliffs of Cape Point, the Cape Peninsula is a scenic sliver of land flanked by the wild, chilly, open Atlantic to the west, and the more sheltered and warmer waters of False Bay to the east. Less than 10km wide for most of its length, but rising to almost 1,000m along the mountainous spine that divides its western and eastern seafronts, this is an area of immense scenic beauty and rare botanical diversity, set at the heart of the Cape Floral Kingdom (see box page 262). Some two-thirds of the peninsula is now protected within the disjointed Table Mountain National Park, of which the most popular sectors are the end-of-the-continent Cape of Good Hope and the penguin-crammed Boulders Beach. Elsewhere, the shore supports a series of small coastal towns and villages whose sleepy, resort-like ambience seems increasingly far removed from the bustle of Cape Town as you head further south. The section below explores the peninsula in an anti-clockwise loop, starting at Hout Bay and ending at Muizenberg, but it could as easily be travelled in the reverse direction.

Cape Peninsula highlights

Western seaboard

Sparsely populated in comparison with the eastern False Bay shoreline, the peninsula's western seaboard is serviced by a solitary

and precipitously scenic road that winds its way from Camps Bay south towards Cape Point. Coming from the city, the first large settlement you reach is **Hout Bay**, which lies 10km past Camps Bay, and whose name – literally Wood Bay – reflects its significance as a source of timber in colonial times. Despite this, there are few buildings of historical significance here, the main exceptions being an 18th-century Cape

Duiker Island is home to a large colony of Cape fur seals. (AVZ)

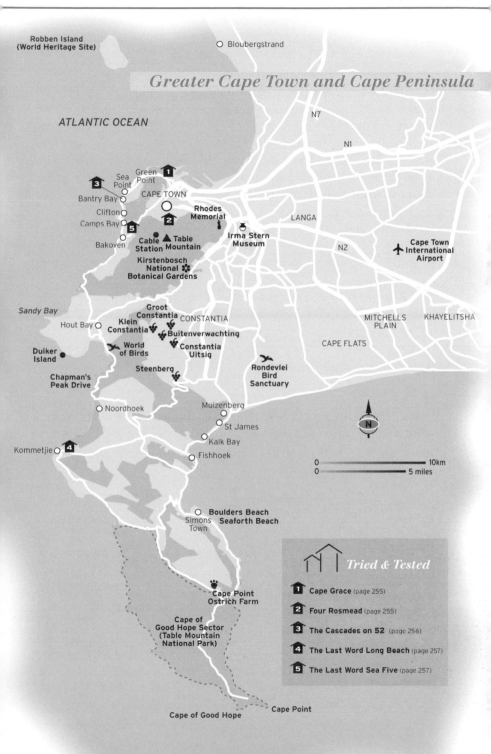

Robben Island
(World Heritage Site)

Blouwbergstrand

Greater Cape Town and Cape Peninsula

ATLANTIC OCEAN

N7

N1

Green
Point

1

Sea
Point

3

CAPE TOWN

Bantry Bay

Rhodes
Memorial

Clifton

2

LANGA

Camps Bay

5

Irma Stern
Museum

Bakoven

Cable
Station

Table
Mountain

N2

Cape Town
International
Airport

Kirstenbosch
National
Botanical Gardens

Sandy Bay

Groot
Constantia

CONSTANTIA

MITCHELLS
PLAIN

KHAYELITSHA

Hout Bay

Klein
Constantia

Buitenverwachting

Duiker
Island

World
of Birds

Constantia
Uitsig

CAPE FLATS

Chapman's
Peak Drive

Steenberg

Rondevlei
Bird
Sanctuary

Noordhoek

Muizenberg

St James

N

Kalk Bay

4

Kommetjie

Fishhoek

0   10km
0   5 miles

Boulders Beach

Simons
Town

Seaforth Beach

Cape Point
Ostrich Farm

Tried & Tested

Cape of
Good Hope Sector
(Table Mountain
National Park)

1 Cape Grace (page 255)

2 Four Rosmead (page 255)

3 The Cascades on 52 (page 256)

4 The Last Word Long Beach (page 257)

5 The Last Word Sea Five (page 257)

Cape of Good Hope

Cape Point

Practicalities

In many respects, the Cape Peninsula functions as a kind of overgrown backyard to Cape Town itself. Surprisingly, perhaps, there are relatively few hotels on the peninsula, and those that do exist tend to be rather good value compared to more central options. However, most visitors opt to base themselves in Cape Town itself, and visit the peninsula as a **day trip**, either driving themselves in a rented vehicle or joining one of the day tours that are offered by operators citywide and can be arranged through any hotel. **Public transport** on the

Accommodation

Exclusive
Twelve Apostles Hotel & Spa South of Camps Bay
⚓ www.12apostleshotel.com

Upmarket
The Long Beach Kommetjie ⚓ www.thelongbeach.com

Moderate
Hout Bay Manor Hout Bay ⚓ www.houtbaymanor.co.za
Quayside Hotel Simon's Town ⚓ www.relaishotels.com
Whale View Manor Simon's Town ⚓ www.whaleviewmanor.co.za

Budget
Lord Nelson Inn Simon's Town ⚓ www.lordnelsoninn.co.za

Dutch homestead called **Kronendal** and the 19th-century **St Peter's Anglican Church**.

The main attraction is **Duiker Island**, home to a large breeding colony of Cape fur seals that can be viewed from a glass-bottomed boat. Trips leave from Hout Bay Harbour throughout the morning (you can book on the spot through any of several kiosks lining the wharf) but infrequently, if at all, in the afternoon. Also popular, especially with children, is **World of Birds** (Valley Rd ☎ 021 790 2730 ⚓ www.worldofbirds.org.za ⏰ 09.00–17.00 daily), which claims to be Africa's largest bird park. The attraction has 400 indigenous and exotic species in the walk-through aviaries, as well as monkeys and a troop of meerkats.

Peninsula is limited, and there is nothing that heads as far south as Boulders or the Cape of Good Hope. However, Metrorail (☎ 080 065 6463 🖰 www. capemetrorail.co.za) operates several trains daily along the (very scenic) line from Adderley Street Station to Simon's Town via Muizenberg, while the Cape Town Explorer (☎ 021 511 6000 🖰 www.citysightseeing.co.za) runs south along the west coast as far as Hout Bay. The usual amenities – shops, ATMs, restaurants – are available in the larger towns along the peninsula, including Muizenberg, Fishhoek, Simon's Town and Hout Bay.

Eating out

Café Pescados (pizza & seafood) Main St, Simon's Town ☎ 021 786 2272 🖰 www.pescados.co.za
Cape to Cuba (Cuban & seafood) Main Rd, Kalk Bay ☎ 021 788 1566 🖰 www.capetocuba.com
Fogey's Railway House (seafood & Cape Malay cuisine) Main Rd, Muizenberg ☎ 021 788 3252 🖰 www.fogeys.co.za
Harbour House (seafood) Kalk Bay Harbour ☎ 021 788 4133 🖰 www.harbourhouse.co.za
Tibetan Teahouse (Tibetan-style vegetarian fare) Sophea Gallery between Simonstown & Boulders ☎ 021 786 1544 🖰 www.sopheagallery.com
Wharfside Grill (inexpensive but very good seafood) Mariner's Wharf, Hout Bay Harbour ☎ 021 790 1100 🖰 www.marinerswharf.com

South of Hout Bay, **Chapman's Peak Drive** (🖰 www.chapmans peakdrive.co.za) is arguably the most spectacular road in the country, having hugged the sheer seaward cliffs of the Constantia Mountains since it was initially constructed in 1915. It re-opened as a toll road in 2004 after a four-year closure for maintenance, but it is worth paying the nominal fee for the stunning views, which can be enjoyed from several demarcated viewpoints. Chapman's Peak Drive terminates at **Noordhoek Beach**, an idyllic 6km stretch of white sand that is usually too cold (and occasionally too rough) for swimming, but is popular with horse riders, kite enthusiasts, surfers and birders – and ideal for a leisurely afternoon beach walk.

The Cape Floral Kingdom

The Cape Peninsula forms part of the Cape Floral Kingdom, which extends along the narrow coastal belt stretching from the Cederberg Mountains in the northwest to the Garden Route in the east. Accounting for a mere 0.04% of the world's surface area, this is by far the smallest of the six globally recognised floral kingdoms, supporting a flora that is strikingly different from the rest of South Africa, due in large part to it having a Mediterranean climate that reverses the trend elsewhere in the country. Most of the rain falls here in the winter months of May to September.

The predominant vegetation type of the Cape Floral Kingdom is an ancient, heath-like cover known as fynbos – literally 'fine bush', a reference to the small, thin leaves typical of many fynbos species. Most fynbos species are subtly coloured and otherwise unremarkable in appearance but there are exceptions, the most notable of which are the shrubby proteas. The largest is the King Protea (*Protea cynaroides*), whose striking salmon-pink flowers have a diameter of up to 30cm. The superficially uniform appearance of many fynbos landscapes often belies their immense biodiversity. More than 9,000 plant species have thus far been described, some two-thirds of which are endemic to the region (that is, they grow nowhere else in the world) and the Cape Peninsula alone supports a greater number of indigenous plant species than the entire British Isles. Little wonder then that the Cape Floral Kingdom has been inscribed as a UNESCO World Heritage Site, and as a key global biodiversity hotspot for its floral wealth, combining eight discrete protected areas, of which the most accessible is Table Mountain National Park.

The Cape Floral Kingdom has a less diverse fauna than many parts of South Africa, but it is rich in endemics, including more than 25 frog species. Large mammals whose range is more or less confined to the region include the Cape mountain zebra, Cape grysbok and bontebok, while other species present on the peninsula include Cape fox, common eland, klipspringer, Chacma baboon, rock hyrax and various small predators. For birders, five species are regarded to be fynbos endemics, most strikingly the Cape sugarbird, a long-tailed nectar-eater often seen feeding on flowering proteas, but also the orange-breasted sunbird, Cape rockjumper, Victorin's warbler and Protea canary. The Cape Floral Kingdom was also the primary habitat of the bluebuck (a sable-like antelope) and quagga (a partially striped zebra) until they were hunted to extinction by the early colonists.

Protea (AVZ)

Cape of Good Hope

📞 021 701 8692 🌐 www.sanparks.org 🕐 Oct–Mar 06.00–18.00, Apr–Sep 07.00–17.00

Set aside as the 77km² Cape of Good Hope Nature Reserve in 1939 and co-opted into Table Mountain National Park 60 years later, the most southerly third of the Cape Peninsula is also the most breath-taking, terminating as it does in a narrow wedge of rocky highlands known as Cape Point. This isn't the most southerly part of Africa (that distinction belongs to the more easterly Cape Agulhas) but it is often touted as such, and is undoubtedly a setting where the innate drama befits an edge-of-the-continent billing.

The main tourist focus is **Cape Point Lighthouse**, set at the top of a precipitous (and often viciously windswept) cliff that rises 250m from the rocky beach below. It was built between 1913 and 1919 using rocks from the present-day car park. If you're reasonably mobile the lighthouse can be reached in 20 minutes along a steep but well-tended stone footpath leading uphill from the car park. Less demanding is the cable-drawn railway, known as a funicular, which undertakes the trip in a couple of minutes. If the walk leaves you hungry or thirsty, the Two Oceans Restaurant, set alongside the car park, serves adequate breakfasts and lunches on a wide terrace overlooking False Bay.

This one grandstand viewpoint aside, the Cape of Good Hope is quieter than might be expected and it wouldn't be difficult to while away a peaceful day or two exploring its lesser-known side roads, walking trails and beaches. An excellent short walk is the 90-minute return trail from the car park to the **Cape of Good Hope Beach** below the lighthouse. Also worth a diversion, **Rooikrans** offers a panoramic view back along False Bay, as well as potentially good whale-watching in season. At rocky

The towering Cape Point Lighthouse (AVZ)

Bordjiesdrif Beach, there are some tidal pools (good for marine life) and an artificial rock pool that's safe for swimming, set below a striking igneous formation called the Black Rock.

The Cape of Good Hope is the best place near Cape Town to see flora and fauna endemic to the fynbos habitat. It is scattered with protea bushes, which bloom in winter and attract nectar-eaters such as Cape sugarbird and orange-belled sunbird. Marine birds are also well represented, including several species of gull and cormorant, and the striking African black oystercatcher. Larger mammals include the Chacma baboon (often very aggressive towards anybody carrying food), Cape fur seals and half-a-dozen antelope species, notably common eland, bontebok, grey rhebok and Cape grysbok. Immediately outside the entrance gate, the private **Cape Point Ostrich Farm** (✆ 021 780 9294 ✆ www.capepointostrichfarm.com ☼ 09.30–17.30 daily) offers affordable half-hour guided tours as well as light lunches.

Simon's Town

The rail service running south along False Bay from Cape Town terminates at Simon's Town, the most characterful town on the Cape Peninsula and the third-oldest in South Africa. It was selected by Simon van der Stel, then Governor of the Cape, as a safe alternative winter harbour to Table Bay back in 1687. Since 1957 it has been the main base of the South African navy, prior to which it was the British regional naval base for 160 years. Today it supports a wealth of Victorian buildings, most notably the long row of façades that comprise the **Historic Mile** along St George's Street, the main thoroughfare through town. Set in the heart of the historic town, palm-lined Jubilee Square and the adjacent Quayside Mall house several eateries overlooking the main harbour and a jetty from where daily boat trips run out into False Bay and Seal Island.

One of Simon's Town's more esoteric attractions is the **South African Naval Museum** (Main Rd ☎ 021 787 4635 ⊙ 10.00–16.00 daily), where a sprawling ragbag of naval artefacts as well as a life-size replica of a ship's bridge, complete with simulated rocking motion, can be enjoyed. The nearby **Simon's Town Museum** (Court Rd ☎ 021 786 3046 ⊙ 09.00–16.00 Mon–Fri, 10.00–13.00 Sat, 11.00–15.00 Sun), which started life as an 18th-century Governor's Residence, has local history exhibits about subjects such as the prehistoric settlement of the Cape and apartheid-era forced removals. It's also a good place to, um, bone up on the life and times of the legendary Able Seaman **Just Nuisance**, a much-loved Great Dane who was formally enlisted into the British navy in 1939 and whose statue now graces Jubilee Square.

Boulders Beach

☎ 021 786 2329 ⌨ www.sanparks.org ⊙ 08.00–18.30 daily

One must-see in the vicinity of Simon's Town is this small enclave of Table Mountain National Park, which lies about five minutes' drive further south. Sheltered by ancient granite boulders, this beach is the site of a famous permanent colony of the endangered African penguin, established by just two breeding pairs in 1982 and now numbering several thousand individuals. There are two main beaches here, connected by wheelchair-friendly Willis Walk, which runs for 600m outside the boundary fence. The more northerly beach is the main breeding site, so it can be viewed only from a network of boardwalks and viewing platforms, which offer great close-up views of these comic creatures as they strut, surf, squabble and sunbathe, occasionally unleashing one of the powerful brays from which derives their alternative name 'jackass penguin'. The more southerly beach hosts fewer penguins and isn't used for breeding, so it is permitted to swim or sun yourself here, joined by the occasional avian wanderer.

(NS/D)

Fishhoek, Kalk Bay and Muizenberg

Set within 5km of each other along the False Bay coastline, this trio of small coastal towns forms a more or less contiguous strip of coastal development serviced by the railway between the city centre and Simon's Town. **Fishhoek**, the most southerly of the trio, offers the least to tourists though it does boast a good beach and is the site of the **Fishhoek Valley Museum** (✆ 021 782 1752 🖳 www.fishhoek.com ◷ 09.30–12.30 Tue–Sat), which displays a collection of stone-age implements and human fossils unearthed at nearby Peers Cave. **Kalk Bay** is popular with Capetonians for its main road lined with antiquarian bookshops, bric-a-brac stores, craft studios and art galleries. More intriguing, however, is the old fishing harbour, with its busy fish market, bargain seafood eateries and resident gang of habituated Cape fur seals.

Muizenberg, situated at the junction of the Cape Peninsula and Cape Flats, was the site of the naval battle that led to the first British occupation of the Cape in 1795. It is also perhaps the most popular swimming and surfing beach on the peninsula, often becoming quite packed over summer weekends and school holidays, but relatively quiet at other times. Muizenberg boasts some interesting buildings dating to the late 19th century, when it was all the fashion for mining magnates and other well-to-do South Africans to build holiday homes here. These include **Rust-en-Vrede**, built by the famous architect Sir Herbert Baker in 1905 for Abe Bailey, and the **Rhodes Cottage Museum** (✆ 021 788 1816 ◷ 10.00–16.00 daily), set in a humble thatched cottage owned by Cecil John Rhodes, who died here in 1902 aged 49. Nearby **Het Posthuys** (✆ 021 788 7972 ◷ 10.00–16.00 daily) is a small maritime museum set in what was originally a lookout post in 1670 and later served as a naval warehouse, pub and private home.

Rondevlei Bird Sanctuary

Perth Rd ✆ 021 706 2404 ◷ Feb-Nov 07.30-17.00, Dec-Jan 07.30-19.00

Situated about 4km northeast of Muizenberg, this 2.2km² sanctuary was set aside in 1952 to protect the largest freshwater wetland site in the immediate vicinity of Cape Town. Serviced by a short walking trail and half-a-dozen hides, it offers perhaps the best general birding in the area, with more than 230 species recorded. Some of the more common sightings are of the great crested grebe, purple gallinule, sacred ibis, great white pelican, greater flamingo, African spoonbill, and various herons, waders and waterfowl. An added attraction is the small but regularly seen population of hippo, introduced in 1982 to help prevent the wetland being choked by floating vegetation.

The Boland, Overberg and West Coast

Cape Town is a convenient base for exploring three other intriguing regions situated a short driving distance from the city centre. The most popular of these, immediately inland of the city, is the **Boland** (literally 'Upland'), where historic small towns such as Stellenbosch, Franschhoek and Paarl lie at the centre of South Africa's burgeoning wine industry. Characterised by lush, vine-planted valleys set below spectacular mountain ranges such as the Simonsberg, Groot Drakenstein and Helderberg, this beautiful area is frequently referred to as the Cape Winelands. Few visitors pass up the opportunity to enjoy a wine tour through some of the more famous estates, many of which also boast world-class restaurants as well as striking examples of Cape Dutch architecture.

Separated from the Cape Peninsula by the Hottentots Holland Mountains and False Bay, the **Overberg** is the most southerly part of Africa, terminating 170km southeast of Cape Point at rocky Cape

Oom Samie se Winkel, one of Stellenbosch's many historic buildings. (AVZ)

Practicalities

Details of getting to the Boland, Overberg and West Coast from elsewhere in South Africa are broadly the same as for Cape Town (indeed, Cape Town International Airport lies alongside the most straightforward route connecting the city centre to Stellenbosch and Hermanus), see page 236. However, all three regions are most often visited as **day or overnight excursions** from Cape Town. **Organised wine tours** out of Cape Town, Stellenbosch or Franschhoek usually take in around five different estates and are widely available and very popular, not least because the self-drive wine-tasting option is in contravention both of common sense and of the law. A longer excursion to the Winelands offers the opportunity to appreciate the region's urban architecture as well as the scenery and wine. Hermanus and the West Coast, though both technically visitable on a day trip out of Cape Town, are definitely more suited to **overnight stays**. Hermanus, Stellenbosch, Franschhoek and most other Boland towns are

Accommodation

For full details of tour operator-recommended accommodation, see pages 274–5 and 280. Here follows a few further suggestions from the author.

Exclusive
Grand Roche Hotel Paarl ⚲ www.granderoche.com
Lanzerac Hotel & Spa Stellenbosch ⚲ www.lanzeracwines.co.za
Le Quartier Français Franschhoek ⚲ www.lequartier.co.za
Marine Hermanus Hermanus ⚲ www.marine-hermanus.co.za

Upmarket
D'Ouwe Werf Stellenbosch ⚲ www.ouwewerf.com
Eendracht Hotel Stellenbosch ⚲ www.eendracht-hotel.com
Old Tulbagh Hotel Tulbagh ⚲ www.tulbaghhotel.co.za
Zewenwacht Country Inn Near Stellenbosch ⚲ www.zevenwacht.co.za

Moderate
Arniston Spa Hotel Near Agulhas ⚲ www.arnistonhotel.com
Franschhoek Manor Franschhoek ⚲ www.franschhoekmanor.co.za
Harbour Vue Guesthouse Hermanus ⚲ www.harbourvue.co.za
Lambert's Bay Protea Lambert's Bay ⚲ www.lambertsbayhotel.co.za

well equipped with ATMs, shops and eateries, but smaller towns in the Overberg and West Coast are less reliable in this respect.

The Winelands is renowned for its cuisine, with tiny Franschhoek at one point accounting for six of the country's top 100 restaurants – and Stellenbosch isn't far behind. You're unlikely to have a problem finding an eatery to suit your taste and budget anywhere in the region, but a few pointers are outlined below.

(AVZ)

Budget

Columbine Beach Camp Columbine Nature Reserve ✥ www.beachcamp.co.za
De Hoop Collection De Hoop Nature Reserve ✥ www.dehoopcollection.co.za
Stumble Inn Stellenbosch ✥ www.stumbleinnstellenbosch.hostel.com
Zoete Inval Lodge Hermanus ✥ www.zoeteinval.co.za

Eating out

Boschendal Restaurant (fine dining & sumptuous lunchtime picnics) Boschendal Estate, R310 between Stellenbosch & Franschhoek ✆ 021 870 4272
D'Ouwe Werf (affordable traditional Cape cuisine) 30 Church St, Stellenbosch ✆ 021 887 4608
Die Strandloper (seafood buffet, booking required) West Coast near Saldhana ✆ 022 772 2490
La Petite Ferme (Mediterranean & fusion) Franschhoek Pass ✆ 021 876 3016
Lady Phillips Restaurant (Continental fine dining) Vergelegen Estate, near Somerset West ✆ 021 847 1346
Seafood at the Marine (seafood) Hermanus ✆ 028 313 1000
The Tasting Room (award-winning, 5–8 course degustation menu) Le Quartier Français, Franschhoek ✆ 021 876 2151
Volkskombuis (Cape Malay) Aan-de-Wagen Rd, Stellenbosch ✆ 021 886 2121

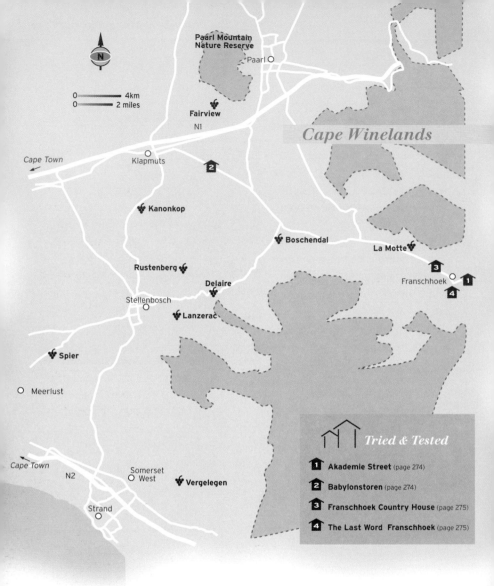

Cape Winelands

Tried & Tested

1 **Akademie Street** (page 274)

2 **Babylonstoren** (page 274)

3 **Franschhoek Country House** (page 275)

4 **The Last Word Franschhoek** (page 275)

Agulhas. The main tourist focus here is Hermanus, an attractive port town famed for its land-based whale-viewing and reached by following the scenic R44 along the mountainous eastern side of False Bay. Somewhat less spectacular, the Atlantic coastline north of Cape Town, usually referred to as the **West Coast**, is home to West Coast National Park and Lambert's Bay, both important sites for marine birds. This little-visited area comes into its own during August and September, when the wildflowers of the West Coast National Park provide a taster for the breath-taking springtime floral displays associated with the Namaqualand region of the Northern Cape.

The Boland, Overberg and West Coast highlights

Stellenbosch

South Africa's second-oldest town, likeable Stellenbosch is named after Simon van der Stel who established it on the north bank of the Eersterivier (First River) in 1679. Today, it doubles as an enclave of venerable Cape Dutch architecture and as the urban centre of Africa's most important wine-growing region. Stellenbosch also hosts an unusually lively café and pub scene, reflecting not only its burgeoning popularity with tourists, but also its status as the home of the Afrikaans-speaking University of Stellenbosch, whose early alumni included four former South African presidents as well as anti-apartheid activists such as Beyers Naudé. One of the most architecturally appealing towns in the country, Stellenbosch definitely warrants an overnight stay, which also allows time to explore the surrounding Winelands and to drive to nearby Franschhoek via the scenic Helshoogte (Hell's Heights) Pass.

Stellenbosch's historic centre, aptly nicknamed Eikestad (Town of Oaks), retains a pleasingly time-warped architectural feel whilst also hosting a good selection of contemporary restaurants, cafés and shops. An oak-shaded village green called **Die Braak** is fronted by

Cape Dutch architecture

Unique to South Africa, the Cape Dutch architectural style took root in the 18th century as traditional Dutch building styles were modified to suit the African conditions. Cape Dutch style is prevalent in the rural Winelands,

Cape Dutch manor house, Boschendal Estate, Franschhoek (AVZ)

where historic estates such as Lanzarac, Groot Constantia, Vergelegen and Boschendal boast large manor houses, along with smaller but similar outbuildings. There are also several more urban examples of the Cape Dutch style, especially in Stellenbosch and Tulbagh. The distinguishing feature of these buildings is the rounded and ornately bordered gable set above the main door, an adornment initially associated with medieval houses in Amsterdam. The classic Cape Dutch building almost invariably has plain, whitewashed walls and a thatched roof, and the finest examples have an H-shaped floor plan wherein the gabled façade is flanked by two perpendicular wings.

an unadorned **Kruithuis** (Powder House) built in 1777, as well as the Cape Dutch-meets-gothic **St Mary's Anglican Church** (1852) and the **Rhenish Church** (1823). A block further south, **Dorp Street** is lined with old Cape Dutch façades. Significant buildings here include the characterful **Oom Samie se Winkel** (Uncle Samie's Shop), founded in 1904, the building that formerly housed Stellenbosch Gymnasium (the precursor of the university, established in 1866), while **D'Ouwe Werf**, a block north on Church Street, is the oldest inn in South Africa, established in 1902.

Running north from Dorp Street along Ryneveld Street, **Stellenbosch Village Museum** (✆ 021 887 2902 ◷ 09.30–17.00 Mon–Sat, 14.00–17.00 Sun) comprises four restored houses – the oldest being the Schreuderhuis, one of the few buildings to survive the great fire of 1710 – representing different phases in the town's development. Directly opposite, the Dutch Reformed **Moederkerk** (Mother Church) is a striking neo-gothic construction whose steeple was completed in 1866. Immediately southwest of the town centre, the **Rupert Museum** (Lower Dorp St ✆ 021 888 3344 ⌘ www.rupertmuseum.org ◷ 09.00–16.00 Mon–Fri, 09.00–12.00 Sat) displays more than 300 works by 20th-century South African artists such as Irma Stern, Moses Kotler and Anton van Wouw.

Franschhoek

Situated in a verdant, vine-planted valley about 25km east of Stellenbosch as the crow flies, pretty little Franschhoek (French Corner) is named for the many protestant Huguenots who settled there in the late 1680s, having fled their homeland to escape Catholic persecution during the reign of Louis XIV. Although these early French settlers had no lasting linguistic impact, they contributed greatly to the growth of the local viniculture, and many of their surnames are still common among Afrikaners – for instance, De Villiers and Malan, or the more bastardised

Franschhoek's attractive Huguenot Monument. (AVZ)

likes of De Klerk and Nel (from Le Clercq and Neél). Franschhoek has a few historic buildings, notably a pastoral Dutch Reformed Church built in the Cape Dutch style in 1848. The town's French roots are reflected in the handsome, arched **Huguenot Monument** built on its outskirts in

Five fine Franschhoek shops

The long main drag through Franschhoek, flanked by some of the country's costliest inland real estate, is known for its selection of independent specialist stores aimed at discerning buyers:

Gallerie Ezakwantu

☎ 021 876 2162 ♁ www.ezakwantu.com
This exclusive ethnic gallery stocks high quality (and accordingly priced) artworks and crafts from all over Africa.

Huguenot Fine Chocolate

☎ 021 876 4096
♁ www.huguenotchocolates.com

Handcrafted Belgian chocolates are the speciality at this cheerful 'Black Empowerment' boutique, established by two Belgian-trained local entrepreneurs.

Touches & Tastes

☎ 021 876 2151 ♁ www.lequartier.co.za
This gift shop in the famous Le Quartier Français was named 'Best Shop in any Hotel Anywhere' by *Tatler UK* in 2005.

Franschhoek Cellar

☎ 021 876 2086 ♁ www.franschhoek-cellar.co.za
This prominent landmark on the Stellenbosch side of town stocks almost every wine produced around Franschhoek, and most can be tasted before you buy.

La Cotte Inn

☎ 021 876 3775 ♁ www.lacotte.co.za
A fantastic selection of South African wines and imported cheeses are on sale at this characterful shop, which also organises regular tasting evenings.

the 1840s, and the adjacent **Huguenot Memorial Museum** (Lambrecht Rd ☎ 021 876 2532 ⊙ 09.00–17.00 Mon–Sat, 14.00–17.00 Sun). Out of town situated on L'Ormarins Wine Estate, is the **Franschhoek Motor Museum** (☎ 021 874 9000), which has a collection of 220 vehicles ranging from an 1898 Beeston motor tricycle to a 21st-century Ferrari. A visit is a must for enthusiasts.

Tried & Tested

Akademie Street
🏠 www.aka.co.za

RAINBOW TOURS

Located in the centre of Franschhoek, just two minutes off the main drag, Akademie Street is a collection of charmingly converted Cape Dutch houses, and is a longstanding favourite. Linked through beautiful gardens to the main house, Twyfeling, where breakfast is served, Akademie Street is a past winner of the coveted AA Accommodation award. The thoughtful staff will help plan your activities, ensuring you are booked into the very best vineyard tours, chocolate and cheese tastings and local restaurants.

Babylonstoren
🏠 www.babylonstoren.com

BRIDGE & WICKERS
travel with experience

In the tranquil heart of the Winelands, beautiful Babylonstoren is a privately-owned, historic wine and fruit farm in the Drakenstein Valley. We love the contrast between the old farm architecture of the 14 guest cottages and the minimalist furnishings; the sensational meals inspired by the kitchen gardens; the garden tours, with the chance to understand gardening in the Cape floral kingdom; and the innocent pleasures of yesteryear – following streams, rowing on the dam and savouring the scenery from the koppie.

Horseriding around Franschhoek (SS)

Franschhoek Country House & Villas
🖑 www.fch.co.za

With a good range of 14 rooms and 12 luxurious villa suites, Franschhoek Country House & Villas is perfect for both honeymooners and families who want a bit of space. We love the grounds nestled in the valley and the sense of space with two swimming pools to relax or play in. And as befits the gourmet reputation of the winelands, the food is outstanding at the award winning Monneaux Restaurant.

Jan Harmsgat
🖑 www.jhghouse.com

Jan Harmsgat Guest House is a two-hour drive from Cape Town, on a working farm in the scenic Klein Karoo winelands region. Guests are treated to understated elegance and comfort In the farm's original slave quarters, two loft rooms and the guest lounge boast expansive mountain views. Relax by the pool with a book from the extensive library or explore the farm and surrounding wine routes, as well as museums and heritage sites in nearby Swellendam and surrounding areas.

The Last Word Franschhoek
🖑 www.thelastword.co.za

The Last Word Franschhoek is an exclusive five-star historic residence in the heart of Franschhoek village, the food and wine capital of South Africa. Beautifully restored in the Cape Huguenot tradition, this intimate hotel is the perfect base to explore the surrounding wine farms and award winning restaurants.
It has been designed with sumptuous home comforts, creating an elegant, sophisticated interior with a handsome mixture of classic and contemporary furnishings. There are six luxurious rooms and all have large en-suite bathrooms.

275

Ten favourite wine estates

Hundreds of wine estates are dotted around the Western Cape, and most offer free or inexpensive tasting facilities. Many are also notable for their Cape Dutch architecture, for restaurants serving Cape Malay or international cuisines, and for their scenic settings. What follows is by no means a definite 'top ten' of estates – no such thing exists – but it does highlight a few exceptional starting points for those with limited time. Opening hours vary, but you can safely assume that any estate will be open for tasting 09.00–16.00 Monday–Friday, and most are also open on Saturday and even Sunday.

Vergelegen Wine Estate (AVZ)

Boschendal
℡ 021 876 3603 🖰 www.boschendal.co.za
Alongside the R312 between Stellenbosch and Franschhoek, this perennially popular all-rounder lies in a green valley flanked by the Groot Drakenstein and Simonsberg Mountains. First planted with vines in 1685, its superb Cape Dutch architecture is reached via a wonderful, tree-lined drive, and the French-style *pique-nique* on the lawn is a must.

Delaire
℡ 021 8885 1756 🖰 www.delairewinery.co.za
Perched on the crest of the Helshoogte Pass between Stellenbosch and Franschhoek, this scenic estate serves popular picnic hampers, ideally accompanied with a chilled, home-grown Sauvignon Blanc.

Fairview
℡ 021 863 2450 🖰 www.fairview.co.za
Children love this unpretentious estate outside Paarl for its laidback farmyard atmosphere. It also gets the thumbs-up from foodies for its above-par wines and superb deli serving a fabulous range of handcrafted cheeses.

Kanonkop
℡ 021 884 4656 🖰 www.kanonkop.co.za
Famed for award-winning Pinotage and red blends, this estate was named after a hilltop canon that was fired to announce the arrival of a ship at the Cape.

La Motte

☎ 021 876 3119 🖱 www.la-motte.com

For serious wine lovers, this consistent performer in the Franschhoek Valley, long famed for its heavy reds and more recently for its organic range, is centred upon an 18th-century farmhouse with an imposing front gable.

Lanzarac

Jonkershoek Rd ☎ 021 886 5641 🖱 www.lanzeracwines.co.za

Founded under the name Scoongezicht (Clean Face) in 1692, this scenic estate within walking distance of central Stellenbosch produced the world's first commercial Pinotage wine in 1959, and its stately Cape Dutch architecture includes a five-star restaurant and hotel.

Meerlust

☎ 021 843 3587 🖱 www.meerlust.co.za

The iconic Rubicon red blend and highly rated Pinot Noir are just two of the excellent reds produced at this historic estate, where the handsome manor house has been in the same family for two centuries.

Rustenberg

☎ 021 809 1200 🖱 www.rustenberg.co.za

This 300-year-old estate on the outskirts of Stellenbosch in notable for its red blends and fine Cape Dutch architecture in the shadow of the Simonsberg.

Spier

☎ 021 809 1100 🖱 www.spier.co.za

This child-friendly estate, on the R310 southwest of Stellenbosch, lacks the stately ambience of many of its older counterparts, but its excellent facilities include a swimming pool, spa, playground, craft shop, cheetah outreach programme and raptor centre. There are also horseback excursions and two onsite restaurants.

Vergelegen

☎ 021 847 1334 🖱 www.vergelegen.co.za

Founded in 1685, Vergelegen, as indicated by its name (roughly translated as 'faraway') was a remote outpost of the Cape Colony until it became the estate of Willem van der Stel (son of Simon) in 1700. The manor house, garden and gnarled camphor trees planted by van der Stel are highlights of arguably the loveliest estate in the Winelands, on the slopes of the Helderberg outside Somerset West. The restaurant and award-winning wines are also exceptional.

Taal Monument (SN/D)

Paarl

Founded in 1720 on the Berg River 30km north of Stellenbosch, Paarl is the largest town in the Winelands, and the least attractive. It sprawls either side of a 10km main road claimed to be longest in the country, and you'd readily agree when there's heavy traffic. The town is named after Paarl (Pearl) Mountain, and is topped by a pearl-smooth granite dome that can be reached via a footpath through the protea-rich slopes of the nature reserve bordering the town centre. As with Stellenbosch and Franschhoek, numerous good wine estates can be visited in the area, and the town itself boasts a smattering of old buildings, notably **Die Ou Pastorie**, constructed in 1787 and now a local history museum (✆ 021 872 2651 ⊙ 09.00–17.00 Mon–Fri), and a Dutch Reformed Church dating to 1805. A more modern landmark is **Drakenstein Prison**, where Nelson Mandela was held towards the end of his term in prison. The **Taal Monument**, built in 1975 to commemorate the centenary of Afrikaans's recognition as an official language, lies on the lower slopes of Paarl Mountain. A 30-minute drive along the R44 north of town will bring devotees of Cape Dutch architecture to the modest **Tulbagh**, where the whole of Church Street was restored in traditional style following a devastating earthquake in 1970.

Hermanus

Situated on Walker Bay 120km southeast of Cape Town, clifftop Hermanus is the main tourist hub in the Overberg thanks to its reputation for offering the world's best land-based whale-watching in season (typically June–November). The town was founded by German settlers in 1855 and is named after the mysterious Hermanus Pieter, reputedly an itinerant shepherd who regularly camped at nearby Kleinmond (the mouth of the Klein (Small) River). Hermanus emerged as a fashionable seaside holiday retreat for wealthy Capetonians in the early 20th century, and it remains to this day something of a resort town, with quaint cobbled alleys, and relaxed seafood restaurants lining the elevated harbourfront.

Whale-watching peaks between September and October, when around 100 southern right whales and a smaller number of humpback whales converge on Walker Bay to calve. At this time of year, a gentle meander along the 10km cliff walk running west from town is almost certain to yield close-up sightings, and whales are

The Old Harbour, Hermanus (AVZ)

often seen breaching and lobtailing immediately below Castle Rock, a 30m-tall vantage point overlooking the harbour. Contact the local tourist office (☎ 028 312 2629 🖥 www.hermanus.co.za) for details of the 'whale crier' (who updates visitors on the latest sightings) and boat-based whale-viewing tours with the only two licensed operators. Also worth a look is the **Old Harbour Museum** (☎ 028 312 1475 🖥 www.old-harbour-museum.co.za), where live whale songs can be heard, beamed through directly from a strategically placed submarine microphone.

On the opposite side of Walker Bay, the modest fishing village of **Gansbaai** (☎ 028 384 1439 🖥 www.gansbaai.com), which was named for the geese that once nested there, is also an excellent spot for whale-watching. It is best known, however, as the springboard for half-day 'shark cage dives' to Dyer Island, home to breeding colonies of African penguin and black oystercatcher, as well as some 30,000 Cape fur seals that are fed upon by a dense population of rapacious great white sharks. Other points of interest around Hermanus include the African penguin colony at **Betty's Bay**, off the R44 towards Cape Town, and the nearby **Harold Porter National Botanical Garden** (☎ 028 272 9311 🖥 www.sanbi.org 🕐 08.00–18.00) on the fynbos-covered slopes of the Kogelberg Mountains.

The peak time for viewing southern right whales in Hermanus is between September and October. (KM/D)

Tried & Tested

Birkenhead House
⌂ www.birkenheadhouse.com

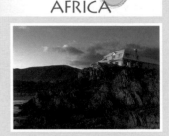

Perched high on the cliffs above Hermanus's most prominent beaches, this boutique hotel definitely has the wow factor. Each of the 11 super-stylish suites are individually decorated and beautifully furnished, and each offers expansive vistas of Walker Bay or the towering Overberg mountains. Enjoy a spa treatment or, from June to October, watch whales from your sunbed by the infinity pool. We think Birkenhead House offers the highest level of accommodation in Hermanus with the most perfect setting. Utterly luxurious.

Cliff Lodge Ocean Front Retreat
⌂ www.clifflodge.co.za

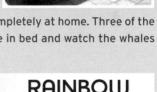

Watch whales from your room at this idyllic ocean front retreat. Cliff Lodge is an award-winning guesthouse with breathtaking views; it's ideal for those looking for an intimate, relaxed atmosphere surrounded by unspoilt nature. There are just five luxurious en-suite rooms, each individually decorated. The owners, Gillian and Gideon, will make you feel completely at home. Three of the rooms are sea facing, allowing you to literally lie in bed and watch the whales go by from June to November.

Grootbos
⌂ www.grootbos.com

Set in acres of reclaimed fynbos with breathtaking views of the dunes and coast, Grootbos Reserve is a haven of rural tranquillity. The 11-suite Garden Lodge and 16-suite Forest Lodge offer activities galore – everything from whale watching, mountain biking and horseriding to beachcombing, bug boxes and quad bikes, with rabbits, tortoises and ponies for the little ones. Brilliant for families and active adults, the food here is to die for, and the Grootbos Foundation's work with the local community is inspiring.

Agulhas and surrounds

East of Hermanus, the somewhat undeveloped new 210km² **Cape Agulhas National Park** (✆ 028 435 6222 🖰 www.sanparks.org) protects the desolate and rocky headland known to the Portuguese as Cabo das Agulhas (Cape of Needles). Not only is this the southernmost tip of Africa, terminating at 34°50′S, but it also has the rather arbitrary distinction of being the official dividing line between the Atlantic and Indian oceans. More than 250 ships have fallen victim to the jagged rocks offshore from Agulhas over the years, and the **Cape Agulhas Lighthouse**, reached via 71 steps, is the country's second oldest.

Running along the coast for 50km east of Agulhas, the underrated **De Hoop Nature Reserve** (✆ 028 542 1253 🖰 www.capenature.co.za ⊙ 07.00–18.00 daily) protects the world's largest remaining block of coastal fynbos, together with an alluring variety of marine and terrestrial wildlife, but it can only be explored properly on foot, with a selection of trails ranging from two hours to five days in duration.

The West Coast

Less popular with international tourists than the Boland and Overberg, the stretch of Atlantic coastline running immediately northwards from Cape Town is not without its charms. A popular excursion here, though actually some 20km inland, is the presciently named town of **Darling**, which pirouetted out of obscurity in 1996 when gay icon Pieter Dirk Uys converted the old railway building into a cabaret theatre and quirky museum called **Evita se Perron** (✆ 022 492 3930 🖰 www.evita.co.za). The name combines that of Uys's Dame Edna-esque alter ego Evita Bezuidenhout with an Afrikaans word for a railway platform, and both

Northern Cape

The West Coast is the gateway to the Northern Cape, South Africa's most arid and thinly populated province, accounting for almost one-third of the country's surface area yet supporting less than 2% of the national population. Few international tourists find their way here, and it's fair to say that these remote badlands of vast, desiccated plains and wide-open blue skies, punctuated by the occasional slumbering *dorp* (village), will hold little appeal to agoraphobics or those seeking slick boutique hotels, tropical beaches, trendy nightspots or any of the other trappings associated with typical tourist resorts. On that level, the Northern Cape doesn't really belong in a Highlights guidebook. But equally, this immense province contains two regions that might easily rank among the country's top ten destinations were they not so remote from any established tourist circuit.

The first and more accessible of these is **Namaqualand,** a highly seasonal destination that can be reached by continuing north from Lambert's Bay along the N7 to the villages of Vanrhynsdorp or Kamieskroon, or the larger town of Springbok. Part of the extensive Karoo ecosystem, Namaqualand is dominated by succulents, and for much of the year its floral diversity is less than apparent to the untrained eye. Between August and September, however, this monochrome landscape of rocky plains and craggy mountains is transformed into a multi-hued carpet of daisies, mesembryanthemums, violets, gladioli and other flowers. It's a wonderful, life-enhancing spectacle that has been cited as the botanical equivalent of the Serengeti migration or the million-strong flamingo flocks that aggregate in the East African Rift.

Altogether more remote is the **Kgalagadi Transfrontier Park**, the South African sector of which is effectively the country's second-largest national park. It protects a wild but fragile dune ecosystem bounded by the normally dry Auob and Nossob watercourses. The environment is harsh and uncompromising, but it is also a place of singular beauty, memorable above all for its red dunes set against a constant blue sky. More surprisingly, perhaps, the game viewing is excellent, with lion, cheetah and leopard all likely to be seen along with the likes of black-backed jackal, bat-eared fox, gemsbok, springbok and eland, while roadside bands of meerkat and ground squirrel captivate with their bipedal posturing. This is the best site in the country for raptors and dry-country birds, most notably the sociable weavers whose immense, labyrinthine communal nests look like scruffy tan lollipops perched precariously on the treetops.

Realistically, the Northern Cape is best viewed as a destination in its own right, one to be explored leisurely over the course of a couple of weeks drive along the N7 and N14 between Cape Town and Johannesburg. Other highlights

The floral diversity in Namaqualand is an incredible natural spectacle to behold. (AVZ)

include the **Kuruman Mission**, which was founded in 1821 by Charles Moffat, and was where the legendary explorer David Livingstone spent his first years in Africa; the defiantly well-groomed town of **Upington** at the centre of the Orange River irrigation scheme (which feeds the world's second-largest wine co-op); and **Augrabies Falls National Park**, where the Orange River tumbles 56m into a spectacular, 18km-long canyon populated by rhino, springbok, gemsbok, kudu, eland and a variety of small, nocturnal predators.

For further details on Namaqualand, you could check out the websites ⌁ www.namaqualand.com and ⌁ www.namaqualand.net, while Kgalagadi and Augrabies are accorded detailed coverage at ⌁ www.sanparks.org.

Tried & Tested

Tswalu Kalahari
⌁ www.tswalu.com

Aardvark
SAFARIS LTD

Situated in the bushveld savannah of the Southern Kalahari, the malaria-free Tswalu is South Africa's largest private game reserve, boasting habituated meerkats, the magnificent Kalahari black maned lion, jaw-dropping scenery, rare wildlife, and truly stunning accommodation. Few properties offer such flexibility and variety, with dedicated guides and butlers on hand to arrange activities from horse-riding to bush breakfasts. Families are welcomed, and – the best bit – Tswalu only accommodates 30 guests, so you virtually have this great wilderness to explore to yourself.

the museum and Uys's satirical one-man show provide a worthwhile if rather irreverent introduction to contemporary South African politics.

The region's largest settlement, 100km north of Cape Town, is the industrialised naval port of **Saldanha**, which services South Africa's deepest natural harbour. Saldanha guards the mouth of **Langebaan Lagoon**, centrepiece of the 330km² **West Coast National Park** (✆ 022 772 2144 🖰 www.sanparks.org), a globally important site for marine birds, some ten species of which have breeding colonies in the area. The park also forms the southernmost reach of the springflower displays for which the Northern Cape is renowned; visit the **Postberg** sector (open only during the flowering season of August and September) to enjoy the surreal site of desert-adapted antelope such as gemsbok and springbok tiptoeing through vibrant fields of colourful flowers!

Protruding westward into the Atlantic some 20km north of Saldanha, the small but lovely **Cape Columbine Nature Reserve** (✆ 082 926 2267 🖰 www.beachcamp.co.za) is a good spot for sea kayaking and it protects an area of coastal fynbos that bursts into spectacular bloom between August and September. Cape Columbine is reached via the characterful fishing village of **Paternoster**, famed for its traditional whitewashed cottages and superb crayfish. Further inland, the 1,600km² **Cederberg Wilderness Area** (✆ 027 482 2403 🖰 www.cederberg.co.za) is a hikers' paradise studded with spectacular sandstone formations and well-preserved prehistoric rock art sites.

Cape gannet (Sa/D)

Further north still, the sleepy port of **Lambert's Bay** has much to offer marine wildlife lovers. The premier attraction, reached via a short causeway from the mainland, is **Bird Island** (✆ 027 432 1000 ☼ summer 07.00–19.00, winter 07.00–17.00), home to a breeding colony of 10,000 Cape gannets as well as smaller numbers of African penguins. The harbour also supports a few resident Cape fur seals, while boat trips out onto the open ocean offer an opportunity to see the rare Heaviside's dolphin and other cetaceans. For foodies this is excellent crayfish territory, and the dozen-odd estates along the underrated **Olifants River Wine Route** include the southern hemisphere's largest single wine producer, **Namaqua Wines** (✆ 027 213 1080 🖰 www.namaquawines.com).

Appendix 1

South African English

South Africa has 11 official languages, of which English is the most widely used in the tourism industry. However, as might be expected, South African English tends to be peppered with words and phrases – many borrowed from Afrikaans, fewer from Zulu and other Bantu languages – that will be unfamiliar or confusing to first-time visitors. Some common examples are listed below:

babalas	hangover
bakkie	a pick-up truck, one of the most popular vehicle types in southern Africa
berg	mountain (range), as in *Drakensberg*, not to be confused with *burg* (town)
biltong	stick of dried, spiced, raw meat, regarded as a delicacy locally
boma	traditional enclosure, but often also the communal area at a safari camp
boerewors	literally 'farmer's sausage'. Good for *braaing*, often referred to as plain *wors*
boet	friendly term of address between males, literally 'brother', the South African equivalent of 'mate'
braai	barbecue; many campsites sell 'braai packs', including a piece of *boerewors* and a chop or steak
bru	variation on boet, used more in the Cape
bush	loosely meaning any woodland or savanna, though 'The Bush' implies an element of wilderness
café	denotes the equivalent of a British corner shop rather than a European-style café
check out	look at
dagga	marijuana
dame/here	ladies/gentlemen; toilets are often signposted *Dame* or *Here*
donga	small ravine, often one caused by water erosion
dop	alcoholic drink, can be used as a verb or noun

dorp(ie)	literally 'village', but applied vaguely disparagingly to any small, quiet town
dumpie	disposable 330ml bottle of beer
fundi	expert
fynbos	the unique, heath-like vegetation of the Western Cape
Howzit?	greeting, abbreviated from 'How is it?'
indaba	meeting or conference
izzit?	conversation interjection much like a non-sarcastic 'really?'
jol	party or good time
just now	a perplexing expression that generally means 'soon', but not immediately
kantoor	any office
kloof	strictly speaking, a gorge, but often used to describe any rocky cliff or slope
koppie/kopje	a small hill or rocky outcrop, this word is used as far north as Kenya
kraal	traditional cattle enclosure, often used simply to mean a rural farm
larney	fancy or smart
lekker	used by English speakers as slang meaning 'nice' or 'good'
location	the rural or small-town equivalent of a township (see below)
mielie	maize, the staple crop of the region, used to make *mieliepap* (porridge)
mlungu	white person
muti	traditional medicine, but often used to describe pharmaceuticals too
oke	man, used in a similar way to 'guy'
robot	a traffic light
rondawel	a traditional round hut of a design that's often mimicked at campsites
sangoma	traditional healer
shame!	versatile exclamation that might as easily be used to woo a cute baby as to express horror or sympathy
shebeen	unlicensed bar
skelm	crook or mischievous person
stad	city, as in *Kaapstad* (Cape Town); street signs for *Stad* point to city centre
stoep	veranda or balcony

tokoloshe	demon who is said to visit homesteads to mischievous ends at night
township	an urban area, such as Soweto, zoned for Black people under apartheid
trek	journey or travel
tsotsi	criminal or gangster
veld	often translated as 'grassland', but in practice use is broader, similar to *bush*
vlei	shallow and often swampy lake, valley or floodplain
voetsek!	go away!
yebo	Zulu word literally meaning 'yes' but often used as a greeting

Greetings

You may also like to know some basic greetings in a few local languages:

	Afrikaans	seSotho	isiXhosa	isiZulu
Hello	Gooie Dag	Lumela	Molo	Sawubona
How are you?	Hoe gaan dit?	Okae?	Unjani?	Unjani?
I'm fine	Goed, dankie	Keteng	Ndiphilile nkosi	Nghikona, ngiyabonga
Goodbye	Totsiens	Sala Hantle	Hamba kakuhle	Hamba kahle
Yes	Ja	Ee	Ewe	Yebo
No	Nee	Tjhe	Hayi	Hayi
Thank you	Dankie	Keleboga	Enkosi	Ngiyabonga

Appendix 2

Selected reading

South Africa has an active local publishing industry, with a strong emphasis on field guides and other titles dedicated to natural history. The country also boasts a well-established literary tradition, having produced two recent Nobel Prize-winners in the form of JM Coetzee and Nadine Gordimer, while its fractious history and contemporary political scene are also addressed in a wide selection of titles. Books about South Africa can be bought through online sellers such as ⁓ www.amazon.com or ⁓ www.amazon.co.uk, which are particularly good resources for locating out-of-print titles. The best bookshop chain in the country is Exclusive Books (⁓ www.exclus1ves.co.za), which is represented at all main airports and in most of the larger shopping malls. Far more widespread is the Central News Agency (CNA ⁓ www. cna.co.za), which has branches in most towns of any substance and sells a good range of current mainstream bestsellers and locally published books, but is hopeless when it comes to anything more obscure. For secondhand books, the cluster of shops in Cape Town's Long Street and the Johannesburg suburb of Melville are good places in which to start.

Wildlife

Southern African Wildlife by Mike Unwin (Bradt, 2nd edition, 2011) is a handy and lavishly illustrated one-stop handbook to the region's mammals, birds and other fauna, aimed specifically at one-off or occasional visitors whose interest in wildlife extends beyond the Big Five but who don't want to carry a library of reference books. In the same vein and also recommended is the more identification-oriented *Wildlife of Southern Africa* by Vincent Carruthers (Struik, 2008).

Mammals

Several options are available. The pick, assuming you want coverage of the entire continent, is Jonathan Kingdon's immensely detailed *Field Guide to African Mammals* (Christopher Helm, 2003), while the same author's *Pocket Guide to African Mammals* (Christopher Helm, 2004) is a more compact, inexpensive title suited to less-dedicated wildlife enthusiasts. For something specific to southern Africa, a good choice is *Smither's Mammals of Southern Africa* by Peter Apps (Struik, 2000) or the more portable and recently revised *Pocket Guide Mammals of Southern Africa* by Chris and Tilde Stuart (Struik, 2011).

Two more quirky reference books are Richard Estes' superb *Behavior Guide to African Mammals*, also known as *The Safari Companion* (Russell Friedman Books, South Africa, 1992), a well-organised and informative guide to mammalian behaviour that might be rather bulky for casual safari-goers, and the self-explanatory *Field Guide to the Tracks and Signs of Southern and East African Wildlife* by Chris Stuart (Struik, 2003).

Birds

Three field guides stand out. These are the recently revitalised *Roberts Bird Guide* by Hugh Chittenden (John Voelcker Bird Fund), *Sasol Birds of Southern Africa* by Ian Sinclair, Phil Hockey and Warwick Tarboton (Struik, 2002) and *Newman's Birds of Southern Africa* by Kenneth Newman (Struik, 2010). All three are comprehensive for the southern African region, and each has its devotees among South African birders, so picking favourites is pointless. Several more lightweight and incomplete field guides are also available, but these tend to be frustrating to use, as do guides that use photos rather than paintings.

Other field guides

For serious tree-huggers, the recently revised, 1,000-page *Trees of Southern Africa* by Meg and Keith Coates Palgrave (Struik, 2003) is the definitive work on the subject, but portability doesn't rank high among its assets. A more realistic option for one-off visitors is the 184-page *How to Identify Trees in Southern Africa* by Piet and Braam van Wyk (Struik, 2007).

Other useful specialist titles include the *Field Guide to Wild Flowers of South Africa* by John Manning (Struik, 2009), the same author's *Field Guide to Fynbos* (Struik, 2007), *Field Guide to Snakes and Other Reptiles of Southern Africa* by Bill Branch (Struik, 1998), *Field Guide to Insects of South Africa* by Mike Picker, Alan Weaving and Charles Griffiths (Struik, 2004), and the out-of-print *Frogs and Frogging in Southern Africa* (which comes with a useful CD of frog calls) by Vincent Carruthers (Struik, 2001).

History, politics, biography and current affairs

Scan the appropriate shelves of an Exclusive Books or CNA, and you'll find them loaded with tomes that pay testament to South Africa's appetite for political navel contemplation. The following are recommended as a starting point:

Ansell, Gwen *Soweto Blues: Jazz and Politics in South Africa* (Continuum, 2004). This history of apartheid-era township jazz places the lives of scene leaders such as Miriam Makeba and High Masakela in the content of the struggle against apartheid.

Krog, Antjie *Country of My Skull* (Vintage, 1999). Winner of multiple awards, this is a highly personal and insightful account of the Truth and Reconciliation Commission hearings chaired by Archbishop Desmond under the Mandela government.

Malan, Riaan *My Traitor's Heart* (Bodley Head, 1990). The quality of the writing makes this autobiographical account of a liberal Afrikaner during apartheid punch above its weight 20 years after publication.

Mandela, Nelson *Conversations with Myself* (Macmillan, 2010). This bang up-to-date and insightful collection of Mandela's correspondence, prison notes and other personal files comes complete with an introduction by Barack Obama.

Mandela, Nelson *Long Walk to Freedom* (Abacus, 1995). The great man's autobiography, published a few years after he was released from prison, also provides a useful overall introduction to apartheid-era South Africa.

Mathabane, Mark *Kaffir Boy: The True Story of a Black Youth's Coming of Age in Apartheid South Africa* (Simon & Schuster, 2006). The subtitle of this riveting autobiography sums up what is at times harrowing subject matter.

Packenham, Thomas *Boer War* (Weidenfeld & Nicolson, 1991). One of the finest historical accounts ever published about Africa, this weighty but highly readable tome provides a definitive overview of the protracted Anglo-Boer hostilities that shaped 20th-century South Africa.

Pakenham, Thomas *Scramble for Africa* (Abacus, 1992). Gripping, 600-page book, aptly described by one reviewer as '*Heart of Darkness* with the lights switched on'.

Reader, John *Africa: A Biography of the Continent* (Penguin, 1997). Perhaps the most readable and accurate attempt yet to capture the sweep of African history for the general reader.

Russell, Alec *Bring Me My Machine Gun: The Battle for the Soul of South Africa, from Mandela to Zuma* (Public Affairs, 2010). This modern history of the ANC – and South African politics in general – builds up to Jacob Zuma's 2009 ascent to the presidency.

Sampson, Anthony *Mandela: The Authorised Biography* (Harper Collins, 2000). Though it's been around for a decade, this is the most thorough Mandela biography in print.

Sparks, Allister *Beyond the Miracle: Inside the New South Africa* (Jonathan Ball, 2003). An adversarial newspaper editor of renown at the height of apartheid, Sparks looks here at a more recent era in South Africa's history, identifying the challenges and successes post 1994.

Thompson, Leonard *History of South Africa* (Yale University Press, 2001). Now in its third edition, this standard work probably provides the best overall compact overview of South African history.

Fiction

The choice is endless, and almost anything by the established literary trio of Andre Brink, JM Coetzee and Nadine Gordimer – who collectively share five Booker nominations and two Nobel awards – is worth reading, but here are a few acknowledged classics and more recent favourites:

Brink, Andre *A Dry White Season* (1979) or *An Act of Terror* (1991)
Coetzee, JM *Disgrace* (1999) or *The Life & Times of Michael K* (1983)
Fugard, Lisa *Skinner's Drift* (2006)
Gordimer, Nadine *The Conservationist* (1974)
Head, Bessie *When Rain Clouds Gather* (1968)
Maart, Rozena *The Writing Circle* (2007)
Mda, Zakes *The Heart of Redness* (2001)
Mhlongo, Niq *Dog Eat Dog* (2004)
Mpe, Phaswane *Welcome to Our Hillbrow* (2001)
Ndebele, Njabulo *The Cry of Winnie Mandela* (2004)
Paton, Alan *Cry, The Beloved Country* (1948)
Scholtz, AHM *A Place Called Vatmaar* (2001)
Schreiner, Olive *The Story of an African Farm* (1883)
van Heerden, Etienne *Ancestral Voices* (993)

Travel magazines

For readers with a broad interest in Africa, an excellent magazine dedicated to tourism throughout Africa is *Travel Africa* (✆ www.travelafricamag.com). Recommended for their broad-ranging editorial content and the coffee table-book standard of photography and reproduction, the award-winning magazines *Africa Geographic and Africa Birds and Birding* can be checked out at the website ✆ www.africageographic.com.

Health

Self-prescribing has its hazards so if you are going anywhere very remote consider taking a health book such as *Bugs, Bites & Bowels: The Cadogan Guide to Healthy Travel* by Jane Wilson-Howarth (1999).

Index

Index

First edition published November 2011
Bradt Travel Guides Ltd
IDC House, The Vale, Chalfont St Peter, Bucks SL9 9RZ, England
www.bradtguides.com
Published in the USA by The Globe Pequot Press Inc,
PO Box 480, Guilford, Connecticut 06437-0480

Text copyright © 2011 Philip Briggs
Maps copyright © 2011 Bradt Travel Guides Ltd
Photographs copyright © 2011 Individual photographers (see below)
Project Manager: Elspeth Beidas

ISBN: 978 1 84162 368 9

British Library Cataloguing in Publication Data
A catalogue record for this book is available from the British Library

Photographs
Aardvark Safaris: &Beyond (&B/Aa), Tswalu Kalahari (TK/Aa); Alamy: Africa Media Online (AMO/A), AfriPics.com (AP/A), Alexander Caminada (AC/A), John Warburton-Lee Photography (JWLP/A), JS Callahan/tropicalpix (JSC/t/A), PCL (PCL/A), Stock Connection Blue (SCB/A); Ariadne Van Zandbergen (AVZ); Crispin Zeeman/Buddha34 (CZ); Dreamstime: Anke Van Wyk (AVW/D), Davidgarry (D/D), Francesco Dazzi (FD/D), Holger, Karius (HK/D), Hongqi Zhang (HZ/D), Inna Felker (IF/D), Karelgallas (K/D), Ken Moore (KM/D), Kevin Brown (KB/D), Lourens Durand (LD/D), Ludwig Kriegl (LK/D), Marietjie Opperman (MO/D), Mark Van Overmeire (MVO/D), Melissa Schalke (MS/D), Mogens Trolle (MT/D), Nico Smit (NS/D), Patrick Allen (PA/D), Riaanvdb (R/D), Rudix (R/D), Sandmanx (Sa/D), Sean Nel (SN/D), Smellme (S/D), Ysbrand (Y/D); FLPA: Chris & Tilde Stuart (C&TS/FLPA), ImageBroker (I/FLPA), Jurgen & Christine Sohns (J&CS/FLPA), Mitsuaki Iwago/Minden Pictures (MI/MP/FLPA), Photo Researchers (PR/FLPA); Gallo Images/Alamy Illustrated London News Ltd/Mary Evans (GI/AILNL/ME); Rainbow Tours: Fugitives Drift (FD/R), Notten's Camp (NC/R); Scott Bennet (SB); SuperStock (SS)

Front cover (Top, left to right) Elephant (SS), Zulu woman (SS), Cheetah (MI/MP/FLPA); (bottom) Clifton Beach (SS)
Back cover Penguin (AVZ); Victorian bathing huts, St James beach, Cape Town (AVZ)
Title page White rhino (SS), House in front of the Drakensberg Mountains (SS), Black-footed penguin (SS)
Part & chapter openers
Page 1: Cape Town (SS); Page 2: Bushmen hunting with bow and arrow, Kalahari, Northern Cape (AVZ); Page 3: Nelson Mandela (GI/A); Page 22: Leopard (AVZ); Page 23: Black rhino (AVZ); Page 56: Elephant (SS); Page 57: Game drive (TK/Aa); Page 81: Waterberg, Marakele National Park (SS); Page 101: Franschhoek (SS); Page 102: (top) Southern masked weaver (J&CS/FLPA), (bottom) Voortrekker Monument, Pretoria (SS); Page 103: City Hall, Johannesburg (SS); Page 128: Blue-eared starling (D/D); Page 129: Zebra (SB); Page 164: Zulu chief (AVZ); Page 165: Royal Natal National Park (SS); Page 200: Public library and statue of Queen Victoria, Port Elizabeth (AVZ); Page 201: Tsitsikamma National Park, Garden Route (SS); Page 230: Victorian Beach huts, St James Beach, Cape Town (AVZ); Page 231: Cape Town (MVO/D)

Maps Artinfusion

Typeset and designed from the author's disc by Artinfusion (*www.artinfusion.co.uk*)
Production managed by Jellyfish Print Solutions; printed in India